Religion in the Twenty-First Century

JONATHAN S. CULLICK
Northern Kentucky University

PEARSON
Longman

New York   San Francisco   Boston
London   Toronto   Sydney   Tokyo   Singapore   Madrid
Mexico City   Munich   Paris   Cape Town   Hong Kong   Montreal

OTHER TITLES IN THE LONGMAN TOPICS READER SERIES

College Culture, Student Success
Deborah Anderson

Translating Tradition
Karen E. Beardslee

Sports Talk
Lisa Beckelhimer

Reading City Life
Patrick Bruch and Richard Marback

Essays On Writing
Lizbeth A. Bryant and
    Heather M. Clark

Diversity: Strength and Struggle
Joseph Calabrese and Susan Tchudi

*Legends, Lore, and Lies: A Skeptic's
    Stance*
Joseph Calabrese

Laughing Matters
Marvin Diogenes

The People and Promise of California
Mona Field and Brian Kennedy

Citizenship Now
Jon Ford and Marjorie Ford

The Changing World of Work
Marjorie Ford

Issues of Gender
Ellen G. Friedman and Jennifer
    D. Marshall

*Youth Subcultures: Exploring
    Underground America*
Arielle Greenberg

Education Matters
Morgan Gresham and Crystal
    McCage

Science and Society
Richard K. Grinnell

*International Views: America
    and the Rest of the World*
Keith Gumery

Listening to Earth
Christopher Hallowell and
    Walter Levy

Chican@s in the Conversation
Elizabeth Kessler and Anne Perrine

Body and Culture
Greg Lyons

Writing Places
Paula Mathieu, George Grattan,
    Tim Lindgren, and Staci Shulty

Peace, War, and Terrorism
Denis Okerstrom

The World of the Image
Trudy Smoke and Alan Robbins

American Dreams
Elizabeth Stolarek and
    Larry Juchartz

Hip Hop Reader
Tim Strode and Tim Wood

The Counterculture Reader
E. A. Swingrover

Discovering Popular Culture
Anna Tomasino

Music and Culture
Anna Tomasino

Ethics in the 21st Century
Mary Alice Trent

Considering Cultural Difference
Pauline Uchmanowicz

Language and Prejudice
Tamara M. Valentine

CyberReader, Abridged Edition
Victor J. Vitanza

For Stephanie and Norma

Senior Sponsoring Editor: Virginia L. Blanford
Senior Marketing Manager: Sandra McGuire
Production Manager: Kathy Sleys
**Project Coordination, Text Design, and Electronic
  Page Makeup:** Karpagam Jagadeesan/GGS Higher Education Resources,
  A Divison of Premedia Global, Inc.
Cover Designer: Margaret Kenselaar
Cover Illustration/Photo: Narinder Nanu/AFP/Getty Images
Manufacturing Buyer: Kathy Sleys
Printer and Binder: R.R. Donnelley & Sons, Inc.

For permission to use copyrighted material, grateful acknowledgment is made
to the copyright holders on pp. 225–227, which are hereby made part of this
copyright page.

Library of Congress Cataloging-in-Publication Data

Cullick, Jonathan S.
  A longman topics reader: religion in the twenty-first century/
Jonathan S. Cullick.
      p. cm.
  ISBN-13: 978-0-205-56779-9 (alk. paper)
  ISBN-10: 0-205-56779-7 (alk. paper)
  1. Religion—History—21st century. I. Title.
  BL98.C85 2009
  200.9'0511—dc22

                                                         2008042636

Please visit us at www.pearsonhighered.com

ISBN 13: 978-0-205-56779-9
ISBN 10:   0-205-56779-7

  2 3 4 5 6 7 8 9 10—DOH—11 10 09

TABLE OF CONTENTS

Preface   x

Introduction   xv

CHAPTER 1   Religion in Personal Writing   1

Introduction: How do individuals write
    about religion?   1

Ranya Idliby, Suzanne Oliver, and Priscilla Warner,
    The Faith Club: A Muslim, A Christian, A Jew—
    Three Women Search for Understanding   3

    Three mothers form a group to learn, and
    to help their children learn, about each other's faith.
    Questions about Content and Rhetorical Analysis

Patricia Monaghan, Physics and Grief   13

    Monaghan struggles to find meaning in the death of
    her husband.
    Questions about Content and Rhetorical Analysis

Lindsey Crittenden, The Water Will Hold You   29

    The writer tries to find comfort in prayer as her
    mother battles a terminal illness.
    Questions about Content and Rhetorical Analysis

Tenzin Gyatso, Freedom in Exile: The Autobiography
    of the Dalai Lama   39

    His Holiness the Dalai Lama describes how
    he became a spiritual leader and what it means
    to him.
    Questions about Content and Rhetorical Analysis

Karen Armstrong, The Spiral Staircase: My Climb
    Out of Darkness   47

    During a trip to Jerusalem, the author discovers
    beauty and compassion not only in her own religion of
    Christianity, but also in Judaism and Islam.
    Questions about Content and Rhetorical Analysis

Connecting the Readings   54
Writing Projects   55

CHAPTER 2   Religion in Sacred Writing   56

Introduction: How do written stories communicate
  religious belief?   56

Judaism, Christianity, Islam: The Abrahamic Faiths   59
Genesis 3: Temptation in the Garden of Eden   61
  Questions about Content and Rhetorical Analysis
Genesis 22: God Tests Abraham   63
  Questions about Content and Rhetorical Analysis

Judaism: The Torah   65
  God commands Jews to remember the story of their
  freedom from slavery
  Questions about Content and Rhetorical Analysis

Christianity: The New Testament   68
  The Sermon on the Mount, How to treat others, and
  the Parable of the Prodigal Son
  Questions about Content and Rhetorical Analysis

Islam: The Qur'an   71
  The story of Joseph, who was sold into slavery
  by his jealous brothers.
  Questions about Content and Rhetorical Analysis

Hinduism: The Bhagavad Gita   79
  The story of Krishna revealing himself to the warrior
  Arjuna.
  Questions about Content and Rhetorical Analysis

Buddhism: The Legend of the Buddha Shakyamuni   85
  The story of Siddhartha's birth, temptation, and
  discovery of suffering in the world.
  Questions about Content and Rhetorical Analysis

Taoism: The Tao Te Ching   90
  The riddles of the Tao: If the Tao can be understood,
  then it is not the Tao.
  Questions about Content and Rhetorical Analysis
Connecting the Readings   93
Writing Projects   93

CHAPTER 3   Religion in Academic Writing   95

Introduction: How do academic disciplines write
about matters of religion?   95

Literary Studies   97
Jack Miles, What Makes God Godlike?   98
The author explores God as a character who is
unlike any other character.

Questions about Content and Rhetorical Analysis

Psychology   102
Steven Pinker, The Evolutionary Psychology of Religion   103
The author explores how the human mind is "wired"
to form beliefs.

Questions about Content and Rhetorical Analysis

Sociology   113
Christian Smith, *Robert Faris*, *Melinda Lundquist
Denton*, and *Mark Regnerus*, Mapping American
Adolescent Subjective Religiosity and Attitudes of
Alienation toward Religion   114
Researchers survey the attitudes of teenagers
and college students.

Questions about Content and Rhetorical Analysis

Economics   123
Laurence R. Iannaccone, Progress in the
Economics of Religion   124
An economist proposes that economics can be used
to understand religious choices and the
"marketplace" of religion.

Questions about Content and Rhetorical Analysis
Connecting the Readings   134
Writing Projects   135

CHAPTER 4   Religion in Public Issues   136

Introduction: How are issues of religion written
about in a pluralistic society?   136

Topic 1: What should the role of religion be
in American society?   138

Jim Wallis, Take Back the Faith   **139**
  Questions about Content and Rhetorical Analysis

Jeff Jacoby, Atheists' Bleak Alternative   **142**
  Questions about Content and Rhetorical Analysis
Connecting the Readings   145

Topic 2: Is the United States a religious nation?   **145**
Robin Morgan, Fighting Words for a Secular America   **146**
  *Questions about Content and Rhetorical
  Analysis*

Student Essay, Is America a Religious Country?   **152**
  *Questions about Content and Rhetorical
  Analysis*
Connecting the Readings   158

**Topic 3: What is our responsibility to the
  environment?**   **158**
Evangelical Climate Initiative, Climate Change: An
  Evangelical Call to Action   **159**

Cornwall Alliance for the Stewardship of Creation,
  The Cornwall Declaration   **164**
Connecting the Readings: Questions about Content and Rhetorical
  Analysis   168

**Topic 4: Is there a "Culture War" over
  Christmas?**   **168**
Adam Cohen, This Season's War Cry: Commercialize
  Christmas, or Else   **169**
  Questions about Content and Rhetorical Analysis

David Frum, "The Lord of Misrule" is Coming to Town   **172**
  Questions about Content and Rhetorical Analysis
Connecting the Readings   175
Writing Projects   175

CHAPTER 5   Religion in Expository Writing   177

Introduction: How are new cultural trends
  changing what we write about religion?   **177**

Popular Culture's Effect on Religion   **178**

Jonathan S. Cullick, The Multimedia Spiritual
  Experience: Popular Culture and Faith   179
  The writer explores the impact of new developments
  such as electronic Bibles, video games, web sites,
  and mega-churches.
  Questions about Content and Rhetorical Analysis

The Growth of Islam in the United States   188
Michael Wolfe, How Does It Feel?   189
  The author describes what life is like for a Muslim in
  the U.S. after 9/11.
  Questions about Content and Rhetorical Analysis

Ingrid Mattson, Discovering (not Uncovering) the
  Spirituality of Muslim Women   193
  The writer reflects upon the spiritual significance,
  and Western misperceptions, of the headscarf
  that many Muslim women wear.
  Questions about Content and Rhetorical Analysis
Connecting the Readings   196

New Discoveries in the Science of Faith   197
Paul Davies, E.T. and God   198
  A scientists speculates: if we find life elsewhere in
  the universe, what effect will that discovery have on
  faith and religion here on earth?
  Questions about Content and Rhetorical Analysis

Paul Bloom, Is God an Accident?   209
  Using neuroscience, genetics, and evolutionary
  psychology, a scientist explores how science might
  discover why belief exists.
  Questions about Content and Rhetorical Analysis
Connecting the Readings   224
Writing Projects   224

Credits   *225*

Amy, an articulate, engaged student, comes to my writing class one day wearing a message of protest, a T-shirt featuring the picture of an upside-down American flag. In a font resembling handwriting, these words appear scrawled in the stripes of the flag:

My kingdom is not of this world

No one can serve two masters

Blessed are the meek

Woe to you who are rich

Blessed are the poor

Love your enemies

An inverted flag is a widely recognizable symbol of distress. When political or religious groups annex that symbol into their messages, the jarring, even transgressive appearance of the image adds urgency to their cultural critique. In this particular flag image, the lines from the Sermon on the Mount and the Beatitudes function as corrective statements that accuse American culture of misplacing priorities, emphasizing wealth over spiritual growth, neglecting the poor, and failing to make peace.

This flag patch, Amy explains to me, is an emblem of the Psalters, which I later discover is an indie punk music group similar to other groups in the alt-evangelical movement. This group's music and punk iconography appeal to those who seek meaning in alternatives to the mainstream religious marketplace. Following a pattern that dates back to the first century A.D., these young believers are finding membership—to borrow Stephen Carter's term from *The Culture of Disbelief*—in a *community of resistance*.

As teachers of writing, how would we react if the student wearing the T-shirt were to use those quotations mentioned earlier to support her thesis in a research paper on poverty in America? Would we assure her that we make no personal judgments about her faith while telling her that such expressions have no place in evidence-based academic writing? Would we tell her that an academic assignment is a rhetorical situation that excludes religious expression? Would we be concerned that her reliance upon a scripture sacred to her might suggest an avoidance of critical thinking? And when she submitted the revised draft with all religious references excised, would we feel confident that she had understood the role of faith in academic discourse? Is it possible that we would also sense that she had excised something of herself from her own writing?

"Faith comes in with the people who populate a composition class," we are reminded in *Negotiating Religious Faith in the Composition Classroom* (Vander Lei & Kyburz 6). It also affects what they write in that class. Like our students' other identities, their religious identities, Lizabeth Rand observes, shape the texts they create. In fact, "spiritual identity may be the primary kind of selfhood that more than a few [students] draw upon in making meaning of their lives and the world" (Rand 350).

Because faith identification has this kind of primacy for our students, we must become more intentional with our responses to the texts they create. Rand suggests, "Even if we don't finally believe in an Absolute Truth or perhaps in a God that asks of us to be 'born again,' we should recognize that many of our students do and that approaching their texts with more knowledge about their religious identities might be the most effective and inviting way to connect with them as people and as writers" (Rand 353). Whether we are adherents of religions different from our students' or adherents to no religion at all, we must become mindful of the ways in which our position as faculty constructs our response.

If we choose to exclude a discourse of religious faith from the classroom with the intent of adopting a position of neutrality, we are taking a position that only validates another normative discourse. "What's the effect of our asking students to keep their faith at home or lock it in the car?" Elizabeth Vander Lei asks. "It suggests to students that to succeed in our composition courses, they must deny who they are: as a result, they may find little reason to engage with either the writing or the other individuals in the composition classroom" (4). That lack of engagement is a high price to pay.

It may also be an unnecessary price. As Amy's T-shirt shows, religious discourse might be a resource that we have overlooked. Her shirt shows that she is intellectually engaged with her world, and her faith is the basis of that engagement. She is concerned about war in the Middle East and keeps herself informed about current developments. She cannot ignore poverty in communities not far from her university campus. She is aware of carbon emissions and the price of oil and wants to be a responsible steward of the environment as a productive contributor to the economy. She takes an oppositional but hopeful stance toward the culture she has grown up in, and the source of that stance is her religious faith. The distressed American flag and the text superimposed upon it are not merely a discursive act from the bohemian margins of popular culture; they are more deeply statements of her core identity, her faith. For students like Amy, faith does not prevent them from thinking critically about social justice. On the contrary, it is the very stuff of their critical thought.

Now, I will not naively argue that faith always works this way in the classroom or in the public square! We certainly see statements of faith employed in political argument as a protective tool to avoid intellectual engagement. But new scholarship in composition pedagogy is suggesting we instructors of writing are avoiding engagement with our students' expressions of faith. Because we want our students to practice the skills of reasoning and analyzing from empirical evidence, those expressions concern us and might even make us feel uneasy or defensive. Sometimes our reactions are valid and appropriate. However, sometimes they are not. New scholarship in our field is challenging the assumption that students using religious discourse are lacking in critical consciousness. Rand argues that "religion, rightfully understood, is a subversive force," a force standing in resistance to the secular world. In modeling skills of critical thought, writing instructors can appeal to that oppositional nature of faith (Rand 361).

We can also begin to strategize ways to negotiate conflicts of religious difference in student writing and classroom discussion. In an article that I highly recommend for anyone who teaches or administers writing courses, Elizabeth Vander Lei and Lauren Fitzgerald recommend ways to resolve misunderstandings that originate from the best intentions of faculty and administrators. In our concern for safeguarding the rights of students and faculty and protecting everyone's privacy, we have disallowed or discouraged discussions about religion in the classroom. Yet the First Amendment neither prevents nor compels such discussion, and many students do want to talk about faith and "apply those intellectual tools [what they learn in school] to the supposedly private aspects of their lives" (190). In our concern for teaching critical thinking skills, we may have created a "false separation of intellect and belief." Instead, "we might consider what possibilities are opened by beginning with students' religious literacies" (189). Vander Lei and Fitzgerald recommend that writing programs create local guidelines for classroom conduct to ensure respect for all faiths. For example, one guideline might stipulate that students and instructors should not attempt to convert or dismiss the beliefs of others (191).

The most engaging point they make addresses pedagogy, empowering instructors to overcome anxiety about responding to statements of faith. They suggest that we *can* critique faith-based arguments or "challenge those who lob religion-based argumentative grenades into public discussion and then retreat behind an imagined 'wall of separation' " (192).

As I have tried to demonstrate in this book, those critiques and challenges might be found in a rhetorical approach to faith-based texts. So, for example, when a student quotes scripture in her essay, we can challenge her to identify and interrogate her rhetorical decisions. We can ask her: Why have you chosen to use this quotation? Is your use of scripture an appeal based in ethos or pathos? If so, who are your readers and what effect might the quotation have upon them? Could the effect be different from what you intend or expect? Is your use of scripture an appeal to logos? If so, what additional or other reasons and evidence would your thesis need? As teachers of writing, questioning our student's faith lies outside the scope of our role, but questioning their use of faith as an act of rhetoric is our responsibility.

This textbook gives teachers a tool for classroom discussions and writing assignments that explore how language determines and shapes the ways we engage with faith. The readings have been selected to invite students to discover how faith and religion are written about in many kinds of texts—personal, sacred, and academic texts—as well as argumentation in the public square and the discourse of popular culture. The questions about content and rhetoric that follow each reading apply critical thinking tools to faith-based texts. The writing projects give students and instructors strategies to explore how faith shapes writing and how writing shapes faith.

ACKNOWLEDGMENTS

I am grateful to have received encouragement and suggestions from several of my colleagues at Northern Kentucky University: Rudy Garns, Danny Miller, Joan Ferrante, Doug Krull, and Peg Adams. John Alberti, our department's assistant chair, deserves special acknowledgement for suggesting that I take a rhetorical approach to religious discourse. I am appreciative to all of my students for exploring these topics with me, especially the students in my Mayerson Student Philanthropy Project classes, the Faith and Philosophy honors learning communities, and the Bible as Literature course. Asra Husejnovic of the NKU Muslim Student Association and Mohammed Abdul Aleem of Islamicity graciously offered me advice, and readers from composition programs and religious studies programs around the country, including Jeffrey P. Cain (Sacred Heart University), Brett McInelly (Brigham Young University), and Richard A. Pruitt (Columbia College), provided invaluable recommendations on the manuscript. At Pearson

Longman, Lynn Huddon helped me to get the project started, Virginia Blanford assisted and encouraged me in seeing the project to completion, and Karpagam Jagadeesan guided me through the production process. My deepest gratitude goes to my wife, Cheryl, whose love, support, and patience made this book possible.

Works Cited

Vander Lei, Elizabeth and Bonnie Lenore Kyburz, eds. *Negotiating Religious Faith in the Composition Classroom*. Portsmouth, New Hampshire: Boynton/Cook Heinemann, 2005.

Vander Lei, Elizabeth and Lauren Fitzgerald. "What in God's Name? Administering the Conflicts of Religious Belief in Writing Programs." *WPA: Journal of the Council of Writing Program Administrators*. 31.1/2 (Fall/Winter 2007): 185–195.

Rand, Lizabeth A. "Enacting Faith: Evangelical Discourse and the Discipline of Composition Studies." *College Composition and Communication* 52.3 (February 2001): 349–367.

JONATHAN S. CULLICK
Northern Kentucky University

INTRODUCTION

WHY FAITH AND RELIGION IN A WRITING COURSE?

What is the purpose of life? How did the world come into being? Does God exist? Why do people suffer? What do I believe? How do I figure out what is right and what is wrong? Where do I stand on today's major social issues? These questions are not electives in your education or extras in your life. After securing the basics of survival, these are, quite simply, among the most essential questions any human being can ask. How we answer these questions determines how we act, the choices we make, the relationships we form, and even the careers we choose.

This book invites you to use some of the most enduring and engaging topics in your writing assignments, research projects, and class discussions. The readings ask you to explore how writing shapes what we believe and how belief shapes what we write. Various kinds of writing are included here—personal stories, sacred texts, and academic essays—as well as writing in the public square and in popular culture.

WHAT IS A RHETORICAL APPROACH TO FAITH AND RELIGION?

Rhetoric is the use of speech or writing to achieve a purpose such as informing or persuading others. Like all other topics, faith and religion depend on language; we encounter them and enact them through written and spoken communication. Whenever we communicate about faith and religion, we decide what to say or what not to say, how to say it or how not to say it. We make decisions about what information to include, what to omit, what order to put it all in, what words to use, and what tone to take. As you read what the writers in this book say, also notice how they say it. Here are just a few examples of the rhetoric of faith.

Personal Writing

Because writing is a tool for exploring ideas, personal writing has always been central to religious faith. As we write, we find out what we think. Three mothers—Jewish, Christian, Muslim—got together to have conversations about teaching their children about their religions. They wrote about their experiences and put their stories into a book. They also created a guide for anyone who wants to create their own "faith club." For these women, the decision to write was a crucial part of understanding their own religions and the religions of others.

Sacred Writing

The writers of ancient texts shaped what they wrote for their audiences. Jesus would often answer a question by telling a story, called a parable, which would communicate a lesson by presenting a situation and calling upon the listener to discover what the story had to teach. The Tao Te Ching, the sacred text of the Asian religion of Taoism, consists of short poems that present images, observations, insights, and even contradictions similar to riddles, which challenge a reader to discover the meaning. In these and other texts, writers shaped their material in ways that would call upon listeners or readers to participate in the lesson.

Writing in the Disciplines

The different methods various academic fields use to write about religion reflect their different approaches to the world. For example, a psychologist who is interested in neuroscience, such as Steven Pinker, explores how the mind is structured or "wired" to adopt beliefs. A scholar in literary studies, such as Jack Miles, will read a sacred text as a work of literature. Miles treats God as a character and analyzes him in relation to the other characters. In his unique perspective, God is unlike any other character in literature because he must create other characters or there will be no story to read!

RELIGION IN AMERICAN UNIVERSITIES

Take this short quiz. Question one, what is the holy book of Islam and who is its prophet? Question two, in what religion will you find the Vedas and Upanishads? Number three, what is Yom Kippur and what religion celebrates it? Four, what is "tao"? Five, who was Siddhartha Gautama? Finally, list all of the Ten Commandments.

How did you do on the quiz? If these questions challenged you, then you are not alone. Students in Professor Stephen Prothero's religious studies course begin every semester with a quiz like this, and he reports that most of them fail. Fortunately, it is not a graded quiz, the purpose being to let the students test themselves. You can read the entire quiz in his book, *Religious Literacy*.

College students are not the only ones who have difficulty with these kinds of questions. Some people in positions of authority, who are responsible for making decisions that affect many others, lack basic knowledge about American and world religions. A reporter with *The Decatur Daily*, M.J. Ellington, contacted ten state senators in Alabama who had co-sponsored a bill to allow the Ten Commandments to be displayed inside the state capitol building. When Ellington asked these legislators to name all of the commandments, only one of them could do so. On his Comedy Central show, Steven Colbert, a comic actor posing as a journalist, gave an on-camera pop quiz to one of the U.S. representatives from Georgia, who co-sponsored a bill to require Congress to display the Ten Commandments in the U.S. House and Senate chambers. Asked to recite the commandments, this politician was barely able to list half of them.

The stakes are higher in foreign policy. Before the U.S. invasion of Iraq, many people who were familiar with the religious history of the Middle East feared that a long period of violence would ignite between Sunni and Shiite Muslims in Iraq. As this prediction became reality, Jeff Stein, the national security editor of the *Congressional Quarterly*, wondered: do government officials responsible for resolving this conflict understand the tensions between the two sides? He contacted some of those officials in Congress, federal law enforcement, and intelligence agencies in Washington, D.C., and he asked them some basic questions: What is the difference between a Sunni and a Shiite? Is Al Qaeda, the terrorist organization that attacked the United States on September 11, 2001, Sunni or Shiite? Is Iran mostly Sunni or Shiite? Anyone involved in Middle East foreign policy should have this fundamental knowledge, yet very few of the officials were able to provide the correct answers.

Some critics hold America's schools responsible for neglecting to teach students about the variety of world religions and the role of religion in world history. Prothero ironically notes that "Americans are both deeply religious and profoundly ignorant about religion," and he recommends that schools add courses about religion to their curricula (1). Critics of higher education have argued that universities, which ought to teach college students about diverse world cultures, have failed to teach them about one of the most important forces that contribute to a culture: religion. In the *Chronicle of Higher Education*, psychologist Robert N. Sollod has observed, "The curricula that most undergraduates study do little to rectify the fact that many

Americans are ignorant of religious and spiritual teachings, of their significance in the history of this and other civilizations, and of their significance in contemporary society." As a teacher, he is concerned that "students with spiritual interests and concerns learn that the university will not validate or feed their interests. They learn either to suppress their spiritual life or to split their spiritual life apart from their formal education."

Many students want to learn and write about world religions and religious issues facing the nation. In one report, "Chaplains, professors and administrators say students are drawn to religion and spirituality with more fervor than at any time they can remember." A 2004 survey of first-year college students by the Higher Education Research Institute at the University of California shows that more than 80 percent believe in the existence of a higher power of some kind, and about 50 percent indicate they want to grow spiritually. Around the country, students are filling courses in comparative religion and the Bible as literature, and they are joining religiously affiliated organizations and residence halls on campuses (Finder 2007).

WHY FAITH IN THE CLASSROOM IS CONTROVERSIAL

A classroom can be a place of struggle. The instructor presents new ideas to students, and students present their opinions to each other and to the instructor as well. Sometimes these ideas and opinions make members of a class uncomfortable precisely because they are unfamiliar and contradict previously held perceptions and values. Because faith is so deeply rooted in an individual's sense of identity and purpose in life, faith may seem to be too "touchy" to bring into this kind of environment.

Consider this typical situation: the use of faith-based evidence in a persuasive research paper. An instructor requires the students to support their opinions by locating and using sources that offer valid, up-to-date, empirical evidence such as real-life examples and statistics from reliable sources. The instructor's job is to challenge students to support arguments more effectively, which might mean raising questions about the reliability or credibility of the evidence. What happens if a student uses, for support, quotations from scripture such as the Qur'an, the Vedas, the Torah, or the New Testament? When the evidence is Holy Scripture, how can the instructor raise questions without offending the student?

Writing instructor Juanita Smart had a student who used religious language that was very judgmental toward others, including the instructor herself. In respect to her student, she did not want to silence or prohibit his efforts. At the same time, she wondered how she could conduct a dialogue with a student who did not think she had anything worthwhile to say because of their differences in faith (18–19). Maybe this is why instructors have preferred to avoid topics of faith. To keep the classroom open to all ideas and opinions, Smart says, "we resist the voice of faith in an effort to prevent alienating and exclusionary rhetorics from dominating the discussion" (22).

At its best, faith is inclusive and life affirming. Faith has helped human beings find purpose and meaning and provided individuals with a code of ethics and courage for humanitarian reform. Religious institutions have played central roles in social justice movements such as the abolition of slavery, reform in the treatment of prisoners, the civil rights movement, and efforts to relieve poverty and end war. But as world history unfortunately demonstrates, too often people have used faith to justify a sense of complacency and self-righteousness, even prejudice and the exclusion of others, and in more extreme circumstances, acts of aggression such as war and terrorism. In trying to keep universities places that are safe for free inquiry, debate, and open expression—all of which are sometimes anathema to systems of certainty and authority—instructors have understandably steered away from issues of faith and their potential to cause offense. The problem is that their efforts, however well intentioned, can make students feel that the university is not open to any expressions of their faith.

USING THIS BOOK

Aware of the potential negatives, a teacher wants to make sure that the classroom is an inclusive environment for students of all faiths and students of no faith. This is where you as a student are responsible for the atmosphere of the classroom. When you write and talk about faith and religion, keep these principles in mind.

- Be respectful.
- Be curious.
- Be mindful.
- Be amazed.

Be Respectful

To be intellectually honest and respectful of others, we must acknowledge that we live in a pluralistic world. The term *pluralism* means the presence of more than one idea, principle, concept, or opinion. Some people fear pluralism and want to limit it. Others find it energizing and want to promote it. Ultimately, pluralism will exist regardless of how we react to it. As long as there is more than one human being in the world, there will be more than one way to think about things.

Pluralism does not mean that all ideas are equally valid. Indeed, you must weigh the reasonableness of every idea you encounter. This is why all people—even those who embrace pluralism—discuss, debate, and argue their opinions. What is important is to weigh those opinions in an open, respectful manner.

P. M. Forni's book, *Choosing Civility*, observes that all people regardless of opinion, creed, religion, belief, culture, or nationality have in common their desire to be treated respectfully and fairly. Forni, a founder of the Johns Hopkins Civility Project, which has studied the good and bad manners of our culture, makes a point that we can apply to a writing course. We may disagree, but we need not communicate our disagreements in a disagreeable manner.

In her autobiography, *The Spiral Staircase*, Karen Armstrong puts this idea into a religious context. After spending many years studying religions of the world, she discovered one concept that all great religions, regardless of their many differences, have in common: the need to overcome self-centeredness, to feel compassion toward others, and to treat others with respect. Considering how much conflict exists on earth, Armstrong argues that the world would become more peaceful if there were less certitude and self-righteousness and more "compassionate action and practically expressed respect for the sacred value of all human beings, even our enemies" (304).

Intelligent, informed, sincere people can and will disagree or view matters differently, but they can agree to talk and write to each other in a civil manner. In so doing, we can all open the doors for agreement or compromise to take place. In class discussion and in all of your writing, including writing assignments, formal assignments, email correspondence, and discussion boards, be respectful and courteous. It is the right thing to do; plus, showing respect to your audience will make you more persuasive.

Be Curious

We all seek certainty and confirmation that our ideas are true and our opinions are valid, but an academic setting provides us with the opportunity to question our own certainties. Learning does not happen when you are presented with ideas or opinions you already possess; it happens when you are offered new concepts and perspectives. A college math or foreign language or writing course would be of little use to you if it did nothing more than review skills you learned in high school.

But learning a new skill has a cost; it requires hard work and patience to overcome the frustration. Discovering a new opinion or concept about religion in a history, literature, psychology, sociology, or biology course may feel awkward. This is normal because the longer we hold an idea in our minds, the more comfortable we become with it. True education challenges you to think critically, creatively, uniquely, and "outside the box." Such a challenge can make you feel uneasy, especially if the idea being challenged relates to deeply held beliefs such as religious faith.

To negotiate this challenge, it may help to think of two types of culture: *the culture of affirmation* and *the culture of inquiry*. These terms are borrowed from an essay by Douglas Downs, a professor of rhetoric and composition. As Downs explains, a culture of affirmation confirms what we believe, assuring us that the views we hold are true. A culture of inquiry questions what we believe; in that culture, we explore and possibly even change or modify what we believe.

A culture of affirmation is a reassuring environment that gives us a sense of community and familiarity. Holidays, celebrations, rituals, and rites of passage such as graduation ceremonies and weddings give us a sense of comfort and direction as we navigate our ways through the major changes of life. Groups such as churches, synagogues, and mosques, or fraternities, sororities, and student organizations give us the security of community. A culture of affirmation confirms the truths we want to live by. In a culture of inquiry, however, that which is believed to be true, valid, and useful is open to question and revision. When a teacher or a spiritual leader challenges our assumptions or previous ways of thinking, we have stepped into a culture of inquiry.

A common example of the culture of inquiry is the ever-changing field of computer science. Academic courses in the sciences teach students the concepts that have progressed through the history of science, but they also teach students how to question those concepts so they can design newer, faster, more efficient software in the future. Similarly, the field of history not only teaches what we currently know but also how to question that knowledge, as historians are always making new discoveries that expand our understanding of the past. The humanities and sciences depend upon foundations of knowledge constructed throughout the past, yet they continue to rebuild those foundations by scrutinizing past knowledge and making it subject to verification or disproof.

In fact, what we think of as common knowledge may have been created in the past by thinkers who questioned the knowledge that came before them.

Historically, the processes of affirmation and inquiry have shaped knowledge about religion. The fields of archaeology, anthropology, sociology, psychology, history, economics, theology, and literary studies have expanded and changed what we know about the development, beliefs, scriptures, and doctrines of religions.

Some students might worry that a culture of inquiry threatens faith. It is true that by questioning and thinking critically, you might begin to alter your beliefs. You might not be the same at the end of the process as you were at the beginning. Learning can be a transformative experience.

But transformation can be more exciting than threatening. You can also come to understand your beliefs more deeply. Francis Collins is a nationally and internationally recognized biologist who was director of one of the most ambitious scientific projects of our time, the Human Genome Project. His book, *The Language of God*, argues that science and faith are compatible and even mutually enhancing. "God's domain is in the spiritual world," he says, "a realm not possible to explore with the tools and language of science" (6). Of course, some scientists—theists and atheists alike—will disagree with this claim, but the point here is that there are writers, such as Collins, who find that it is possible to work for re-conciliation and harmony between seemingly opposing ideas.

Astronomer Carl Sagan saw no disparity between having a sense of the sacred and questioning everything. He believed that the world is much greater than the ability of human beings to understand it, and this gives us a sense of the divine. Because our understanding of the world is always partial, he argued, we must be humble about what we think we know. Remembering him lovingly many years after his death, his wife recalls, "He never understood why anyone would want to separate science, which is just a way of searching for what is true, from what we hold sacred, which are those truths that inspire love and awe" (xi). Sagan called science "informed worship": the act of using our natural, intellectual gifts to explore, appreciate, and be amazed by the world we live in.

Be Mindful

Being mindful means being aware of what you are doing when you write. It means making conscious, deliberate decisions.

When we feel strongly about a topic, we might feel tempted to argue our opinion passionately, even to the point of attacking anyone who disagrees. That strategy might give us a sense of self-satisfaction, but if our goal is to be persuasive, it will fail. Think for a moment about a time when someone tried to persuade you to change your mind about something. Did they insult you, throw sarcasm at you, accuse you of being ignorant, or imply that you were somehow not a good person or a loyal citizen? If they did that, how did you react? You probably did not say, "Thank you for insulting me and calling me names. You have helped me realize that I was wrong. You have convinced me to change my mind!"

Many cable television personality shows, radio talk shows, blogs and other web sites yell and rant, accuse and insinuate, and imply or declare that their opponents lack intelligence or morality. The intended audience for these sensational kinds of media is most likely an audience that already agrees with them. They are not likely to convince an audience that disagrees.

Addressing a sympathetic audience does not require much skill. Winning the support of an audience that is ambivalent or not in agreement takes more careful and sophisticated effort. It requires balance and nuance. In your college writing assignments, assume that your audience is well informed, reasonable, and diverse in backgrounds, values, and opinions. If you practice making effective decisions to pull that kind of audience toward your way of thinking, you will be able to rise to more occasions and address yourself to more people, which will ultimately make you more persuasive. You will have what Shannon Carter calls "rhetorical dexterity," the ability to communicate in a variety of situations whether in school or in a religious community.

Being convincing to those who do not see the world as you do is not just a matter of being right or having valid reasons. It also depends on communicating in a way that makes others want to listen to you. Shane Claiborne, an evangelical minister who has been appealing to college students and other young people, puts it this way:

> If there is anything I've learned from both conservatives and liberals, it's that we can have all the "right" answers and still be mean. And when you're mean, it's hard for people to listen to, much less desire, your truth. We have nothing to fear from people who disagree with us. Folks who see things differently from us are our best teachers.

Writers like Claiborne have realized that they can be much more effective if they can understand their audience and speak or write in a way that will appeal to those they wish to address. They try to respect the people they talk to. They avoid statements that might alienate those they want to reach. They use language that will appeal to their listeners' values.

The instructor mentioned earlier, Juanita Smart, had a student who may have meant well, but the language he was using created distance, making communication less effective. "What seems so clear to me, but what my student may not yet understand," Smart observes, "is that much of the religious discourse he invokes is verbal code that can be estranging to an audience not conversant in that code", (Smart 18). Many religious people believe in sharing their faith with others as an act of love. The desire to enlighten or empower someone with faith, especially someone who is going through hard times, may be well intended. However, despite those good intentions, other people, who embrace their own faiths, may feel offended or alienated by such an attempt. When writing to an audience with similar beliefs, the writer has less to worry about in appealing to beliefs. That situation changes when writing to a diverse audience—and diversity means not only people of different religions but also people with different ideas about the same religion. In these situations, using religious appeals or scriptural quotations could potentially make an argument less effective.

A conscientious writing instructor knows that a writer using appeals to religion might be less effective with some audiences. The instructor must point this out to the student because teachers of writing are responsible for preparing students to write successfully as members of diverse campuses, work places, and civic communities.

A writer who cares about what she is communicating will invest herself—her values and her faith—into her writing. At the same time, an effective writer will always consider the possible consequences of her writing. She will consider whether or not her writing will have the desired effect upon the reader. She will try to learn about her audience's experiences, values, and beliefs. She will shape what she is writing so it will have the maximum effect. Anything less will make the writing less effective in accomplishing the writer's goals. It is therefore important to keep in mind that an instructor who challenges the way you are writing about a particular topic is helping you become more persuasive about matters of faith.

Be Amazed

Carl Sagan, the astronomer mentioned earlier, was not only a respected scientist, he was also a superb writer. He could describe a solar system's movements or a star's birth so vividly that reading his work is like reading an action-adventure story set in the heavens. The key to his success as a scientist and as a writer is probably that he chose to spend his time studying and writing about things that fascinated him. Then he shared that fascination with his readers. "By far the best way I know to engage the religious sensibility, the sense of awe," Sagan said, "is to look up on a clear night" (2). That sense of awe could be a model for all students in a writing class. Be alive with curiosity. Search for answers. Courageously question what already seems answered. Finally, to be the best college writer you can be, write about the things that amaze you.

Answers to the Questions

1. The Qur'an (Koran) is the holy book of Islam, and Muhammad is the prophet.

2. The Vedas and Upanishads are collections of sacred writings in Hinduism.

3. Yom Kippur is the "Day of Atonement," a major holiday of Judaism.

4. "Tao" is the power of the universe and source of life, literally the "way" or "path," central to Taoism.

5. Siddhartha Gautama was the Buddha, who left the life of privilege he was born into so he could seek enlightenment.

The order and wording of the Ten Commandments differ slightly according to different religions and translations of the Bible, but generally they consist of these:

1. I am the Lord your God, you shall not have any other gods before me;

2. You shall not make graven images (idols);

3. You shall not take the name of the Lord in vain;

4. Remember the Sabbath day and keep it holy;

5. Honor your parents;

6. You shall not kill;

7. You shall not commit adultery;

8. You shall not steal;

9. You shall not bear false witness against (or tell lies about) your neighbor;

10. You shall not covet (or desire) anything that belongs to your neighbor.

Works Cited

Armstrong, Karen. *The Spiral Staircase: My Climb Out of Darkness.* New York: Random House, 2004.

Douglas Downs: "True Believers, Real Scholars, and Real True Believing Scholars." Vander Lei and Kyburz 39–55.

Carter, Shannon. "Living Inside the Bible (Belt)." *College English* 69.6 (July 2007): 572–595.

Claiborne, Shane. "Don't Fear Disagreement." God's Politics: A Blog by Jim Wallis and Friends. February 8, 2008. April 29, 2008. http://blog.beliefnet.com/godspolitics/2008/02/dont-fear-disagreement-by-shan.html.

Collins, Francis. *The Language of God.* New York: Free Press, 2006.

Ellington, M.J. "Thou Shalt Debate: Lawmakers Wrestle with Issue of Displaying Commandments." *The Decatur Daily*, 31 July, 2005. http://www.decaturdaily.com/decaturdaily/news/050731/debate.shtml.

Finder, Alan. "Matters of Faith Find a New Prominence on Campus." *New York Times*, May 2, 2007. www.nytimes.com May 2007.

Forni, P. M. *Choosing Civility: The Twenty-Five Rules of Considerate Conduct.* New York: St. Martin's Press, 2002.

Prothero, Stephen. *Religious Literacy: What Every American Needs to Know—And Doesn't.* New York: Harper Collins, 2007.

Sagan, Carl. *The Varieties of Scientific Experience: A Personal View of the Search for God.* Edited with an introduction by Ann Druyan. New York: Penguin Press, 2006.

Smart, Juanita M. "Frankenstein or Jesus Christ? When the Voice of Faith Creates a Monster for the Composition Teacher." Vander Lei and Kyburz 11–23.

Sollod, Robert N. "The Hollow Curriculum: The Place of Religion and Spirituality in Society is Too Often Missing." *The Chronicle of Higher Education*, March 18, 1992. www.chronicle.org 12 April 2007.

Stein, Jeff. "Can You Tell a Sunni from a Shiite?" *New York Times*, October 17, 2006. http://www.nytimes.com.

Steinfels, Peter. "Beliefs: When Higher Education Lost Its Bearings, It Might Also Have Forfeited Its Primacy in American Life." *New York Times*, July 8, 2006. www.nytimes.com, May 2, 2007.

Vander Lei, Elizabeth and Bonnie Lenore Kyburz, eds. *Negotiating Religious Faith in the Composition Classroom.* Portsmouth, New Hampshire: Boynton/Cook Heinemann, 2005.

Religion in Personal Writing

How do individuals write about religion?

BACKGROUND

Religion has always been a cornerstone of communities. Buddhists come together in a sangha to listen to dharma talks and meditate. Jews meet in temples and synagogues to study and worship. Muslims worship together in mosques and gather in large numbers for the annual pilgrimage to the Ka'ba in Mecca. Christians congregate in churches for worship and fellowship. People of faith throughout the world form communities to support the study and practice of their religious traditions.

As much as religion is a characteristic of community, and as much as community is a characteristic of religion, so too is faith a personal matter. Although individuals are often deeply influenced by the faiths of their families and neighbors, the decision to adopt a particular faith is ultimately a matter of personal choice. World history shows that people under dictatorial powers can be coerced to conform outwardly or forced to perform religious practices, but no one can be coerced or forced into inwardly adopting a form of faith. As a matter subject only to the individual's mind, heart, and conscience, faith is always deeply personal.

Because each person comes to her own faith in her own way, there is a long history of writing about faith. One of the earliest and most celebrated of these narratives is the *Confessions*, written by Augustine, Bishop of Hippo, in the fifth century C.E. A famous episode in Augustine's narrative occurs in his youth, when he joins other boys in stealing pears from a neighbor's yard. As he describes the incident, they steal the fruit not because they are hungry but simply because it is wrong. He wants to do something forbidden precisely because he wants to feel some exhilaration from violating another person's property. However, instead of feeling good, he feels guilty, and more than that, he feels a sense of failure. Stealing is easy, he realizes, because it means surrendering to temptation. Respecting others would bring him a true sense of self-worth. At this moment he becomes aware of something greater than himself, a sense of higher morality that guides the thoughts and actions of all humanity. For Augustine, this incident becomes an opportunity for self-reflection and ultimately conversion and faith. Augustine wanted his readers to use his story to learn about themselves and to explore their own sense of faith.

Augustine's *Confessions* became a kind of touchstone for future writers of personal, spiritual narratives. To this day, it is possible to survey autobiographies in the religion section of book-stores and find many personal narratives about spiritual struggles. Readers enjoy autobiographies because they enable us to learn about the lives of those who have overcome crises. We may read the life story of a famous politician, athlete, scientist, inventor, or business leader as a way of considering how we, too, might resolve problems. So, too, we can read spiritual autobiographies to learn ways we might deal with problems that challenge our faith.

Before the personal narrative reaches the reader, it serves a purpose for the writer: it allows the writer to explore his or her own spiritual journey. If you have ever kept a diary or journal, if you have ever sent a text message or email to ask a friend about a prob-lem you were dealing with, or if you have ever taken part in an online chat room for people looking for advice, then you know how writing can help individuals find solutions to problems. When we write, we must search inside ourselves for a way to express ideas that sometimes seem inexpressible because they may be upsetting or confusing. Once we write those ideas down, they begin to take form. We can look at them on the computer or cell phone screen, and because they now exist not only in our minds but also outside ourselves, we can deal with them more objectively. As we revise our ideas, we delete words or move words around on the screen, which gives us real power over those ideas. Writing in any form is an instrument that can help us address and resolve challenges. When we write our spiritual autobiographies, we are using writing as a tool to work out solutions to situations that have challenged us.

AS YOU READ

In the autobiographical narratives below, writers describe their beliefs and tell the stories of how they arrived at their beliefs. Like Augustine, several of the writers refer to events in their childhood. Some of them describe times when they were challenged to find something larger than themselves to believe in. Some of them describe relying on the faith they inherited from their families or communities. Some of them describe moments of crisis or opportunity when they felt compelled toward a unique sense of faith.

You will notice many apparent differences among these selections because the writers come from various places, backgrounds, and time periods. So as you read, notice any threads of commonality running through the stories of these writers who come from such different faiths and backgrounds. You could take notes by creating a chart. Use the "table" function in your word processing program, or just use pen and paper. At the top of the page, write the name of each writer. Between each writer's name, draw a vertical line down to the bottom of the page. Now draw several horizontal lines across the page, to create a grid of rows and columns.

During your reading, notice certain traits of the narratives, such as "childhood experiences." Write those traits down the left column, and put check marks in each writer's column when you recognize that trait in a writer's spiritual narrative. As you read each passage, you may find yourself discovering a certain trait that also appears in a previous passage. In addition to putting a check mark in a cell, you could also jot down notes about how that particular aspect shows up in the writer's narrative. In the end, your chart will help you to compare and contrast the writers at a glance, and your chart may give you plenty of ideas for writing your own personal narrative.

The Faith Club:
Three Women Search for Understanding

Ranya Idliby, Suzanne Oliver, and Priscilla Warner, respectively Muslim, Christian, and Jewish, are mothers who came together out of a common concern for their children. Wanting a peaceful world for their children to thrive in, these women discovered that parents of all religions have much in common.

Worried about religious conflict in our world after witnessing the September 11 terrorist attacks and their aftermath—especially after the Muslim mother's children began to ask tough questions—these mothers wanted to teach their children about their religions. The result was the creation of what they decided to call a "faith club," a group formed for the purpose of interfaith dialogue.

They wrote about their experiences, and the result was collaboration on a book titled The Faith Club: A Muslim, A Christian,

A Jew—Three Women Search for Understanding. *This book tells the story of their conversations with each other, their questions, their debates, and their mutual concerns. The book is full of instructions for the reader. It includes "How to Start a Faith Club" with a guide of steps to follow, helpful hints to keep in mind, and discussion questions that faith clubs can use to engage in meaningful conversation. The book also provides descriptions of each of the three religions—their main beliefs, holy books, worship, prayer, rituals, and holidays.*

The web site that supplements the book, www.thefaithclub .com, features information about the book (excerpts, reviews, a reading guide), biographies and scrapbooks by the authors, resources for starting your own faith club (including a faith club kit and flyers), a blog, and a page of links to interfaith and informational web sites. You will find this page of links especially useful for research.

In the selected passage that follows, the authors write about getting together for the first time. As you read, notice what they say about their expectations and fears before that initial meeting.

---- ✦ ----

PREFACE

Meet the Faith Club. We're three mothers from three faiths—Islam, Christianity, and Judaism—who got together to write a picture book for our children that would highlight the connections between our religions. But no sooner had we started talking about our beliefs and how to explain them to our children than our differences led to misunderstandings. Our project nearly fell apart.

We realized that before we could talk about what united us we had to confront what divided us in matters of faith, God, and religion. We had to reveal our own worst fears, prejudices, and stereotypes.

So we made a commitment to meet regularly. We talked in our living rooms over cups of jasmine tea and bars of dark chocolate. No question was deemed inappropriate, no matter how rude or politically incorrect. We taped our conversations and kept journals as we discussed everything from jihad to Jesus, heaven to holy texts. Somewhere along the way; our moments of conflict, frustration, and anger gave way to new understanding and great respect.

Now we invite you into our Faith Club to eavesdrop on our conversations. Come into our living rooms and share our life-altering experience. Perhaps when you're finished, you will want to have a faith club of your own.

IN THE BEGINNING

Ranya

The phone rang on the morning of September 11th. It was my husband, screaming for me to turn on the TV. With sheer horror, I watched as the second plane hit the World Trade Center.

"Please don't let this be connected to Islam," I thought desperately.

As the city began to mourn, churches and temples opened their doors for worship and emotional support. I longed for a mosque, or a Muslim religious leader, an imam, who could help support my family during this horrific time. I needed a spiritual community, a safe haven where we could seek comfort.

Back then, I knew of no alternative Muslim voice that could represent the silent majority of Muslims, no nearby place where we could congregate. I did not feel comfortable at the mosque in our neighborhood, where women prayed separately from men. I wanted to feel respected. I longed to enter a mosque on an equal footing with Muslim men, to be treated as an equal, as I know I am in the eyes of God.

Tensions rose, and as some Muslims, or those mistaken for Muslims, were attacked or rounded up for questioning, I began to feel self-conscious about our Muslim identity. I was concerned and fearful for the security of my children as American Muslims. I avoided calling my son by his Muslim name, addressing him in public only by his nicknames, Try and Timmy. When my grandmother came to visit, I asked her not to speak Arabic in public. And when my parents were in New York, they were approached by a stranger who advised them not to speak Arabic on the street. A well-meaning friend, trying to make me feel better (and warning me not to "take it the wrong way"), told me that my family and I "don't look Muslim." This, she thought, might protect us from discrimination. What were Muslims supposed to look like, I wondered?

My husband and I were challenged on both fronts, by Muslims abroad who questioned the very possibility of a future for our children as American Muslims of Arab descent, and on the home front, by the stereotypes and prejudices that were heightened by the attacks of 9/11. On street corners, people joked about Muslim martyrs "racing to heaven to meet their brown-eyed virgins," a supposed reference to the Quran, but something I had never heard before. While we took heart from our president's visit to the mosque in Washington, D.C., we were also aware of the voices within his own administration who felt he had gone too far and who maintained that, at its core, Islam was a militant and dangerous religion. I wondered who was representing my faith.

Although my husband and I had at first chosen to spare our children the details of the attacks, we soon found out that our kindergarten-age daughter, who was the only Muslim in her class, was learning a great deal from friends at school. We explained to her that evil men who were Arab and called themselves Muslim had performed an evil deed. Since her only experience of the Arab world overseas had involved her grandparents, she anxiously asked if her grandmother knew these men or was involved in any way.

Soon thereafter, my daughter came home from school and asked me a simple question: "Do we celebrate Hanukah or Christmas?" Her friends at school wanted to know I wasn't sure how to respond. I worried that the reality of 9/11 had made it unworkable for my children to be both Muslim and American. Would their sense of belonging be compromised? Would they as Americans feel burdened by their religion and heritage? So far I'd tried to raise my children with moral character and pride in their Muslim heritage despite the fact that we did not practice many specific religious rituals or worship at a mosque. We do celebrate a commercial kind of Christmas. But we're Muslims. We believe Jesus was a prophet, not the son of God. How could I give my daughter an intelligent, clear answer that she could confidently deliver to other kindergarteners? Was there such an answer? As a concerned parent I created a challenge for myself: If I was unable to give my children good reasons why they should remain Muslims, other than out of pure ancestral loyalty, I would not ask them to remain true to Islam, a religion that had come to seem to me to be more of a burden than a privilege in America.

A student at heart, I started researching Islam looking for possible answers for my concerns. Soon, I stumbled upon the story of Muhammad's night flight journey and ascension to heaven, essentially an inter-faith vision in which Muhammad rides a magical winged horse ridden before him by Jesus, Moses, and other biblical prophets. As he ascends a jeweled staircase to the threshold of the kingdom of God, Muhammad is welcomed by various prophets as a fellow brother and prophet. Along with Jesus and Moses, he stands at the Temple Mount in Jerusalem for communal prayers.

My heart raced with excitement as I read all this. I was dumbfounded. Why weren't Muslims telling the world this story? It was the perfect way to share the beauty and true voice within Islam when so many, including many Muslims, were so desperately looking for answers. The terror of September 11th turned my alienation and frustration into anger at those who had invoked Islam to justify such heinous crimes. I felt an urgent need to do something. I could no longer be apathetic; I could no longer resign myself to just accepting the prevailing image of Islam, if only for the sake of my children. Wouldn't it be wonderful,

I thought, to find a Christian and Jewish mother to write a children's book with me that would highlight the connections within Judaism, Christianity, and Islam.

Suzanne

In the fall of 2001, I was an ex-Catholic, happily participating in a vibrant Episcopal church in New York City, when that cozy, homogeneous community was confronted in very different ways by Islam and Judaism. First, terrorists calling themselves Muslims crashed into the World Trade Center killing our neighbors, colleagues, and one parishioner. Then, days later, our neo-gothic, beautifully adorned church closed for renovation, and our Sunday services were moved to a modern synagogue, which had offered to share space with us.

As the 9/11 bombing challenged our perceptions of Islam and Muslims, our church's relocation to a temple tested our relationship with Judaism and Jews. Many of our church members went elsewhere rather than attend Sunday services there. To some, the setting was off-putting, to others a barricade-protected temple felt like a dangerous place in the aftermath of 9/11.

At the time New York was a city on high alert. Everyone speculated about how and when the terrorists would strike again, but we didn't have enough information to make an informed judgment. Who were these people? And why did they hate us? My book club started selecting books on the Middle East, and as I began my reading, I thought of a woman I greeted each morning at the school bus stop. Our daughters were in the same kindergarten class. I didn't know her background. She looked like a stylish blend of Europe and the Middle East, and her name, Ranya Idliby, sounded Middle Eastern to me.

One morning as we waited for the bus together, I asked her where she was from, and she told me that her parents were Palestinian refugees and that she was born in Kuwait and had grown up in Dubai and in McLean, Virginia. I had never heard of Dubai, but I nodded my head anyway. After hearing about Ranya's family history and her experience studying Middle Eastern politics, I invited her to join my book group discussion. To my surprise, a Jewish member of my book club then declined to host the next meeting. But the book club went on without that hostess, and Ranya and I started to become friends.

As our children played together we shared conversations about Islam, and I became intrigued by the roots Ranya said our religions shared. One afternoon she mentioned to me her idea to bring together a Muslim, a Jewish, and a Christian mother to write a children's book of miracles, and I jumped at the chance. The intent of the book—to educate children about our common heritage—seemed a necessary and noble goal in the months after September 11th. So I told Ranya I'd love to be part of her trio and offered to find a Jewish woman to join us. A friend recommended Priscilla Warner for our project. She had two sons and experience writing children's books.

It was an awkward first call. "Hi, Priscilla. I'm calling because you're Jewish; you're a mother; and you write." But the idea of talking religion with a Palestinian Muslim and a Christian didn't frighten Priscilla, and we made a date to meet.

I walked into our first meeting, my stiff new notebook in hand, ready to share stories of religious inspiration. I was comfortable in my own religion, having made a difficult decision to leave the Catholic Church of my parents for the relative liberalism of the Episcopal Church. After twelve years in Catholic schools, I was finally going to get an interfaith education. That education, however, proved not to be as neatly packaged as I had anticipated. It came with the messiness and complications of the real lives and perspectives of three women with very different relationships to their religions.

Priscilla

When Suzanne Oliver called me, she wasn't looking for just any children's book writer. She was looking specifically for a Jewish mother who wrote.

I had never really defined myself in those terms. I was a writer. And most definitely a mother. But a Jew? Religion wasn't my field of expertise. Deflecting pain with humor was. I'd joked all my life about being a "neurotic Jew."

I knew a fair amount about my religion, thanks mostly to my father, who came from a family of conservative Jews and exposed me to Judaism early in life. I knew the rituals and stories of my religion. I had attended a somber interfaith service at my suburban reform temple on September 12, 2001, where my rabbi, along with other local clergy, tried to make sense of the unfathomable events of 9/11. The temple was overflowing that night as people spilled out onto the steps, down into the street, where policemen stood watch. (It occurred to me later that no imam had been present.)

I was comforted by the words of the moving service and the fact that so many people of different faiths had gathered together to support one another. But despite the fact that I prayed along with others to God that night, I wasn't sure whether I really believed God existed.

Where was God on September 11th? I wondered for weeks afterward. The horrifying images of the World Trade Center attacks played over and over in my head, and I had a persistent fear that New York City would be attacked again. This time, I worried that my husband, who worked in lower Manhattan, wouldn't be fortunate enough to survive. Would the next attack be a nuclear one? Although my family was alive and well, safe in the suburbs, the horror of 9/11 had hit close to home. Our son's basketball coach, a kind, compassionate father of four, had died that day and a close friend's husband had escaped the South Tower just minutes before it collapsed.

For thirty-five years, I'd suffered from severe panic attacks. And after the events of September 11th, I was thrown into one long, never-ending state of low-grade panic. But I tried to keep my fears to myself. I didn't want to scare my kids. I wanted them to know and love New York as I did. So a couple of weeks after the attacks, I started bringing them back into the city. They wanted to come, and I pretended to be calm. I tried to convince myself New York was still alive and well as I talked to them.

"Look around you," I said to my children. "Look at all these people" We were in the middle of Times Square. People of all shapes, sizes, colors, and ages were streaming past us. "We come from all over the world!" I said. "We're the best of America! Look what people can do here! They can do anything they want. They can be anyone they want to be. They can worship wherever they want, whenever they want. New York is the very best of what America stands for."

Although I fantasized about moving my family to a "safer" city, I was still smitten with New York, the city I loved too much to flee.

So when Suzanne Oliver called me, I was eager to collaborate on a children's book that would bring children hope. And bring me hope. I waned to try to explain the inexplicable to my kids. And to myself. To allay the fears everyone had. The fears that were overwhelming me.

A MUSLIM, A CHRISTIAN, AND A JEW WALK INTO A ROOM . . .

Priscilla

Ranya opened the door to her home for our first meeting, and I was immediately intrigued. There was so much to look at: beautiful artwork on the walls, sensual fabrics and furnishings. The space felt both familiar and exotic to me at the same time. Ranya and I both own lush, color photographs by the same photographer. The identical chandelier illuminates the main room of both our homes. I felt that was an unusual omen.

I had never met a Palestinian woman before, but have always had both Jewish and Christian friends. So I focused on Ranya in particular at that first meeting. Suzanne was less mysterious to me, and Ranya was, well, Palestinian. I'm not sure how I expected a Palestinian woman to look or act, but I was intrigued by Ranya as a person. She was beautiful, smart, sophisticated, and warm. She was confident, but refreshingly self-deprecating, one of my favorite traits in any person. I felt an immediate connection to her.

Ranya spoke eloquently about the unique position she was in as a Muslim mother in New York, particularly after the attacks on the World Trade Center. "My daughter's confused," Ranya explained. "She knows she's different from the Christian and Jewish children she's surrounded by, and I feel it's time to educate her and my son about what it means to be a Muslim in America today." This was a difficult challenge for Ranya since Islam now had violent and confusing connotations for most Americans.

I'd never interacted so intimately with a Muslim woman, I kept thinking as I listened to Ranya speak about her concerns. This was going to be an interesting meeting. The air felt charged. Partly because I didn't know these women and we were getting into personal issues, partly because I didn't know, as a Jew, what political direction a conversation with a Palestinian woman might take. But primarily the air was charged because I was in a room with two substantial, intelligent women who felt an urgent need to connect and produce something meaningful out of that connection.

I asked Ranya where her family was from, and she told me and Suzanne, in vivid detail, the story of her family's history in Palestine. I was riveted. Ranya talked with passion and sensitivity. I was hearing the story of a displaced Palestinian family, told to me not by an angry person with a political ax to grind, but by a loving mother with a family and a story to tell. It was as simple as that.

In retrospect, I guess I had been expecting a woman straight out of the evening news shots of anguished Palestinian mothers in refugee camps. A woman who would never sit down and talk to me, face to face, so calmly.

Ranya

The morning of our first meeting, I lit a scented candle, fussed with the cushions on my couch and waited for Priscilla and Suzanne to arrive. I was not nervous about meeting a Jewish woman. Unlike Priscilla, who was meeting her first Palestinian woman, I had met many Jewish people representing an array of political opinions. Even before I'd moved to New York City ten years earlier, I'd had many Jewish friends. Still, I knew it was possible that Priscilla and I could clash. Palestinians and Israelis were at war. And while I may suffer less than those in refugee camps, my identity is tied up in my family's displacement from our ancestral home half a century ago.

As soon as I met Priscilla, her eagerness to connect was evident, and, I hoped, an indicator of the warmth and generosity of her spirit. Priscilla was a reform Jew, and in my mind she represented the great Jewish liberal tradition of debate and free thought. As she confirmed later in our discussions, a large part of the Jewish theological tradition is based on the commentaries, which represent centuries of ongoing debate and interpretation of the Jewish Holy Books. The fact that I was able to talk so freely to Priscilla and Suzanne served as a sad reminder to me of the lack of debate in Islam today.

I had grown up hearing of a legendary time in history when the door was closed on Islamic theological debate (*Ijthihad*). So as Priscilla explained the evolution of the reform, conservative, and orthodox branches of Judaism in America, it occurred to me that Islam needed a parallel experience. America is a country that was built on the principle of freedom of worship, and in America today Islam needs an American journey.

When I shared my family story with Priscilla, although I felt self-conscious of such instant intimacy and a little awkward about sharing my family's sense of loss and victimhood, I felt that I was in the presence of someone open to meaningful dialogue. While Priscilla accepted my story at face value, she told me later that some of her friends were skeptical.

Suzanne

From the time I discovered Ranya was Muslim, I was intrigued. I wanted to understand the basis of her faith and how she reconciled her modern, Westernized life with what was widely viewed as an unenlightened religion of the developing world. My knowledge of Islam was meager. I knew Muslims followed the teaching of an Arab called Muhammad, that they worshiped in mosques, that they had a holy book called the Quran, and that they were obliged to make a pilgrimage to Mecca once in their lifetime.

I had visited mosques in Istanbul, and I had heard the enchanting Arabic calls to prayer of the muezzin throughout Turkey and Morocco. But I held an image of Islam as a violent religion controlled by men to promote the continued hegemony of men, a religion of mistreated women, polygamy, and an "eye for an eye" justice system. All of these images fit with stereotypes popularized in books I'd read, like Jean Sasson's *Princess*, and were supported by reports in the American media at various times—stories about women being stoned, about the 9/11 attackers being inspired by the Quran, about the death sentence placed on author Salman Rushdie by the Iranian Ayatollah Khomeini.

During my own travels in Muslim countries, I had seen women treated as second-class citizens. They covered their heads with scarves or even their entire bodies in shapeless cloaks. In Istanbul, I was shooed out of the courtyard of a mosque while I could see men prostrating themselves in prayer inside. One man quickly emerged and waved me out of the mosque's gates. I was not allowed to look.

I had left the Catholic church to become an Episcopalian, in part because Catholics don't allow women to become priests, so I was curious to learn how Ranya could reconcile her modem life with Islam. After all, she did not wear a head scarf. She drank alcohol. And she wasn't fighting a jihad against the West, at least as far as I could tell.

In retrospect, Ranya was on a jihad—a word I later learned to mean an inner struggle. She was struggling to define her Muslim faith. And she was struggling to have this faith recognized in the West.

Questions about Content

1. What was Ranya personally worried about on September 11 and afterward? Would you agree that she had cause to worry about her family? How did Suzanne and Priscilla respond to September 11? Were their worries more similar to Ranya's, or did their different backgrounds result in a different kind of worry?

2. How does the fact that the writers are mothers make their club unique? How could the club have been different if it had included fathers or women with no children or men with no children?

3. Which of the three women seems to be at the "center" of their first meeting? What are the other two members of the group thinking as they prepare to meet this woman?

4. Using the story of these women's initial meeting, consider how familiarity changes our preconceptions of people we have not known before. In your classes or residence halls or neighborhoods, have you had opportunities to meet people of religions different from yours—Muslims, Jews, Buddhists, and so forth? What about nonreligious people or agnostics or atheists? How have those meetings changed your perceptions of those religions or philosophies?

5. Think of someone you have not yet had an opportunity to meet—a Muslim, a Jew, a Buddhist, a Hindu, and so on. How might your feelings about a religion change if you could have an opportunity to get to know someone who practices that religion?

Questions about Rhetorical Analysis

1. The writers agreed to begin their book by writing about their fears on September 11. Why did they choose this strategy?

2. The title of the first passage is "in the beginning," an obvious reference to the first three words of the Bible. What effect might these three writers—Muslim, Jewish, and Christian—have been trying to achieve by deciding to start with these words?

3. The title of the second passage is "A Muslim, a Christian, and a Jew Walk into a Room." When you read or hear a statement like that, what do you think is going to follow? What effect are the writers achieving with this title?

4. Whenever writers collaborate on a project, they must decide how they will work together. Rather than writing one text as a group, they decided to write their stories individually and then put these stories together to form chapters. Why do you think they decided to create chapters made up of individually written stories?

Physics and Grief
PATRICIA MONAGHAN

A member of the faculty at DePaul University's School for New Learning, Patricia Monaghan teaches ecological sciences and writing. She earned her B.A. and M.A. degrees in English at the University of Minnesota, an M.F.A. degree in creative writing at the University of Alaska, and her doctorate at the Union Institute, where she wrote a dissertation exploring the unity of science and spirituality in American poetry. She has a great interest in mythology, spirituality, and poetry. The widow of science fiction writer Robert Shea, she now lives in Chicago with her husband, Michael McDermott, a physician. Her web site, www.patricia-monaghan. com, provides biographical information as well as descriptions of her writings, lectures, interests, and other activities.

There is probably no experience that can test faith or reinforce faith more than the death of a loved one. In the story, "Physics and Grief," Monaghan describes how she dealt with the intense grief she endured upon the death of her husband. She finds great comfort in the science of physics, leading to the realization that there is a kind of unity in science and faith. Through physics, she says, "I did not have to believe. I only had to wonder."

◆

*In nature nothing remains constant. Everything is in a
perpetual state of transformation, motion, and change.
However, we discover that nothing simply surges up out
of nothing without having antecedents that existed before.
Likewise, nothing ever disappears without a trace, in the
sense that it gives rise to absolutely nothing existing in
later times.*

—DAVID BOHM

"Actually," Dan said. "I've been reading a lot of physics." He looked down at his empty paper plate and shrugged one shoulder, then the other. "I don't suppose that makes any sense."

Dan had not spoken to me in almost a year. We'd seen each other occasionally; we had too many common friends for that not to happen. But when it did, Dan made certain to stay on the other side of the room, to find himself in need of a drink when I came near, to turn suddenly away when I tried to catch his eye.

That was the year when I was a new widow, and Dan was about to become one, his partner, Steve, descending into a hell of lesions and pneumonia and fungal invasions of the brain. Even in the blur of my loss, I felt no anger toward Dan—though anger is so predictable a part of grief—for avoiding me. I knew the cause: I already was what he most feared to become.

Six months after I was widowed, Dan joined me in that state. Steve gave up his obdurate struggle to remain alive, asking to be kept home when the next crisis hit. It was only a week. Friends told me that Steve's death was gentle and that Dan bore up as well as could be expected. Dan dropped from sight for a time, disappearing into memories and pain.

Now it was summer, and we were sitting under blue canvas at an outdoor festival. Dan had approached me with an apology for his actions. I had embraced him with understanding. We were sitting companionably together, catching up on each other's lives, when I asked him what most helped him deal with his grief.

Physics.

Dan met my eyes, and his brows came together, then raised. "Relativity. Quantum mechanics. Bell's Theorem. You know?" I think he expected me to be surprised. But I was not. It had been the same for me.

To explain how physics came to be important on my journey of grief, I have first to describe the problem with my keys. There were five of them, bound together with a wide steel ring: a big silver skeleton key, for the embossed brass Victorian lock on the front door; a round-headed key that opens the more modern deadbolt; a little golden key to the garage; an institutional "do not duplicate" key to my office; and a black-headed key to the Ford station wagon.

I remember the day—the hour—that the keys disappeared. It was late spring, less than three months after Bob died. Walking out the door to go shopping, I had reached into my jacket pocket, where I always kept my keys.

They weren't there.

At the instant, it seemed inconsequential. I'd mislaid keys before; hasn't everyone? I was inside the house, so I had used the keys to enter. They were, therefore, somewhere in the house with me. I merely had to look carefully and I would find them.

I was unperturbed. I did what I did whenever I had mislaid something. I looked in all the logical places: in my coat's other pocket; on the shelf near the front door; next to the telephone; in the kitchen near the sink. Nothing.

I was still not overly concerned. I must have been distracted when I entered, I reasoned with myself, I must have put the keys in some unlikely spot. So I began methodically searching the house. Entry hall. Living room. Pulling out furniture, looking under pillows. Nothing. Dining room. Kitchen. Opening cabinets, reaching to the back of shelves. Nothing.

Okay, then, I must have carried them upstairs. Guest room. Bathroom. Moving around each room slowly, looking especially in places where keys were unlikely to be. Behind pictures. In rarely-opened drawers. Study. Nothing. Linen closet. Nothing.

In my bedroom, I suddenly grew frustrated. I needed my keys! The only key to my car was on that ring; I could not go to work without it. What would I do without my keys?

I started to cry.

I had been crying for months, ever since Bob had finally died, fighting cancer to the last. The six months before his death were exhausting. For three months I was his sole caregiver; then, during his final hospitalization, I visited him two, three, even four times each day. Economics forced me to continue working, so I had neither physical strength nor emotional resources left when he died.

In the days before Bob's death, I had been with him constantly, telling him stories of the future we should have had, praising his work and his son to him, reminiscing for him about happy times when he could no longer speak. I did not sleep for perhaps forty-eight hours as I held vigil by his bedside, leaving only for necessary moments, for he had been shatteringly fearful of being alone at the moment of death. And so I was with him when that moment came, holding his hand as his breathing slowed, singing old songs to him, stroking his face through its paralysis.

It was the hardest thing I have ever done, witnessing as he "departed from this strange world a little ahead of me," as Einstein said when his oldest friend, Michele Besso, died. When I left that hospital room, bearing with me the amaryllis that had bloomed only the day before, I felt that I was leaving all happiness behind, that my world had changed unutterably, and only for the worse.

I lived the months afterward in a trance of grief. There was a memorial service that I planned, I remember that. I remember a brick meeting hall with red tulips, a jazz pianist, readings from Bob's novels, visitors from many states. For the rest, I barely recall anything. I apparently kept working, and doing laundry, and feeding the dogs, and planting the garden. My body kept moving through the Midwestern spring. But my soul was in the desert, in winter.

That day in May, the loss of my keys reduced me to tears, though of course I was weeping for my greater loss, which every other loss would now reflect. Possibly I wept for hours; I did such things at that time. Finally the storm passed. I got up and set determinedly about to find the keys. To survive, I had to work. I needed to drive to my office. I could not manage without my keys. I would find them. I had to.

And so I repeated my search. I must have missed the keys the first time, I told myself. I started again at the front door and scoured the downstairs. Living room: no. Kitchen: no.

And so it went. After an hour or so, I found myself again in the bedroom, still keyless.

I began to weep again. This time, my desolation seemed endless. I could not stop crying. I lay on the bed, sobbing and flailing my arms. I soaked several handkerchiefs. I buried my head in pillows and drenched them with tears.

Then I became enraged. I got up from the bed and began to scream at Bob, furious at him for dying and leaving me so helplessly besieged by grief. I screamed that he was cruel and heartless, that I'd been there in his hour of need, and where was he when I needed him? I raged and wept, wept and raged.

I had not, before Bob's death, spent much time thinking about the question of whether or not there is an afterlife. I had been brought up with a conventional picture of heaven and hell. And I had studied enough other religions to realize that many wiser than I believed in some kind of survival after death. I had read believable-enough accounts of those who claimed to have been contacted by the dead. But the possibility of an afterlife was not something I dwelt upon. I did not wish to make moral decisions by weighing the possibilities of future reward or punishment for myself. Nor did the survival of my own small person seem especially important in comparison with the universe's vast majesty.

So, for myself, what happened or did not happen after death was not a very important question.

Bob, by contrast, had been quite clear about his beliefs. A natural mystic, he had practiced Zen for twenty years. But he was also an unrelentingly hard-headed empiricist who believed the universe to be a mechanistic place in which consciousness was only a byproduct of the body's functions. Thus, when the body died, consciousness ceased as well. Bob believed, as Fred Alan Wolf put it in describing the Newtonian worldview, that mind—or soul, or spirit, whatever you call it—was just "a convenient byproduct of the physiology of . . . the mechanisms of the brain, down to the remarkable electrical and mechanical movements of the nerve firings and blood flows."

He never changed his belief once he entered the hospital that final time, even though I, desperate for some reassurance that our love could continue after he faded from this life, talked to him about reincarnation and other possible survivals. But Bob would be no foxhole convert; he marched gamely toward that abyss which he saw as the likely end of his being. Death was painful to him; he had much to live for; but he would not grasp at hope of continued life just to ease his pain. Unless he had time to ponder, unless he could become completely convinced, he would believe as he always had. Happy lies held no appeal for him.

One thing I loved about Bob was this: he had more integrity than any person I'd ever met. That integrity remained to the end. He met his death with his long-held beliefs intact. He was frightened, but he was very, very brave.

Because I had no personal convictions on the subject, I held true to Bob's beliefs after he was gone. It was a way of remaining close to him. I, too, would refuse to grasp at imaginary straws just to ease my pain. If Bob believed that all traces of his consciousness would evaporate at his death, that only his physical works would remain, then I would loyally uphold that belief.

And so I lived in the desert. Life has never seemed so dry and meaningless to me as it did then. I would watch lovers kiss in a coffee shop and a whirlpool of pain would open beneath me, as I thought of one of them holding the other as they parted forever. I would stare at parents playing with their children near the lake and imagine sudden illnesses and accidents, wondering how life could create such joy only to obliterate it. I wept constantly: when I heard beautiful music, when I saw painful news, when I saw new flowers, when I went to bed, when I woke up.

But I adamantly refused to settle for those happy visions that religion held out, of dreamy heavens full of harps, of other lives to come, of eventual reunion in some cosmic void. I even rejected nonreligious spiritualism. When friends said they had dreamed of Bob, or felt him near, I received the information in silent disbelief. It was their need of solace, I told myself, that caused these apparitions. They had just imagined them. I, loyal to Bob's beliefs, would nor settle for such self-deluding comfort. I would tough it out, looking reality right in its cruel face.

But the day I lost my keys, I could not be brave like Bob, not any longer. Seeing those loving eyes go dim had been the single most painful moment of my life. The idea that the universe could so wantonly create beauty, could bestow upon our lives the kind of love that seems like ultimate meaning, only to destroy it in a breath, had finally become too much for me.

I wanted so desperately to believe that Bob, and Bob's love for me, still existed somewhere in the universe, that in my furious pain I flung down a challenge. Standing in the middle of the bedroom, I demanded that he come back. Find my keys, I insisted. Find my damned keys! If there's anyone there, if there's any love left in this universe for me, find my keys!

After the fury had passed, I felt mortified. I had been screaming at a dead man. Standing in my room alone, screaming at a dead man.

Worse, it was all so trivial. If I were going to throw down the gauntlet to the universe about whether there is life after death, couldn't I have chosen something more important as proof? World peace? Personal economic security? A beatific vision?

But I'd spoken. I'd insisted that Bob prove his continuing existence by finding my keys.

Even writing about that day, I feel embarrassment cover me. It was such an excess of emotion about such a small matter, about such a minor inconvenience. Why had I broken down over such a silly thing? Why had I challenged the universe over something as unimportant as a key-ring?

But break down I had, and challenge the universe I had. And I could not bear the answer to be silence, negation, the absence of Bob forever, anywhere. Now I truly had to find the keys. So I resolutely began, yet again, to search. I started once more in the front hallway. But this time, I took a new tack. I might as well do spring-cleaning, I decided. I'd clean the entire house, front door to attic, and in doing so I would certainly find the keys.

There was more than a bit of desperation about all this. If I did not find the keys, all was indeed lost. If I did not find the keys, there was no vestige of Bob in the world. If I did not find the keys, I was alone in the cruelest universe imaginable.

Three days later, I was back in the bedroom. Except for that one room, the house was now clean, ammonia-and-paste-wax clean.

I had taken down curtains and washed them, cleaned out closets, pulled up rugs. I had upended sofas and searched their bowels. I had repotted plants. I had pulled books from shelves and dusted both. The house sparkled, indeed. But I had not found the keys.

The bedroom was the final outpost of possibility. From the first corner around to the last, then spiraling in to the center, I cleaned and searched. I opened drawers and rearranged them, shaking out their contents on the floor. I moved pictures and dusted their frames. I worked slowly, with mounting despair, for the keys had still not appeared. I moved the bed and polished the floor under it. I shook out the bedclothes and aired out the mattress.

Finally, I was finished.

There were no keys.

I collapsed. This time my grief truly knew no bounds. I had asked for an answer from the universe, and I had—I believed—received one. Bob had been right. Consciousness was a byproduct of our body's functioning, and now that the ashes of Bob's body sat on the bookshelf in a white box, there was nothing, anywhere, left of the curiosity and passion and brilliance and love that had been him.

The depression that began that day incapacitated me. I was unable to work for nearly a week. Finally, however, I called the car dealership and got new car keys. I found the spare house keys. I began to reconstruct the openings to my life. I knew now that I was indeed alone, that I could not call upon Bob for help, that he was no longer present anywhere, in any form. It was a bleak and cruel universe, but at least I knew the truth of it.

What I experienced during that next year was more than simple grief and certainly more than emotional depression, although I suffered from both as well. It was stark existential despair. Life had no meaning, much less any savor. I tried to find what comfort I could in friendship, in earthly beauty, in art, in learning. But at my center was an abyss of meaninglessness. I could as easily have gambled all my resources away as built a garden; as easily have crashed my car as driven it safely across the Midwest; as easily have drunk slow poison as cocoa for breakfast. That I did one thing rather than another seemed only an arbitrary choice.

At last, however, I began to awaken from my coma of sorrow. I began to argue with Bob in my mind. As I gardened, I noticed again the resilient connection of matter and energy, how nature never destroys but only transforms. As I walked in the woods with my dog, I saw spring flowers emerging from the withered leaves of autumn. What hubris, I began to think, to imagine that human consciousness is the only thing this universe cares to obliterate. Surely we are not that important.

But these were fleeting thoughts, unconvincing, evanescent, ideas which did not in any case reach to the root of my grief. It was easy to accept that Bob's body would eventually nourish other beings, through the cycle of decomposition and recomposition. But it was Bob's self that I'd loved—not only his body, though certainly that. And although I knew and accepted, with piercing pain, what had happened to his body, that told me nothing about where the unique energy went that had invigorated it.

Every once in a while, I would think of the lost keys and sigh. I had, after all, asked for a sign, and I had been given one.

That was when I began reading books on physics. I had been reading a lot of spiritual literature, looking for answers to the appalling questions life presented. But I only grew more isolated, angry at the serenity that seemed forever beyond my grasp, despairing at my continuing inability to find any sense in death's senselessness. It was not that the answers which spiritual literature offered seemed implausible or incorrect; it was simply that I could not believe them, could not make the leap into not-doubting. The more rigidly codified the religious insight, the more it seemed to exclude—even to mock—my anguished confusion.

I can't remember exactly which book, which author, brought me to physics. Most likely one that pushed the boundaries of science to include spirituality. Fritz Capra, perhaps, or Gary Zukov. One of those wild minds who saw bridges where others saw barricades. But it wasn't the spirituality that gripped my attention. It was the science.

Where religion had failed me, being so certain of itself, physics offered paradoxes and complexities so bizarre that my hatred and fear of the universe began to be replaced with what can only be called awe. I'd known Newtonian physics before, from my days as a science reporter, but I had never ventured into quantum mechanics. There I found the most astonishing ideas, ones which smashed the clockwork universe just as Bob's death had torn apart mine. Ideas that read like Bob's beloved Zen koans, statements that strained the limits of my linear thinking. "Our universe seems to be composed of facts and their opposites at the same time." I read in Louis de Broglie's work, and "everything happens as though it did not exist at all."

Such statements seemed eminently sensible, reasonable, even straightforward. Yes, I responded passionately. Yes, the universe was that strange, that indescribable. Death is not an equal and opposite reaction to life; consciousness is not some strange form of inertia. I needed a new physics to describe the wild movements of my grieving soul. And a new physics I found.

Like my friend Dan, I found quantum theory immeasurably consoling. With an uncertainty-loves-company kind of logic, I lost myself in Heisenberg and the reassurances of the Uncertainty Principle. If we cannot conceivably know everything about the physical universe, then the abyss of doubt whereon I stood was as good a standpoint as any from which to view life. If we cannot know something as simple as two aspects of a subatomic particle's motion simultaneously, how can we know for certain that there is no life after death—or that there is? If our measurements may alter the reality that we measure, could not consciousness be a form of measurement, subtly altering the universe?

My deepest consolation, however, was not in speculating about whether a consciousness suffused, as mine was, with grief altered the world in a different way than one flooded with happiness. Rather, I drew solace from the dumbfounding absoluteness of Heisenberg's theory. We could not know everything, not ever, because in the moment of such knowing we may change what we know. I could not know—I could never know—if or where Bob existed, for each time I sought for him—each time I measured this universe in terms of Bob's existence or nonexistence—I was perhaps changing the conditions of the very universe through which I sought. It was as though Heisenberg, by enshrining uncertainty at the center of perception and knowledge, made anything and everything both possible and impossible at once.

Suddenly the world seemed to make sense again, although in a deeply paradoxical way. Where religion's certainties had left me bitterly bereft of comfort, quantum uncertainty allowed for unimaginable possibilities. Whatever measurement I took of the universe, I understood now, could be only partial. There would always be something that eluded my grasp. This was an enormous comfort.

It was not only uncertainty that captured me. Because this new physics was all about time and space, Einstein spoke to me like a voice from a burning bush. I, who lived in a time and space from which my love had disappeared, found respite in considering the ways that time and space were linked. "Any two points in space and time are both separate and not separate," David Bohm said. What salvation that seemed! As incomprehensible as this new spacetime was, it was more lively with possibilities than linear and planar realities. My separateness from Bob was real, but in some way, we were also still together.

In some way—this was most important to me. For this was not a metaphoric togetherness, a trick of language. This was science, after all. And not just science but the queen of sciences, physics. Physics which did not ask me to believe, did not ask me to have faith. Physics which observed and experimented. Physics which offered a description of the world, admittedly bizarre but as accurate as blundering language could make it.

I did not have to believe. I only had to wonder.

The fact that, as Max Born pointed out, the quantum world is utterly unvisualizable presented no problem to me. Visions of the subatomic world were metaphors, whose richness and limitations I amply understood. But unlike religion, which seemed hypnotized by its own articulations of the ineffable, physics acknowledged that any picture we hold of the subatomic world is by definition inaccurate, limited, inexact. No one has ever seen a quark, much less a Higgs boson. But they act; we see their traces. Such quantum strangeness spoke to my condition. I had witnessed something deeply incomprehensible when Bob died. Studying what Bohm called the "unanalyzable ways of the universe" mirrored that experience.

My grief did not disappear, for grief is a chronic disease which exists in the body. My body would still regularly writhe with sudden memories: when I automatically reached for Bob's favorite juice at the Jewel, when I passed the lake where we had taken out last walk, when someone uttered a phrase he had relished. The tape-loop of his last hours ran constantly in my mind, so that I would see the doctor, my friends Natalie and Barbara arriving, Bob's son Michael leaving, the amaryllis. Bob's paralyzed face, the doctor, Natalie, the amaryllis, the doctor. . . .

Because of the power of these death-watch memories, relativity especially absorbed me. The paradoxes of time preoccupied me for days on end. Einstein had seen the connection between the study of time and awareness of death's approach, arguing that death really means nothing because "the distinction between past, present and future is only a stubbornly persistent illusion." I envisioned those points in the universe where radio waves of Bob's voice, from a long-ago interview, were still new and bright. I invented scenarios in which I stretched time out like taffy, making Bob's last days as eternal as they had subjectively seemed. I relished that consoling insight that Einstein's equations were time-reversible, that perhaps time does not move in one direction but can flow backward as well as forward. I imagined moving backward through time, intersecting with a healthy Bob and recreating our life, always hopping back on the time machine before the diagnosis, living those happy times over and over and over. I knew these were fantasies, but I also knew that I no longer knew what time really was. There, once again, were limitless possibilities.

If my grief did not disappear, that crazed existential doubt did. Life no longer was so utterly senseless. It made sense again, but in a more marvelous way than I'd ever imagined. I found myself staring at graphs of the Schroedinger wave collapse, imagining a cat alive, dead, alive, dead, all at the same time—imagining Bob's continued existence as such a wave. I pondered the complementarity between particles and waves, especially the way an observer seems implicated in the emergence into reality of each. Particles dancing and leaping in a virtual world, flickering in and out of measurable existence. Or perhaps they were not even particles at all, but what Henry Sapp called "sets of relationships that reach outward to other things." To David Bohm, too, particles exist not so much as nuggets of virtual and actual matter, but as "on-going movements that are mutually dependent because ultimately they merge and interpenetrate."

Matter disappeared, at this scale, into flashing energy, particles into momentarily observable comets of being. Bob had been composed of these miraculous particles, these miraculous relationships reaching outward toward me, these mutually dependent and interpenetrating movements. And perhaps he still was, in some way, in some unmeasurable place. Our lives together had been lived in a space and a time, within a universe through which the mighty and unfathomable river of spacetime flows. Were we still connected, as Bell's Theorem hints, in some intricate and inexpressible way? Was I somehow still affected by the changes that he experienced—in whatever state those blinking-into-existence particles that had been Bob were now? And did my changes affect him still as well?

Far from compelling me toward certainly about where and how Bob still existed, quantum theory removed from me any urge toward stapling down reality within one interpretation. In the quantum world, Nick Herbert has pointed out, there are at least eight possible pictures of reality, any of which is more consoling than the Newtonian vision of the universe. Maybe there is an "ordinary reality," as de Broglie and Einstein believed; in that case the hard stuff that made up Bob is somewhere still in existence, and even now I am breathing atoms that had been part of him during his life. But the Copenhagen hypothesis of Bohr and Heisenberg questions whether there is any such "reality" at all. In their view, Bob and I had lived something like a dream together, and that dream had as much reality without him as it had with him. An alternative reading of the Copenhagen hypothesis is that we create our own realities, that reality exists only as we observe it doing so; in that case, I could create the reality of his continued existence by believing strongly enough.

These were only some of the possibilities. There was David Bohm's theory of the implicate order, which argues that there is an undivided wholeness that could wrap both Bob and me, in our varying current states, in what he called "indivisible quantum processes that link different systems in an unanalyzable way." There was the fantastic many-world hypothesis, which permitted me to envision that Bob and I still lived happily in another space-time, after he had survived cancer; in that reality, we are writing an essay together, perhaps this very one.

Or possibly, the quantum world is based upon no logic that we would recognize. In that case, life's either/or does not exist, and Bob's apparent lack of existence is no more true than his apparent existence had been. Or perhaps I created him, or he me; perhaps neither of us existed before we met, we came into being complete with memories when we created each other, and thus he continues in me, his creation. Perhaps, as Fred Alan Wolf has argued, the mind does not "exist in the physical universe at all. It may be beyond the boundaries of space, time and matter. It may use the physical body in the same sense that an automobile driver uses a car."

Or maybe all of this is simultaneously true. Maybe this world is so full of mystery that we cannot ever grasp its actual probabilities and probable actualities.

I pondered these extraordinary possibilities as I moved through my ordinary life. Slowly, the pain of my loss began, not to diminish, but to find its place in my life. If I did not feel joy, at least my pain had become a familiar companion. I continued reading physics, but with less crazed compulsion. I even began to accept the cruel existence of thermodynamics, with its arrow of time that threatened my happy time-travel imaginings, once I realized how connected to the richness of chaos it was.

Every once and again, I thought of the lost keys. In fall, as I was raking the front yard, I imagined that perhaps I had gone to the car for something, that spring day, and had dropped my keyring into the crowded bed of hosta by the door. But no. In winter, when I decided to move the piano, I thought that perhaps I had missed the hidden keys during my frenzied cleaning by not moving that massive upright. But no. That next spring, after preparing for a dinner party, I sat in Bob's recliner and noticed a side pocket I had missed. There? But no: the keys were not there either. The seasons passed, and the keys remained lost.

Each time this happened, I thought to myself that finding the keys no longer mattered. That I had moved beyond the challenge I had flung out to Bob, to the universe, on that wild sad day. That unless the keys found their way back to me in some utterly strange way, I could not regard it as an answer to my desperate plea. I said to myself that finding the keys would be—just finding the keys. That if I found them in some ordinary way, it would prove nothing, one way or the other: I lost the keys, I found them, there was no connection.

And then I found the keys.

Friends were coming to dinner, and I was sitting in my study feeling sad, as I often did, and thinking of Bob, which I always did. I wistfully imagined him being with us, thought how much he would have enjoyed it. I felt my loss again, but poignantly this time, as a sad melody rather than as painful cacophony.

Then, for no special reason, I looked at the door of my study. It was open after having been closed all day. I kept it closed to keep my dog out and to keep visitors from wandering into my private space. That door had been opened and closed scores of times in the preceding year. When I entered, nothing unusual had caught my eye.

My study door is decorated. There is a Celtic knocker in the shape of a squirrel, a St. Bridget cross made of Irish rushes, and a poster. The poster, mounted on heavy blue cardboard, is a memento from the publication of my first book. Issued by my publisher for promotional parties, it shows the book's cover, my name, and the huge black words "it's here!"

The door is one of those old wooden doors with six deep panels. The poster is tacked tightly to the middle of the door, covering the two center panels and resting on the lower. The edges of the poster are flush against the door, especially at top and bottom, with the exception of two areas on each side, halfway down the cardboard, where small gaps exist.

From one of these gaps, I noticed a key coyly poking out. I walked to the door and pulled sharply. Immediately, out tumbled the entire missing set.

I held the keys loosely in my hand and stared at them. I looked up at the poster, with its emphatic proclamation. And then I smiled and said aloud, "You always did have a great sense of humor, Bob Shea."

It would make a good story to say that everything suddenly fell into place, that all my questions dissolved, that I was somehow transported to a place of certainty and confidence in life's meaning. That I no longer felt that the universe was a place of uncertainty and chaos. That I recognized and accepted the proof of Bob's continuing existence.

But that would not be true. What I felt was bafflement and curiosity, together with a startled amusement. This could not be the answer to my crazed prayer. No. There had to be some other, more commonsense answer. The keys were behind the poster: effect. Someone must have put them there: cause. I had been alone when the keys disappeared. Ergo, I had put the keys behind the poster. I did not remember doing so; it must have happened accidentally. Somehow, it was clear, I must have dropped the keys behind that poster, that day a year previously when I'd lost them.

I set out to prove my thesis. I tried to drop the keys behind the poster. I stood at the door, held the keys up in my right hand, and dropped them on the door. They caught at first on the cardboard's edge, then bounced off the door mounding and slid down to the floor.

I tried throwing the keys at the poster from a few feet away. The same thing happened: they slid down and did not hold. I tried walking past the door with the keys dangling from my hand, to see if they would catch in the poster and hold. They did not catch and hold.

There was only one way to get the keys into the position I had found them. I had to pull the poster forward, push the keys along a little groove in the door, and shove the poster back in place. Anything else would result in the keys either not lodging behind the poster at all, or dropping out as soon as the door was moved.

I spent a half-hour trying to make the keys stay behind that poster. Natalie, when I told her the mystery of the found keys, did the same. We stood in the green-carpeted upstairs hallway, two grown women flinging keys at a door, over and over. Thinking of more and more peculiar ways that the keys might have wound up resting on that hidden shelf. Unwilling at first to accept that only careful, conscious effort could bring the keys to rest as they had been, but unable lo find any other way to make the keys stay in that place.

A year previously, the answer that I had wanted was a simple one: that Bob still existed and, hearing my call for help, would return my keys to me. But once this particular and peculiar miracle had occurred, I resisted accepting it as an answer to that crazy challenge. I attempted to catalog all possibilities. I had gone into a fugue state, placed the keys behind the poster, and forgotten all about them. A visitor had found the keys and whimsically placed them behind the poster. A worker—the plumber, say—had found the keys and hid them rather than giving them to me.

These scenarios are possible, though fairly unlikely. Were this a court of law, I would argue that there was no motive for anyone else to hide the keys, and no evidence that I have either before or since gone into a state of mindless fugue. That my beloved Bob had somehow answered my request seems as likely as any of these interpretations. Also: Bob had a unique sense of humor, and he tended to procrastinate. So it would be in character for him to have taken a year to get around to giving me the keys back, and then it would be in a suitably clever fashion.

I have, many times since the keys reappeared, asked myself how I would have responded had I found the keys, in exactly the same place, during my original frenzy of grief. I would, I think, have accepted it as a dramatic proof of Bob's continued existence. Look, I would have said to myself, he returned to me in my hour of need. He loved me still; I could still call upon him and rely upon him; there was life after death. In retrospect, I am glad that I did not find the keys then. Although my pain might have been greatly lessened at the start, I would have been left with only an odd anecdote which, over time, would have grown less and less vital, would have held less and less consolation.

Instead, the loss of the keys had propelled me into discovering a way to live with the unresolvability of our most basic questions. During my period of grief, I became familiar—even comfortable— with relativity and uncertainty. Indeed, those theories polished the world so that it shone with a strange and compelling luster. The world could never again be ordinary once I had plummeted through the rabbit-hole of quantum mechanics. If there was uncertainty at the basis of the universe, there was also a ravishing mystery.

After the keys reappeared, as I considered the various possibilities for how they got where they did, I did not feel compelled to prove any one or another. I did not call every visitor and worker who had entered the house in the previous year; I did not have myself examined for unsuspected fugue states. Neither did I convince myself that I had proof of life after death. I was, and I am, willing to live with all the possibilities. I will never know exactly how those keys got on my door, but it does not matter. The loss of the keys did not pose a question to me; it set me on a journey. Finding the keys was not an answer to my question; it was just another station on the way.

I once asked a techno-junkie friend where my email is stored. I think I pictured a huge computer somewhere, where I had the electronic equivalent of a little mailbox. I think I pictured that mailbox sometimes full with mail, sometimes empty. But where on earth was the mailbox?

My friend guffawed. "There's no big computer," she said, "it's all in the fiber-optic network."

This answer was utterly mysterious to me. In the fiber-optic network? Where is that? How can messages be in a network, rather than in a place? My mind boggled.

But quantum theory teaches us that this is not, ultimately, a universe of hard mechanistic reality where mail has to rest in mailboxes. It is a universe of connections and relations, of particle-waves in spacetime where order explicates itself in form and enfolds itself in pattern. The universe is not a great machine, Jeans said, but a great thought. A great thought that expresses itself in matter and energy, ceaselessly changing places.

Whatever part of that great thought once appeared as Bob Shea still exists, I now believe, somewhere in the network of this universe. He has only "departed from this strange world a little ahead of me." Perhaps, as Einstein said, "That means nothing.

People like us, who believe in physics, know that the distinction between past, present and future is only a stubbornly persistent illusion." If I cannot access the codes to find Bob in the universal network, it does not mean that he has ceased to be. But "being" in that other world must surely be something beyond our imagining in this one, something as different as messages surging through networks are from little meal envelope-filled boxes.

I am comforted by having my keys again. We live in story, and the story of the keys now has a pleasing symmetry. But I do not know what that story means. Or, rather: I know that it can mean many things, some contradictory, but perhaps all true at the same time nonetheless. And I am most deeply comforted by knowing that I cannot ever truly know, that the universe is so far beyond our understanding that miracles, even peculiar and rather silly ones like this one, are very likely to keep occurring.

Questions about Content

1. Monaghan says that she will "explain how physics came to be important on my journey of grief." How did physics inform her faith and help her in her grief?
2. What does Bob believe about the universe even to the moment of his death? What are Patricia's beliefs, and what ultimately causes her to question them?
3. The initial loss of the keys causes her to cry. Later in the story, the moment of her deepest grief comes because of the keys. Why does she keep reacting to the loss of the keys this way?
4. "Where religion's certainties had left me bitterly bereft of comfort, quantum uncertainty allowed for unimaginable possibilities. . . . This was an enormous comfort." Why does she say science, not religion, brought her comfort?
5. Ultimately, what do you think finding the keys means for her?

Questions about Rhetorical Analysis

1. Throughout the narrative, the writer tells the story of her keys. What role do the keys play in the story?
2. Notice how the narrative is structured. The writer begins with her conversation with Dan. Then she describes the loss of her keys. Then she describes Bob's final days. Notice where she goes from there, and write a list, a brief outline, of what happens after that. What is the effect of her sequencing the narrative this way?
3. Who seems to be the reader Monaghan has in mind: A scientist? Someone who has lost a loved one? A deeply religious person? What traits do you find in her story to suggest who her intended reader is?
4. Nearing the end of the narrative, Monaghan writes, "It would make a good story to say that everything suddenly fell into place, that all my questions dissolved, that I was somehow transported to a place of certainty and confidence

in life's meaning. . . . But that would not be true. What I felt was bafflement and curiosity." Does this ending offer resolution or uncertainty, and does it fit her definition of a "good" story?

The Water Will Hold You
LINDSEY CRITTENDEN

Lindsey Crittenden is the author of two books: The Water Will Hold You: A Skeptic Learns to Pray *and a collection of short stories titled* The View From Below. *Her essays, stories, and articles have appeared in publications such as* The New York Times, Real Simple, Bon Appétit, *and the popular series,* Best American Spiritual Writing. *She lives in San Francisco and teaches at the University of California Berkeley Extension. Her web site, www.lindseycrittenden.com, provides more information.*

Crittenden's article, "The Water Will Hold You," is a memoir of her relationship with her mother and her relationship with prayer. As she matures and develops a greater understanding of one relationship, so does she better understand the other one. Throughout her personal story, notice how she uses the image of water as a metaphor of those relationships.

◆

I knew nothing of prayer when, as a child, I watched my mother disappear. Sitting next to me on a wooden pew in St. Stephen's Episcopal Church, she leaned forward to pull down the prayer bench, slip onto her knees, press her palms together, and bow her head. Her wool dress and stockings, her black patent-leather purse upright and open next to her in case she needed to reach for a pressed handkerchief, her shoes and hair and arms all remained recognizably *Mommy,* but with her face hidden—she didn't rest her head against her hands as much as *in* them, to shut out everything else—she became other. No longer mother or wife or Sunday school teacher, but her *self,* gone somewhere else, somewhere that—it seemed—had nothing to do with me.

She went there again, years later, when she was upset and I tried to comfort her. Weeping in a deck chair, she pushed my arms away and clutched her hands to her chest when I bent to hug her. She and my father had argued, I recall; I don't remember the specifics, but their disagreement would have played the recurring tape loop I'd heard my whole life—she was oversensitive and he was callous, she was a spoiled little girl and he an unfeeling boor. She wanted, now, to be alone. "Leave me be," she said, and hunched further into herself.

She went there, too, the summer she was dying, as we both stood in the shallow end of my parents' swimming pool and she mentioned how, sick with tuberculosis at age nineteen, she'd been sent to a chiropractor by my grandmother. "My God," I said. "Why?"

"Oh, I've told you that before," she replied, splashing water with her hands.

"No, Mom, you haven't. And whenever you say you've told me something before, it's something you never have."

"Oh." She leaned back on the steps and kicked her legs. "Aren't you funny."

She distrusted hovering concern, loathed wringing hands. The worst word, I learned early on, wasn't a four-letter curse or the taking of the Lord's name in vain (whatever that meant). No, the word that our household, under her domain, did not allow, was *pity*. My mother didn't want any, and—she'd announce, in case you had any doubt—she wouldn't be handing any out, either.

I remember my confusion: did pity differ so from sympathy, from kindness, from letting me stay home (as I craved) to hide out from fourth grade? On days I was sick with a sore throat or a tummyache, she made me cinnamon toast and dealt Double Solitaire on top of the bedcovers and rubbed my back. But on days I was nervous about having to Steal the Bacon in P.E. or face down the fifth-grade toughs who'd been teasing me the day before, her message consisted of "No one ever said life was easy. Off you go." From her big-boned hands, capable of wiping spills, soothing tears, and dealing with spider in the bathtub (a swoop of her hand, a crunch of paper towel, and *There*: the bug was dead), to her exclamatory voice and effusive enthusiasms, my mother was indomitable, her strength a force of nature that shaped my world.

From a young age, I wrote stories and drew pictures, and my mother would go through *Wizard of Oz* garbage can to find out— she told me years later—what I was thinking.

"Why didn't you just ask me?"

"I don't like to pry," she said.

An adult by then, I didn't remember throwing my creations away—but I did remember the impulse, even at age four or five, to keep things to myself, to hide from my mother my inner world.

She had no boundaries with the people she loved. "My mother," I once told a friend, "could take the weather personally." When she saw signs in me of vulnerability or insecurity or anger, she couldn't let me linger there. And she often turned my enthusiasms into her own property, as I learned when, high on painkillers after having my wisdom teeth pulled, I showed her my yearbook and the photo of my longterm crush, only to listen the next day as she told a friend over the phone, "Some boy named Chris who looks like he never combs his hair."

"I can't handle this upheaval," she announced one Thanksgiving after I admitted I didn't want to see my brother—he'd been lying, stealing, doing drugs—because I wasn't sure I could sit across the table from him without throwing something breakable. "I have a turkey to worry about."

After being voted "prettiest hair" in her high school yearbook and getting an A in Mark Schorer's English 1B at U.C. Berkeley, my mother had to cut her social life and college education short when she was diagnosed with TB. She survived the TB and nine months of hospitalization and several years of follow-up treatment by not feeling sorry for herself, not getting depressed—by hardy German strength and will, by suppressing her vulnerability. There were places she didn't want to go—and if on occasion she had to, she went alone.

The first time you dive into a swimming pool, you're told the water will hold you—but *still*. You stand on the edge, toes curled, unconvinced. The object of your hesitation and longing lies before you, discrete and intact. And then you're in. You slip right through, feeling the water slide against your skin. You can't grab hold, but maybe you don't need to. It holds you.

Each day, as I sit down to pray, I negotiate that scrim between my morning—coffee cup, unmade bed, weather outside—and the deep inner space offered by prayer, by listening. Prayer is a dive, yes—but it is also an excavation. It is bold impulse, pure throw of yourself into the unknown, and premeditated, intentional methodology. We divide space into a grid and begin, carefully, in one corner, to dig and turn over, to examine and consider. We pick up the prayerbook, hold the rosary, determine what it is we want to ask or thank God for on this day. And yet, for all our planning, we still have to leap.

Open my lips, O Lord, and my mouth shall proclaim your praise. Closing my eyes, I see a void shot through with dots and dashes of light, untempered by time or space, as if the universe had turned itself inside out through my mouth. "I had a pit inside me," a friend said, "and then I saw it was a galaxy." *Create in me a clean heart, O God, and renew a right spirit within me.*

At St. Stephen's Episcopal Church, on Christmas Eve and Easter and every Sunday until our priest went through a divorce in which my parents sided with his wife, I swung my legs and put my quarter in the collection plate and watched my brother squirm and my father take him outside and my mother disappear into her hands. Prayer, like dress-up, held mystique and allure—as well as the notion that I'd figure it out some day. In the meantime, I blew bubbles with my saliva, secure at least that *that* wasn't it.

Then, when I was ten, my cat was hit by a car, and I discovered that prayer is born out of desperation. I clutched my pillow every night for a week and promised God that if He let her live, I'd do whatever He wanted. God kept His end of the deal, returning my cat with a rattling purr and one cloudy dead eye but otherwise the same. I felt grateful, but had no idea how to pay Him back.

When I turned to prayer as an adult, at age thirty-five, I was desperate again—but much less spontaneous. I woke every morning at three or four to lie awake for hours. I tried warm milk, I tried melatonin and Tylenol PM. I tried turning on the light and reading. I tried turning it off and imagining myself on a tropical beach. I got up at dawn to dry heaves and diarrhea. I had trouble concentrating. I rarely smiled, and when I did, my cheek muscles ached. Those things I'd kept to myself for so long—my enthusiasms and my doubts, my fear of exposure, the adult writer's equivalent of the, fourth-grader's dread of P.E. class—began to clamor. I wanted to speak them. I wanted to be heard. I wanted pity.

Prayer, I figured, couldn't hurt. But I didn't know to begin. "Our father" and "Now I lay me down to sleep"—the extent of my formal repertory—didn't name what I needed. Without believing myself heard, though, I'd been saying *Help* and *I hurt*, pleas that, like toads and worms in a children's fairy tale, had needed to escape. A priest I spoke with said those were a good start, and steered me to a few more—"You are here, I am here," "Have mercy on me," and the Daily Offices of the Book of Common Prayer. I started praying in bed, at the gym, in the car, and as I grew used to the words and the way they stretched my mouth, I realized that the words didn't matter as much as the saying of them. Words, like kneeling or sweeping hands over candles, provide a miner's lamp lighting the path, a voice for the ineffable. A way in.

My mother wasn't particularly interested in the details of how I found my way back into the Episcopal fold. She reminded me how, at age four, I had responded to her description of the Easter resurrection by saying, "Maybe someone in our family will do that." Now she asked, as if I'd been not to 10 A.M. mass but to a cocktail party, "Meet anyone interesting?" When I recounted to her my first foot washing as part of Maundy Thursday services, she shuddered; "Touching my feet—I wouldn't like that one bit."

But that, to me, was the whole point. Maundy Thursday, as my high church parish celebrated it, had moved me so much I wept I wanted to explain to her the experience of intimacy I felt I'd shared with God and my priest as my priest had sponged and toweled my bare feet. I started to describe the tradition that Jesus had begun with his disciples. "Well," she sniffed. "I certainly don't have all that background. I don't remember that from Sunday school."

In that way, she silenced me. And how often I wished to silence her! When she repeated the tale of my brother climbing out of his crib at nine months; when she turned potentially confrontational topics into commentary on flower arrangements; when she told me once again that life wasn't easy. And yet my mother, who deftly deflected so much, pondered deeply. She and I didn't always meet in our distinctions of what merited further consideration: "What a silly thing to wonder about," she'd say, or "You think too much." I felt the chill of her disinterest, the hurt in those replies.

And yet she loved to tell how she'd overheard me tell a playmate, after disagreeing about whether babies came out of the tummy or out of down there (I argued the latter), "My mommy never lies." (She set us both straight; Sera's mother had had a caesarean.) She repeated with pleasure and pride how she once responded to a friend's announcement that "I'm so lucky, my children believe everything I tell them" with "I'm so lucky, mine don't believe a thing I tell them." My mother fostered independent thinking, contrariety, good solid rebuttals—and any anecdote that planted her in the camp of open-mindedness. "My daughter, the family Democrat," she used to refer to me—frequently, I suspected, to shock her more conservative friends. "For your eighteenth birthday," she announced excitedly in the car one day, "let's get high!" And, one night when I defended France's record in feeding its people and tilling its fields during the 1920s to my father's comment disparaging the Maginot Line, "Good for you!" If I learned anything at the dinner table and in the station wagon of my youth, I learned to argue, to wonder—and, when my mother looked hurt or disapproving, to pull back.

My mother liked to say that she had little respect for organized religion—she'd known too many hypocrites, cared nothing for the trappings of power—and found God in nature and art and books. She'd converted from Presbyterianism to Episcopalianism to marry my father, whose mother cared a lot about such distinctions, but used to say, "It's all one God, whatever you call it." She didn't care about incense and stained-glass and sermons, as I would when I joined a high church parish at age thirty-five, but stopped speechless with her hand on her heart at the sight of Monet's water lilies when we visited the Jeu de Paume galleries in 1982 and repeated with wonder her hairdresser's tale of tripping on acid and watching a rose open in 1969. And yet she taught me to dress (skirt, pressed blouse, leather shoes, purse) for church, for lunches downtown, and for airplane travel ("After all," she'd say, "you'll be arriving somewhere"). Today, when I remove my wristwatch in the evenings, whether or not I'm going out, I hear her voice telling me, with only a touch of amused irony, "Ladies don't need to know the hour after sundown." She cared about appearances, but dismissed what other people thought. Unless she loved them, and then they could wound her to the quick.

My depression wounded her. Unlike my father, who was able to recognize my symptoms—listlessness humorlessness, heaviness of tread and affect—and listen to me without feeling threatened, my mother couldn't take my depression any way but personally. "How do you think that makes *me* feel?" she cried out after I'd told her I felt so bad sometimes I thought about suicide. I'd been co-opted, my despair having to make room for worry about her. Feeling unmet, as flat as my voice sounded, I told her, "Don't worry, Mom. I won't do anything." "I just don't know what's bothering you so much," she said, as though I were making it all up.

I hurt, I hurt, I hurt. This phrase resonated throughout my day, from earliest waking consciousness through footsteps, ringing phones, and lifting a fork to my mouth. Food lost its taste, books their pleasure. I'd been to college, I'd been in therapy. I knew how to think, to reflect, to articulate. I spoke to friends, I wrote in a journal. I couldn't shut my mind up. I stopped trying to talk to my mother about how I felt. *This is,* I told her, *not about you.*

Instead of retreating inward for safety, I became trapped there and didn't feel safe at all. When my own thoughts became too circular, I found myself thinking, *Maybe I should pray.* And so I would. I whispered in the produce aisle, yelled in the car, screamed underwater in the swimming pool. I learned the prayer in silence, in breathing, in saying "Okay okay" as steadily as a metronome. A woman at church introduced me to the Anglican rosary, and I strung my own, repeating certain phrases—the Twenty-third Psalm, the morning Daily Devotion from the Book of Common Prayer, images from a haiku I wrote—as I fingered the blue glass beads. I carried the rosary with me, the touch of which through the fabric of my pocket seemed in some moments prayer enough. I would always be a ponderer, but I found ways to quiet the voices, to loosen the tight skein of anxiety. I did not feel instantly better. But I did, over time, believe that I was met by a presence larger than myself, a presence that told me I wasn't alone. I found security in prayer, in returning to a space that wasn't about isolation or retreat from my strong, effusive, passionate, judgmental, exasperating, generous mother, but that offered a way to hold onto myself and to my growing experience of God.

When, in November 1998, my mother was diagnosed with endometrial cancer, I did what I do when I'm scared. I tucked in.

I worried. And then I started reaching out by phone and e-mail. Prayers were offered, even by friends who would not describe themselves as devout. "I'll be thinking of her," they told me. "And of you." My mother had a radical hysterectomy, and the pathology report came back negative. She was walking in three days and home in five. But even before the good news that they'd caught it all and it had not spread, I felt one morning gratitude and love so strong that I knew myself carried. Prayer had become palpable.

Just as it had a few weeks later when, overwhelmed and lonely, I went for a run. I came home as taut and tense as when I'd set out, and then I flopped onto a yoga mat to stretch. I began, "The Lord is my shepherd," and before I hit the word *want*, I felt release. The tight box I had been in collapsed—not suddenly and jerkily and violently, but smoothly and almost sensuously, like melting chocolate. The walls were down, and I was surrounded by light and air, by love.

Seventeen months later, driving down Ashbury Street on my way to my parents' house, I remembered that sensation of spaciousness and support and I asked, as blatantly as I could, for God to hold us all in it again: "We're really going to need you now." I'd just hung up from talking to my mother, who'd phoned to tell me the lump on her neck was cancer—this time lung cancer, metastasized to her lymph nodes, liver, and (we would find out, in the weeks and months to come) bones and brain.

Prayer didn't save my mother the way I'd believed, when I was ten, that it had saved my cat. But it did something else. Praying is nothing if not paying attention, for without attention, the dive becomes sloppy, the dig a waste of time. Without attention, prayer becomes rote and meaningless. During my mother's illness, I paid a lot of attention—to every word the doctor said, to every movement of his face as he felt her tumor each week, to how her skin tightened and her rings loosened on her fingers and her ankles swelled and her lips chapped and her smile took up ever more of her increasingly gaunt face. By giving me a place to fall apart—to scream and weep and plead and, yes, to disappear—prayer gave me strength.

"You're my strength," she told me in August, when there were only two months left. "I have to lean on you."

"Of course, Momma. Of course."

Since the diagnosis, in April, I'd felt focus and purpose. Anxiety and uncertainty, second-guessing and wondering, all blew away in the gale force of caring for my mother, helping to watch over my nephew, relieving my dad. Life cinched in tighter—and with more meaning—in the last months. Everything outside of love and care, friendship and prayer and intimacy, felt extraneous. I became more forthright and independent, more blunt and direct. You're not a grownup until you lose a parent, the cliché goes, and I found it true. "What's wrong with me?" I asked my therapist. "I actually feel good."

"You are doing something for your mother," he said. "You are doing something with enormous meaning."

"My mother is dying," I said.

"Exactly."

Even in the beginning, when she told me I wasn't needed, I went with her to her oncology appointments and took copious notes, asked question that made her sigh in irritation. When I had to miss an appointment, I phoned the doctor to ask what he thought, even though she'd told me not to bother him, he was a busy man. When he kept us waiting almost forty minutes for an appointment, she fussed about my being late to work until I told her I wasn't worried so she shouldn't worry for me. When he told me, one Saturday when I called him on his cell phone, that she might not live past the end of the year, I told him that he needed to tell her that. And when, two weeks into the third chemo cocktail, she found a new lump on her chest, she handed me the phone: "Call Dr. Smith," she told me. "That's not good news," he said, and I hung up and told her that. At the very end, as she lay dying on a hospital bed in our dining room, I phoned him and told him he needed to come tell her that she'd fought the good fight and could let go. "She needs to hear it from you," I said. I would never have believed I could have done these things, until I had no choice and did them.

I sat next to her when the doctor slid the first drip of Taxol and carboplatinum into a vein on the back of her hand, and I shaved her head and giggled with her about how she needed a black leather jacket to complete the look. I wiped urine from the back of her legs and rubbed ointment onto her slack buttocks to prevent bed sores. I watched the radiation oncology technicians draw crop marks on her abdomen, and I stared at the thickness of the door as they shut it and left her inside. I lifted her from bed to wheelchair to commode and in and out of deep armchairs when she had no lower-body strength, when she suddenly could not raise her foot. "Lindsey," she'd say to my father or the nurse, "let Lindsey do it," and she'd lift her arms to me. "Don't worry, Momma," I'd say, bracing my feet and bending my knees the way the PT had shown me, "I've got you."

We bickered over which nurse had night duty, and whether or not she'd taken her four o'clock meds. When she frowned and spoke about Janet's doctor putting a button in the drawer *over there*—and lifted her shaking and slightly yellow hand to point *over there* and then, exhausted by effort and frustration, dropped it on the third clean sheet that day—I said, "Okay, Mom." I had no idea what she was talking about, and she knew it. She narrowed her eyes and pulled her hand out of mine and whispered, as loudly as she could with a tumor pressing on her voice box, "No!" My mother dying was more than ever my mother—and knew when she was being lied to, or pitied.

After the hospice nurse told her (she'd asked him, as soon as she felt the stethoscope on her chest) that she had only a day or two left, I told her we knew what was happening.

"It's awful," I said. My face was close to hers, but she was still a blur through my tears. "I don't know what we'll do, but I don't want you to worry. We'll be okay. We'll be okay, Mommy."

"Thank you," she whispered, and pressed my face against her neck, against the smooth flesh and musky smell that had been my earliest experience of another and without which I couldn't imagine the world. I smoothed her brow and gripped her hand. She gripped back, and we sat like that for a long time. Even after she was too weak to speak or move, her hand never let go. Her strength—and with it her vulnerability, the flip side of the same coin, no longer something to hide or tuck away or be alone with—passed into me. The boundaries blurred completely, grief and loss having opened up the essence of love. When I look at my hands now, moving on the keys, I know it grips me still.

When the task of choosing the readings for her memorial service fell to me, I selected Paul's first letter to the Corinthians, chapter thirteen. My mother had little patience for clanging gongs or clashing cymbals, and—as I'd seen through her fight with cancer and our loss of my brother, six years earlier—infinite love and hope, so the passage seemed right. Also, as my nephew said, "It's easy to understand." From the lectern in Grace Cathedral, I read the words I'd practiced the night before. I made it through without breaking down. I knew I could: I was doing it for her. It wasn't until a few days later, writing in the journal I'd been keeping since her diagnosis, that I realized what I'd really done for her.

My mother, you see, had one story in particular among those she liked to tell. One *über*-story, if you will, of wonder and aliveness. She told it many times, the last of which I recall as a summer day on the deck at my parents' house in Sonoma. I probably have a sigh, steeled myself for yet another recounting of something I'd heard a zillion times before: Mom and her friend Jackie in high school on "the river," where they'd hold their hands overhead to tan and lean out of windows at night to hear boys sing to them from the driveway. This story, though, took place when she was ten or so, lying awake on a sleeping porch and looking at the night sky scattered with stars. *Who am I?* she thought, and *How do I fit into all that? She* described her experience in a voice throbbing with intensity and openness, her face rapt with mystery and the divulgence of self. Her directness and passion embarrassed me, and I responded as I had many times before—as though I wasn't really listening. *Mm*, I said, and reached for another tomato. I knew what she was talking about but didn't want to hear about it, any more than she'd wanted to hear about my experience of Maundy Thursday. What, out of self-protection, had we kept from one another? What, if she hadn't gotten sick, would we still be keeping from one another?

I knew, as I wrote in my journal, that I'd chosen a passage that addressed what my mother had been talking about on the deck that day: the limitation of human sight, the knowledge in part. "For now we see through a glass, darkly," Paul wrote, speaking of the mystery she'd glimpsed that night in 1940 on the Russian River. On the other side of that dark glass now, she saw face to face. My choosing 1 Corinthians 13 didn't just speak to those of us left behind. *Mommy*, it said, *I was listening all along.*

Underwater, we see how the sky looks from beneath a wavering scrim, feel how it is to be held by something we can't hold onto. Underwater, we're the same composition of matter and mind, cells and neurons—but we move in ways not possible on dry land. In the pool at the health club, when I've finished my round of businesslike, adult laps, if I have the lane to myself, I float on my back the way I did when I was a child, my face an inch or two beneath the surface, to look up through the squiggles of light and water that always mesmerize.

Each time we dive, we stretch our bodies, suspended for the briefest of instances between dry land and water. When we pray, we float between who we are to the world and who we are to God. It may look, in both, like we're disappearing. And in a sense, we are. When I finish praying and emerge to the surface of morning and bed and desk and work, I know I've been somewhere else. I blink to hold onto the internal spaciousness, the glimpse of transcendence, the wonder of love. That's where she went, that night on the Russian River when she was ten, and—I like to think—all those years later, sitting next to me in St. Stephen's Episcopal Church, and at the very end, gripping my hand. And in going there, made me long to follow.

Questions about Content

1. Crittenden's memoir begins, "I knew nothing of prayer when, as a child, I watched my mother disappear." At the end of the first section, she writes, "There were places she didn't want to go—and if on occasion she had to, she went alone." What are those "places" her mother disappears to?

2. How do the swimming pool and prayer present similar experiences to Crittenden? What does she mean by, "Prayer is a dive"?

3. In the second section, Crittenden describes her journey in prayer. For her, how is praying as an adult different from praying as a child, and what do you think might cause that difference?

4. Describe how certain moments in their lives affected Crittenden's relationship with her mother: their discussions or disagreements about religion, Lindsey's diagnosis of depression, and her mother's diagnosis of cancer.

5. What does Crittenden expect prayer to do, and what does she ultimately discover about it?

Questions about Rhetorical Analysis

1. Notice the places in the narrative that mention water. What role does water play in the narrative?

2. Crittenden's narrative is not about just one journey; the writer joins together her thoughts about prayer, her mother, and water. How does the writer work elements together in the narrative? How would the narrative have been different if the writer had written about only one of these elements in her life and not the others?

Freedom in Exile
The Autobiography of the Dalai Lama
TENZIN GYATSO

A lama is a type of Buddhist monk in Tibet, and the "Dalai Lama" is the leader. Tenzin Gyatso, His Holiness the Fourteenth Dalai Lama, is the current Dalai Lama of Tibet; he is considered to be the leader, both governmental and spiritual, of the Tibetan people. A recipient of the Nobel Peace Prize and numerous other prestigious awards from governments and human rights organizations around the world, he writes and speaks to audiences and political leaders internationally about world peace, civil rights, and social justice.

Exiled from his native country by the invading Chinese Communists in the 1950s, he lives in Dharamsala, India, and acts as the leader of the Tibetan government-in-exile. He is the author of many books about Buddhism, Tibet, and life in contemporary society. In books such as Ethics for the New Millenium *and* The Universe in a Single Atom: The Convergence of Science and Spirituality, *the*

Dalai Lama has attempted to offer inter-religious, international solutions, based in reason rather than dogma or coercion, to what he sees as a world in need of spiritual nourishment and compassion. He was selected as the fourteenth Dalai Lama by a group of monks who, through traditional rites, identified him as the reincarnation of the thirteenth Dalai Lama.

The Dalai Lama's web site, www.dalailama.com, contains a wealth of information about his life, work, and teachings as well as historical background into the political issues of Tibet. The site includes a biography, a list of all prior dalai lamas, a chronology of events concerning Tibet, a list of awards and honors he has received and dignitaries he has met, descriptions of his numerous publications, information about his travels, and several web pages providing the texts of his messages, speeches, and teachings.

The passages below come from three sections of his autobiography. In "The Prologue," Tenzin Gyatso begins by establishing his self-identity and exploring what it means to be called "Dalai Lama." In "The Lion Throne" he recounts his teenage years, when he was being educated to assume the role for which he had been chosen. "Invasion: The Storm Breaks" introduces the great crisis that would consume his attention for a lifetime, the invasion of Tibet by the Chinese army, an event that pushed him onto the world stage at the age of fifteen. As you read, notice how much of his concerns involve not so much a spiritual journey as involvement in the immediate affairs facing his life and his country, and notice his reason-based approach to problem solving.

◆

PROLOGUE

Dalai Lama means different things to different people. To some it means that I am a living Buddha, the earthly manifestation of Avalokiteshvara, Bodhisattva of Compassion. To others it means that I am a "god-king"! During the late 1950s it meant that I was a Vice-President of the Steering Committee of the National People's Congress of the People's Republic of China. Then when I escaped into exile, I was called a counterrevolutionary and a parasite. But none of these are my ideas. To me "Dalai Lama" is a title that signifies the office I hold. I myself am just a human being, and incidentally a Tibetan, who chooses to be a Buddhist monk.

It is as a simple monk that I offer this story of my life, though it is by no means a book about Buddhism. I have two main reasons for doing so. Firstly, an increasing number of people have shown an interest in learning something about the Dalai Lama.

Secondly, there are a number of historical events about which I wish to set the record straight.

Because of constraints on my time, I have decided to tell my story directly in English. It has not been easy, for my ability to express myself in this language is limited. Furthermore, I am aware that some of the subtler implications of what I say may not be precisely what I intended. But the same would be true in a translation from Tibetan. I should also add that I have at my dis-posal only limited resources for research and my memory is as fallible as anyone else's.

Dharamsala
May 1990

• • •

THE LION THRONE

Up until my early twenties, when I began to remain there perma-nently, I moved each year to the Norbulingka during early spring, returning to the Potala around six months later with the onset of winter. The day that I quit my gloomy room in the Potala was undoubtedly one of my favourite during the whole year. It begin with a ceremony that lasted for two hours (which seemed like an eternity to me). Then came the great procession, which I did not much care for. I would rather have walked and enjoyed the coun-tryside, where fresh outpourings of natural beauty were just beginning to show themselves in delicate shoots of green.

The diversions at the Norbulingka were endless. It consisted of a beautiful park surrounded by a high wall. Within this there were a number of buildings which were lived in by the members of staff. There was also an inner wall, known as the Yellow Wall, beyond which no one but the Dalai Lama, his immediate house-hold and certain monks were allowed. On the other side of it lay several more buildings, including the Dalai Lama's private resi-dence which was surrounded by a well-kept garden.

I happily whiled away hours in the park walking though the beautiful gardens and watching some of the many animals and birds that lived there. Amongst these were, at one time or another, a herd of tame musk deer; at least six *dogkhyi*, enormous Tibetan mastiffs which acted as guard dogs; a Pekinese sent from Kumbum; a few mountain goats; a monkey; a handful of camels brought from Mongolia; two leopards and a very old and rather sad tiger (these last in pens, of course); several parrots; half-a-dozen peacocks; some cranes; a pair of golden geese; and about thirty, very unhappy Canada geese whose wings had been clipped so that they could not fly: I felt very sorry for them.

One of the parrots was very friendly with Kenrap Tenzin, my Master of the Robes. He used to feed it nuts. As it nibbled from his fingers, he used to stroke its head, at which the bird appeared to enter a state of ecstasy. I very much wanted this kind of friendliness and several times tried to get a similar response, but to no avail. So I took a stick to punish it. Of course, thereafter it fled at the sight of me. This was a very good lesson in how to make friends: not by force but by compassion.

Ling Rinpoché had a similarly good relationship with the monkey. It was friendly only with him. He used to feed it from his pocket, so that whenever the monkey saw him coming, it would scamper over and start delving amongst the folds of his robes.

I had slightly better luck in making friends with the fish which lived in a large, well-stocked lake. I used to stand at the edge and call them. If they responded, I rewarded them with small pieces of bread and *pa*. However, they had a tendency to disobedience and sometimes would ignore me. If this happened, I got very angry and, rather than throw them food, I would open up with an artillery barrage of rocks and stones. But when they did come over, I was very careful to see to it that the small ones got their fair share. If necessary, I would use a stick to prod the larger ones out of the way.

Once whilst I was playing at the edge of this lake, I caught sight of a lump of wood floating near the edge. I started to try to sink it with my fish-prodding stick. The next thing I knew, I was lying on the grass seeing stars. I had fallen in and started to drown. Luckily, one of my sweepers, an ex-soldier from far western Tibet, had been keeping an eye on me and came to the rescue.

Another attraction of the Norbulingka was its proximity to a tributary of the Kyichu river, which lay a few minutes' walk beyond the outer wall. As a small boy I used to go out incognito quite often, accompanied by an attendant, and walk to the water's edge. At first, this practice was ignored, but eventually Tathag Rinpoché put a stop to it. Unfortunately, protocol regarding the Dalai Lama was very strict. I was compelled to remain hidden away like an owl. In fact, the conservatism of Tibetan society at that time was such that it was considered improper for senior government ministers even to be seen looking down on to the street.

At the Norbulingka, as at the Potala, I spent a great deal of time with the sweepers. Even at a very young age, I had a dislike of protocol and formality and much preferred the company of servants to that of, say, members of the Government. I particularly enjoyed being with my parents' servants, with whom I spent a lot of time whenever I went over to my family's house. Most of them came from Amdo and I liked very much to hear stories about my own village and others nearby.

• • •

INVASION: THE STORM BREAKS

On the day before the opera festival of summer 1950, I was just coming out of the bathroom at the Norbulingka when I felt the earth beneath my feet begin to move. The tremors continued for several seconds. It was late evening and, as usual, I had been chatting to one of my attendants whilst I washed before going to bed. The facilities were then situated in a small outbuilding a few yards from my quarters so I was outside when this happened. At first, I thought we must have had another earthquake as Tibet is quite prone to seismological activity.

Sure enough, when I went back inside, I noticed that several pictures hanging on the wall were out of alignment. It reminded me of the time I was in my rooms on the seventh storey of the Potala during a quake. Then I had been extremely scared. But, on this occasion, there was no real danger as the Norbulingka consists of only one- and two-storey buildings. However, just then, there was a terrific crash in the distance. I rushed outside once more, followed by several sweepers.

As we looked up into the sky, there was another crash and another and another and another. It was like an artillery barrage—which is what we now assumed to be the cause of both the tremors and the noise: a test of some sort being carried out by the Tibetan army. In all, there were thirty to forty explosions, each appearing to emanate from the north-east.

Next day we learned that, far from being a military test, it was indeed some sort of natural phenomenon. Some people even reported seeing a strange red glow in the skies in the direction from which the noise came. It gradually emerged that people had experienced it not only in the vicinity of Lhasa but throughout the length and breadth of Tibet: certainly in Chamdo, nearly 400 miles to the east, and in Sakya, 300 miles away to the south-west. I have even heard that it was observed in Calcutta. As the scale of this strange event began to sink in, people naturally began to say that this was more than a simple earthquake. It was an omen from the gods, a portent of terrible things to come.

Now from very early on, I have always had a great interest in science. So naturally, I wanted to find a scientific basis for this extraordinary event. When I saw Heinrich Harter a few days later, I asked him what he thought was the explanation, not only for the earth tremors, but more importantly for the strange celestial phenomena. He told me he was certain that the two were related. It must be a cracking of the earth's crust caused by the upward movement of whole mountains.

To me, this sounded plausible, but unlikely. Why would a cracking of the earth's crust manifest itself as a glow in the night sky accompanied by thunderclaps and, furthermore, how could it be that it was witnessed over such immense distances? I did not think that Harrer's theories told the whole story. Even to this day I do not. Perhaps there is a scientific explanation, but my own feeling is that what happened is presently beyond science, something truly mysterious. In this case, I find it much easier to accept that what I witnessed was metaphysical. At any rate, warning from on high or mere rumblings from below the situation in Tibet deteriorated rapidly thereafter.

As I have said, this event occurred just before the opera festival. Two days later, the omen, if that is what it was, began to fulfill itself. Towards evening, during one of the performances, I caught sight of a messenger running in my direction. On reaching my enclosure, he was immediately shown in to Tathag Rinpoché, the Regent, who occupied the other half. I realised at once that something was wrong. Under normal circumstances government matters would have had to wait until the following week. Naturally, I was almost beside myself with curiosity. What could this mean? Something dreadful must have happened. Yet being still so young and having no political power, I would have to wait until Tathag Rinpoché saw fit to tell me what was going on. However, I had already discovered that it was possible, by standing on a chest, to peep through a window set high up in the wall separating his room from mine. As the messenger went in, I hoisted myself up, and, holding my breath, began to spy on the Regent. I could see his face quite clearly as he read the letter. It became very grave. After a few minutes, he went out and I heard him give orders for the *Kashag* to be summoned.

I discovered in due course that the Regent's letter was in fact a telegram from the Governor of Kham, based in Chamdo, reporting a raid on a Tibetan post by Chinese soldiers, causing the death of the responsible officer. This was grave news indeed. Already the previous autumn there had been cross-border incursions by Chinese Communists, who stated their intention of liberating Tibet from the hands of imperialist aggressors—whatever that might mean. This was despite the fact that all Chinese officials living in Lhasa had been expelled in 1949.

It now looked as if the Chinese were making good their threat. If that were so, I was well aware that Tibet was in grave danger for our army mustered no more than 8,500 officers and men. It would be no match for the recently victorious People's Liberation Army (PLA).

I remember little else of that year's opera festival, save for the desolation I felt in my heart. Not even the magical dances performed to the slow beat of drums could hold my attention, the players in their elaborate costumes (some dressed to look like skeletons, representing Death) solemnly and rhythmically following an ancient choreography.

Two months later, in October, our worst fears were fulfilled. News reached Lhasa that an army of 80,000 soldiers of the PLA had crossed the Drichu river east of Chamdo. Reports on Chinese Radio announced that, on the anniversary of the Communists coming to power in China, the 'peaceful liberation' of Tibet had begun.

So the axe had fallen. And soon, Lhasa must fall. We could not possibly resist such an onslaught. In addition to its shortage of manpower, the Tibetan army suffered from having few modern weapons and almost no training. Throughout the Regency, it had been neglected. For Tibetans, despite their history, basically love peace and to be in the army was considered the lowest form of life: soldiers were held to be like butchers. And although some extra regiments were hurriedly sent from elsewhere in Tibet, and a new one was raised, the quality of troops sent to face the Chinese was not high.

It is useless to speculate on what might have been the result had things been otherwise. It is necessary only to say that the Chinese lost large numbers of men in their conquest of Tibet: in some areas, they did meet with fierce resistance and, in addition to direct casualties of war, they suffered greatly from difficulties of supply on the one hand and the harsh climate on the other. Many died from starvation; others must certainly have succumbed to altitude sickness, which has always plagued, and sometimes actually killed, foreigners in Tibet. But as to the fighting, no matter how large or how well prepared the Tibetan army had been, in the end its efforts would have been futile. For even then, the Chinese population was more than a hundred times larger than ours.

This threat to the freedom of Tibet did not go unnoticed in the world. The Indian Government, supported by the British Government, protested to the People's Republic of China and stated that the invasion was not in the interests of peace. On 7 November 1950, the *Kashag* and the Government appealed to the United Nations Organisation to intercede on our behalf. But sadly, Tibet, following her policy of peaceful isolation, had never sought to become a member and nothing came of this—nor from two further telegrams sent before the year was out.

As winter drew on and the news got worse, there began to be talk of giving the Dalai Lama his majority. People started to advocate my being given full temporal power—two years early. My sweepers reported to me that posters had been put up around Lhasa vilifying the Government and calling for my immediate enthronement, and there were songs to the same effect.

There were two schools of thought: one consisted of people who looked to me for leadership in this crisis; the other, of people who felt that I was still too young for such responsibility. I agreed with the latter group, but, unfortunately, I was not consulted. Instead, the Government decided that the matter should be put to the oracle. It was a very tense occasion, at the end of which the *kuten*, tottering under the weight of his huge, ceremonial head-dress, came over to where I sat and laid a *kata*, a white silk offering scarf, on my lap with the words *"Thu-la bap"*, "His time has come."

Dorje Drakden had spoken. Tathag Rinpoché at once prepared to retire as Regent, though he was to remain as my Senior Tutor. It remained only for the state astrologers to select the day for my enthronement. They chose 17 November 1950 as the most auspicious date before the end of the year. I was rather saddened by these developments. A month ago I had been a carefree young man eagerly looking forward to the annual opera festival. Now I was faced with the immediate prospect of leading my country as it prepared for war. But in retrospect, I realise that I should not have been surprised. For several years now, the oracle had shown undisguised contempt for the Government whilst treating me with great politeness.

● ● ●

It was to be a splendid occasion with the entire Government present, along with the various foreign officials resident in Lhasa all attired in their most formal and colourful regalia. Unfortunately, it was very dark so I was unable to see much detail. During the ceremony, I was handed the Golden Wheel symbolising my assumption of temporal power. However, there is not much more that I remember—save an insistent and growing need to relieve my bladder. I blamed the astrologers. Their idea of giving me an apple to eat was clearly at the root of the problem. I had never had much faith in them and this reinforced my bad opinion.

I have always felt that since the most important days of a person's life, those of their birth and death, cannot be set in consultation with astrologers, it is not worth bothering with any of the others. However, that is only my personal opinion. It does not mean that I think that the practice of astrology by Tibetans should be discontinued. It is very important from the point of view of our culture.

Anyway, my situation on this occasion went from bad to worse. I ended up by passing a message down to the Lord

Chamberlain begging him to speed things up. But our ceremonies are long and complicated and I began to fear it would never end.

When eventually the proceedings drew to a close, I found myself undisputed leader of six million people facing the threat of a full-scale war. And I was still only fifteen years old.

• • •

Questions about Content

1. How does the Dalai Lama identify himself in the prologue? How would you compare or contrast this self-description with the way other spiritual leaders might describe themselves?
2. Consider how his character in the prologue compares with the way he describes his later experiences, especially the final paragraph of "The Lion Throne" and the final six paragraphs of "Invasion: The Storm Breaks." Do his actions and thoughts in those paragraphs match his description of himself in the prologue?
3. The first six paragraphs of "Invasion: The Storm Breaks" narrate the story of a mysterious thunder. How do the Dalai Lama's reactions to this thunder differ from those of other religious people around him? Considering that he is a man of deep faith and leader of a religion, do his reactions surprise you?

Questions about Rhetorical Analysis

1. Several of the Dalai Lama's early memories of his childhood in the Norbulingka involve animals. Considering that the Dalai Lama became world famous, why would he retain these memories and put them into his autobiography? Why do they have significance for him?
2. The Dalai Lama understands that most of his readers around the world do not share his religious beliefs. How does he appeal in his writing to readers of various faiths? What choices does he employ in his writing to invite those readers to consider his point of view?

The Spiral Staircase
My Climb Out of Darkness
KAREN ARMSTRONG

Karen Armstrong has written many books about world religions including A History of God: The 4,000 Year Quest of Judaism, Christianity, and Islam; Holy War: The Crusades and Their Impact on Today's World; The Battle for God: A History of

Fundamentalism; Jerusalem: One City Three Faiths, *as well as introductory books on Buddhism, Islam, and the Prophet Muhammad. Her books have been translated into more than forty languages, and she has participated and appeared in several television documentaries, conferences, and panels, around the world, including the Bill Moyers public television series and book,* Genesis.

Armstrong spent seven years as a Roman Catholic nun but left her order in 1969. She received her Bachleor's degree in literature at Oxford University and taught literature at the University of London and a public girl's school. After she published the story of her life in the convent, she became much in demand as a writer and broadcaster on religious issues. She regularly contributes articles to newspapers and journals.

The following passage, taken from Armstrong's spiritual autobiography, The Spiral Staircase: My Climb Out of Darkness, *describes her first trip to Jerusalem. Because this city plays a central role in the founding of the three Abrahamic faiths of Judaism, Christianity, and Islam, adherents of those faiths have long considered a visit to Jerusalem as a kind of pilgrimage. Armstrong enjoys a similar experience, but for different reasons. As one who calls herself a "freelance monotheist," believing in God and rooted in her Christian tradition but not embracing any particular creed or church, Armstrong discovers something meaningful, beautiful, useful, and essential in all of the world's religions. As much as the creeds, traditions, rites, and rituals of religions of the world diverge from each other, Armstrong discovers that they all share at least one characteristic in common: the belief in replacing egotism and pride with selflessness and the sense of a larger purpose in life. The practice of compassion and ethical action, she believes, stands at the core of all great world faiths.*

✦

. . . This was a homecoming, after all. I had a strange sensation of being physically present in a place which had for so long been part of my inner landscape, a province of my own mind that now took on an objective life of its own. I could feel my personal geography shifting to take in this new reality, and yet also sensed that I had somehow caught up with myself and was about to discover something important. When we caught a glimpse of the golden Dome of the Rock, I involuntarily but audibly caught my breath, and as we veered away from the walls, I turned back to Joel to thank him. He was watching me and, almost in spite of himself, was smiling.

The purpose of this first visit was to find a way of putting my inevitably abstract, theological, and historical ideas into a visual form suitable for television. The most important task right now was to find locations where I, as the presenter of the series, would film my "pieces to camera," speaking directly to the audience. These had to be chosen with care. Each place had to have a clear relevance to the subject matter of the presentation delivered there, and our choice would affect the shape of our six hour-long films. Every morning Danny and Joel would collect me from the American Colony Hotel for a day's tour in Jerusalem or the surrounding countryside, visiting places that Joel thought I should see; during the second week we spent a few days in Galilee, in the north of Israel, looking at the sites connected with Jesus' ministry. Joel could not drive. He was a recovered alcoholic and had lost his license, but I would sit in the front of the car with Danny while Joel directed our tour from the backseat. There was no small talk, however. On the first morning, while we were driving out to the Mount of Olives, I had made another attempt at polite conversation, twittering in my English way to fill the awkward silence. After he had endured my pointless remarks—"How beautiful the light is! How long have you lived in Jerusalem, Joel? And where do *you* live, Danny?"—for about ten minutes, sighing heavily and answering in curt monosyllables, Joel's patience finally came to an end.

"Karen," he growled, "if you have something to say, say it! If not, *sheket!*" The last word clearly meant "Shut up!" I looked back at Joel inquiringly, surprised to find that I did not feel at all offended. Joel grinned. "You are not in England now!"—a phrase that would often fall from his lips during the coming months. "There is no need to be a polite lady here in Israel. We are not formal people. There is no point to speak if there is nothing to say."

Curiously, I found this liberating. After years of deference and formality, it was strangely peaceful to abandon these codes of politeness, at least for a while. I was quite content to sit in the car and gaze enthralled at the biblical scenery without having to think of stimulating topics of conversation. For the first two days of my stay, the weather was cold. It didn't snow, after all, but there was a sharp wind and a sleety rain. But even though this didn't fit my expectation of sun-baked deserts, the sense of walking in an already familiar landscape persisted. It was like stepping into a myth. Here were the places I had struggled to imagine during all those meditations: the Garden of Gethsemane, the Via Dolorosa, and Ein Karim, the home of John the Baptist. Jesus had probably walked up those steps leading to the temple mount. He had certainly walked right here beside the Sea of Galilee. This was the best sightseeing I had ever done in my life. I was not simply letting the sights and sounds of the Holy Land sweep past me in an impressive panorama, but was in search of Jesus and Paul, trying to fit my thoughts and ideas with the landscape and the convoluted history of its famous sites. In the process, these holy places entered my mind and heart in a way that they had never done when I had tried to re-create them in the "composition of place" during meditation. I could understand why so many people felt possessive about the Holy Land. I was beginning to feel that it was *mine*, too.

And yet the land was also a challenge, because the reality was nothing like my pious imaginings, nor would either Paul or Jesus have recognized it. When I had made the Stations of the Cross in the convent, I had never in my wildest dreams thought that I would one day sit at the fourth station—where Jesus had met his mother on the road to Calvary—eating hummus and pita bread. But that is what we did one day when Joel stopped at an Arab restaurant on the Via Dolorosa. Ahmed, a Palestinian who was taking us to Bethlehem and the West Bank, joined us there. Later that day we sat on the roof of the Basilica of the Nativity, drinking Arabic coffee, which Ahmed had brought in a flask, and smoking cigarettes, looking down on Manger Square below. My religious order had been dedicated to the infancy and childhood of Jesus. Bethlehem had been a constant symbol of our spiritual quest like the Magi, we were to follow the star that would lead us to the holy child and his mother. Each one of our convents was a Bethlehem. But here I was, laughing with Joel and Ahmed, neither of whom had any time for religion, and having an impromptu picnic on the site of Jesus' birth. It showed me how far I had departed from those old ideals, and I could almost see my former self looking at this profane scene in astonishment.

I had a similar experience when Ahmed and his Jewish Israeli wife picked me up at my hotel at five o'clock one morning and drove me down to Jericho. This was probably the road that Jesus had described in the parable of the Good Samaritan. Now, sitting between Ahmed and Miriam, watching the sunrise over the desert hills, with the Mendelssohn violin concerto blaring from the car radio, I felt happier than at any time in my life. Again, there was no polite conversation to break the mood. With my ears popping as we passed sea level and continued our descent to the Dead Sea, the deepest spot in the world, I gazed at the extraordinary beauty of the desert and felt moved as I had never been before by any landscape. I could not drag my eyes away from it and felt a great silence opening within me. There were no words and no thoughts; it was enough simply to be there. Perhaps other people had found this quietness in prayer, but there was no God here and nothing like the ecstasies experienced by the saints. Instead there was simply a suspension of self.

Later we sat with a Bedouin family who lived in the ruins of the deserted Palestinian refugee camp outside Jericho. Abu Musa gave Miriam and me a breakfast of pita bread and sour melted butter, while Ahmed rode the horse that the Bedouins looked after for him into the mountains. Then we had to drive home quickly, snaking swiftly up that mythical road, so that I would be ready to start work with Joel at nine o'clock. We reentered Jerusalem, turned a corner, and there on our right was the Dome of the Rock, blazing in the sunlight. Not only was it perfectly at one with the hills and stones, it seemed to bring all the elements of the environment together, completing them and giving them fresh significance. "Strong!" Ahmed said briefly, and we all nodded. That was exactly the right word.

It was not simply my personal circumstances that had changed, but my religious landscape was also being transformed. In my convent meditations, Jews had scarcely figured in the scenes that I had tried so hard to conjure up. They were marginal figures, lurking in the wings in a rather sinister way. At best, they were simply foils to Jesus' superior insight: they asked Jesus trick questions but failed to catch him out; they made obtuse and heartless remarks, which showed how impervious they were to true spiritual values. But now that I was thinking about these scenes in modern Israel, Judaism had moved from the periphery to the foreground, and made sense of the lives and careers of both Jesus and Paul. When we visited the Western Wall, the last relic of the temple planned by King Herod, which was nearing completion in Jesus' lifetime, I stared fascinated at the crowds who were pressing forward to kiss the sacred stones. There were black-caftaned Orthodox, with their earlocks and huge fur hats, as well as men and women dressed in ordinary casual clothes. I watched a young Israeli soldier bind his tefillin to his arms with a thick strap as he bowed and prayed before the wall. Judaism was not the superseded faith of my blinkered meditations. It had a life and dynamism of its own, and was as multifarious as Christianity. It had continued to grow and develop, in ways that I had never considered, since Jesus had died in this city, some two thousand years ago.

As I worked on the scripts, I was entering more and more deeply into a Jewish perspective. I was now engrossed in the books that Hyam Maccoby had recommended, trying to imagine the religious ambience which Paul and Jesus had imbibed. There were elements that were both familiar and, at the same time, revealingly different. Hyam had been right, of course. This truly was a religion of doing rather than believing, and the discipline of living according to the Law was, I could see, very similar to our observance of the rule in the convent. Or rather, in both cases, the *ideal* was the same. The 613 commandments of the Law brought God into the minutiae of daily life, whether one was eating, drinking, cooking, working, or making love. No activity, no matter how mundane, was without religious potential. Each was what Christians called a sacrament: it was an opportunity to encounter the divine, moment by moment Every time a Jew observed one of the commandments (*mitzvoth*), he or she was turning toward God, giving daily life a sacred orientation. Certainly, the Law could seem oppressive. Paul seemed to have found it so; it had ceased to project him into the divine presence, just as my convent rule-had seemed stifling to me after a time. But the Law could also bring joy. This was clear in the psalms that described the Law as luminous and liberating. I was beginning to understand why Jesus' first disciples had been so angry when Paul, the brilliant newcomer, told them that God had now abrogated the Law and that Jesus had become God's primary revelation of himself to the world. They did not feel that Jesus had set them free from the Torah, but had experienced Paul's vision as a potential deprivation. They were fighting for something very precious that gave meaning and value to their lives.

I was also intrigued by the role of study in the religious life of Jews. As a woman, I could not visit the Orthodox yeshivas in Jerusalem where Jews studied Torah and Talmud, but Joel had some film of these noisy, lively sessions, which we were going to use in our series. I watched the men bent over the scrolls, swaying rhythmically in prayer, as they spoke the sacred words aloud and argued passionately with one another. Those gospel scenes suddenly sprang into new life. Those "scribes and Pharisees" excoriated by the evangelists were not simply trying to trap Jesus when they questioned him about the greatest commandment of the Torah, about what Moses would say about paying tribute to the Romans, or about Sabbath, observance. They were like these modern Jews in the yeshivas. This argumentation was a form of worship. Certainly the rabbis who compiled the Talmud, some or whom were Jesus' contemporaries, insisted over and over again that "when two or three study the Torah together, the Divine Presence is in their midst"— words that were strangely echoed in one of Jesus' own maxims. Study of the Law was not a barren, cerebral exercise. It brought Jews into the presence of God. I might have liked that, I reflected as I watched those films. Studying in that intense way might have suited me a great deal better than Ignatian meditation.

It seemed suddenly shameful to me that I had grown up in such ignorance of Judaism, the parent faith of Christianity. The more I read about first-century Judaism, the more intensely Jewish Jesus appeared; and even Saint Paul, who was such a rebel, was really arguing about a New Israel, a fresh way of being Jewish in the modern world of his day. I knew that because of this project, I would never again be able to think about Christianity as a separate religion. I would have to develop a form of double vision. Increasingly, Judaism and Christianity seemed to be one faith tradition which had gone in two different directions.

But there was a third factor. Every time we visited the Western Wall, my eyes were drawn upward to the golden Islamic dome on the site formerly occupied by Herod's temple, which had been destroyed by the Romans. The Dome of the Rock, I was told, was the first major building to be constructed in the Muslim world. Here was another faith that, in its earliest days, had been proud to declare to the world that it was firmly rooted in Judaism. Ahmed and his family took me up to the Dome one Saturday, and I stared at the rock from which the prophet Muhammad was said to have ascended to heaven. It was also the rock on which the prophet Abraham had offered his son to God, Ahmed explained. Again, I felt ashamed of my ignorance. I knew nothing—nothing at all—about any of these traditions. I had had no idea that Muslims venerated Abraham, but now Ahmed told me that the Koran revered all the great prophets of the past, even Jesus. And when we visited the Mosque of al-Aqsa at the southern end of Herod's huge platform, I felt immediately at home. There were light, space, and silence. A bird flew in from outside; the mosque seemed to be inviting the world to enter, instead of shutting the profane world out. I watched Muslims sitting on the floor, studying the Koran—looking remarkable like the Jews studying. Torah in the yeshiva as their lips mouthed the sacred language. This, I realized, was a form of communion. By repeating words that God had in some sense spoken to Muhammad, Muslims were taking the Word of God into their very being. By doing what God had somehow done, they were symbolically positioning themselves in the place where God was.

My project, of course, demanded that I concentrate on Judaism and Christianity. I had no brief as yet to study Islam, but I found that in Jerusalem it was impossible to ignore this third member of the Abrahamic family. On my very first morning, I had been torn violently from sleep at dawn by the ear-splitting call to prayer, which exploded at dawn from the minaret beside the American Colony Hotel. I had sprung up in bed, dry mouthed, with my heart beating wildly. Islam had erupted into my world as a reality that was raw, alien, shocking, intrusive, and wholly unexpected. But after that first morning, the muezzin never woke me again, though the dawn call was still issued at exactly the same number of decibels. I had somehow managed to absorb and accommodate it. Indeed, I soon learned to love the strange Arabic chant as it echoed through me streets of Jerusalem and filled the valleys and hills around the Old City. The call to prayer was a constant reminder that whether Christians or Jews liked it or not, Islam was a part of their story too. Perhaps we were talking about a tradition that had gone not in two directions but in three.

Questions about Content

1. Armstrong does not identify herself as Jewish, Christian, or Muslim, yet in the first four paragraphs she describes her trip to Jerusalem as a "homecoming." Why does she use that word?
2. Despite her sense of coming home, she also feels out of place. Why?
3. In paragraphs five through seven, how does the scenery of the place alter her outlook? In paragraph eight, she says, "It was not simply my personal circumstances that had changed, but my religious landscape was also being transformed." What is happening within her?
4. Explain how Armstrong's previous ideas about Judaism are being challenged in paragraphs eight through eleven, and how her previous ideas about Islam are being challenged in the final two paragraphs.

Questions about Rhetorical Analysis

1. Why does Armstrong tell us the story of her trip to Israel? Why doesn't she just explain her perspectives of Judaism, Christianity, and Islam? What does the narrative of her visit to Jerusalem provide to the reader?
2. Some of Armstrong's readers will be devout Jews, Christians, and Muslims with strong beliefs. What choices does Armstrong make in her writing to encourage all of those readers to consider her perspective?

Connecting the Readings

1. Based upon the personal narratives in this chapter, what seem to be characteristics that personal narratives of faith have in common? Consider elements such as the topics the writers address, the images they use, the ways the writers organize their material or put events into sequence, and the kinds of words they use.
2. Compare and contrast the journeys that Patricia Monaghan and Lindsey Crittenden take. Both of their narratives involve loss by death. Are the objectives of these writers similar or different? Do they end up with the same conclusions? Using these or other combinations of writers in this chapter, explain the similarities and differences using specific examples from their writings to support your response.
3. Does the writing of so many different personal narratives imply the struggle to come to terms with religious truth is universal? Or are the journeys unrelated, each unique unto itself? Are some of these writers describing a personal struggle *about* a particular kind of faith or a personal struggle *with* faith in general?
4. Some writers, such as Karen Armstrong, suggest that various world religions are different paths toward the same truth. In *Religious Literacy*, Stephen Prothero disagrees, saying that various religions "aren't even climbing the same mountain" because they define the problems of the world so differently and look for such different solutions (Prothero 121). Reviewing the

writers in this chapter, which of these points of view seems to be more valid? Do these writers have more in common or more that separates them? Are these writers finding different roads to the same destination, or are they seeking completely different destinations?

Writing Projects

1. If you have enjoyed reading personal narratives, find another, book-length spiritual autobiography. You could read all of Karen Armstrong's book or the Dalai Lama's autobiography, or you could select a new one from your library or bookstore. In what ways is the autobiography similar to or different from the writers in this chapter? What do you learn from the much longer narrative of a book?

2. Using Armstrong as your model for research, explore a church, synagogue, temple, mosque, or other house of worship that is completely unfamiliar to you. If you wish, you could observe a service or interview the spiritual leader or other affiliated persons. Write a profile of your visit and the person(s) you talked to. Describe your perceptions of that religion before your visit, what you observed and learned during your visit, and how your perceptions have changed as a result of your journey. As Armstrong's research gave her a wider perspective, how does your research enlarge your understanding of your own position on faith and religion?

3. As a first-hand research project, explore the perspective of someone who comes from a belief (theist or atheist) that is not your own. For a couple of days, as you read newspapers and magazines, listen to music, and watch television news and other shows, consider: How would all that you read and listen to be different if you were a believer of that belief? How does the world seem to perceive people of that religion or nonreligion? What are some ways in which other people misunderstand that faith? What would you need to know to understand how a believer of that religion sees the world? What are the challenges of trying to view the world from that point of view even for a few days?

4. Write a profile of a person from a belief or religion that is not your own. Interview someone of that religion to learn about how their beliefs shape their values, choices, and actions. Then write a profile of that person. Who are they and what is their history? What do they believe, what are their ethics, and what draws them to this belief? What points of common ground have you found with this person?

Religion in Sacred Writing

How do written stories communicate religious belief?

BACKGROUND

Adam and Eve in the Garden of Eden. The Buddha at the Bodhi Tree. Noah's Ark. Mohammad's Night Journey. Moses Parting the Red Sea. Jesus' Last Supper. Even if you have never read these stories, they might be familiar to you. They are the kinds of writings that have defined the religious identities of people throughout history. The stories found in the Bible, the Qur'an, and other sacred books express relationships among human beings, the world, and a sense of the divine. Beyond the differences, these stories or narratives have one thing in common: they come to us as written texts.

Writing plays a central role in world religions because faith takes shape in the writing of *scripture*. Originating in the ancient Latin word *scriptura* (meaning something that is written), scripture usually applies to a piece of writing that is considered sacred. A scriptural text is considered to be written by a prophet who received the words from God or an angel, or by someone who had a divine revelation, inspiration, or insight.

Because sacred texts are among the most treasured writings in all cultures, scholars take them seriously, studying them to deepen their knowledge about them. Archaeologists locate ancient texts, and by examining the condition of a document as well as the area in which it was found, they identify the time, place, and culture that produced the text as well as the purposes and uses of the text. Historians study the content and language of the document, comparing it to other documents to determine its historical accuracy and to find out what it might contribute to our knowledge about the earlier time period. Literary scholars study the text as a literary form. Many sacred books such as the Bible are anthologies of history, myth, biography, legend, fable, parable, short story, lyric poetry, epistle, apocalypse, and proverb. The literary approach explores how a text has been constructed and shaped by human ingenuity. Through these methods of study, scholars enable us to have much greater understanding, appreciation, and reverence for these unique ancient texts.

Scholars acknowledge that each scriptural text is a document that has gone through a writing process. It was created in a particular time and place by an author or authors struggling with questions about existence and responding to social, economic, ethical, and political circumstances. The author might have been the originator of the words or, if the words were first transmitted orally, the author might have been the first person to put the spoken words into writing. The document might have been altered by subsequent authors, revised by later editors, and translated numerous times, all of which affect the way readers interpret the original text. The sacred document is ultimately selected for inclusion in a *canon*, the collection of writings approved by ecclesiastical or political authorities as authentic or acceptable.

THE READINGS

Following are narratives from the scriptures of several major world religions. These stories are not intended to represent each religion fully or even partially. That would be impossible because these short selections come from much longer chapters, books, or collections of books. The only way to learn fully about a religion is to read and explore as much of its scriptures as possible. The passages here have been selected only to provide examples of the kinds of writing valued in religious traditions.

Every religion in the world represents humanity's search for truth, meaning, and purpose. That search takes many paths. Religions around the world differ from each other in many respects: their understandings of God and interpretations of God's presence in the world, the history of their community and their relationship with God, and the outward forms of rituals and practices they have developed to embody and express that relationship. The various religions do share a crucial feature: each one values ethical behavior and respect for others, empathy and care for those who are in pain, and charity for all who are in need. As much as the passages below illustrate the differences, you might discover ideas that unite them.

Each narrative shows or suggests a conception of God. In the Genesis passage, for example, the way God speaks to Abraham suggests something about God's character. In the Taoist scripture, *Tao Te Ching*, the way the writer describes life and reality suggests a very different conception of what God is. Each passage suggests a practical application of that relationship to the divine; it shows human beings deciding how to act.

AS YOU READ

1. **Analyze.** Look for certain elements in each passage. Whenever we read a historical narrative or a fictional story, all narratives have certain elements in common that you can identify as you read:
   - *Setting*, the time and place where the action occurs;
   - *Characters*, the actors playing major or minor roles;
   - *Plot*, a sequence of events told in a deliberate order, chronological order (each event relating to the others according to when they occur in time), and causal order (each event being the cause and consequence of other events);
   - *Narrator*, the person—real or fictitious, a character in the narrative or a voice outside of it—who tells the story;
   - *Theme*, one or more meanings that are illustrated or expressed by the other elements and overall structure of the narrative;
   - *Audience*, the listener or reader who understands the narrative, learns from it, analyzes it, questions it, finds the significance in it, and responds to it.

2. **Listen.** Many scriptural texts originated from an *oral tradition*. They were spoken aloud and passed on from person to person and from generation to generation within families and communities until eventually they were recorded in written form. Because they were meant to be heard, part of the beauty and power of any work of scripture is the way it sounds, the rhythms of its sentences and tones of its words. In fact, some religions consider God and spirituality to be present in the sounds of the words themselves. For this reason, many traditional Muslims continue to recite the Qur'an aloud in the original Arabic language, and many orthodox and conservative Jews read the Torah aloud in ancient Hebrew. They all continue to place great value on the experience of hearing the text. Even to someone who does not follow a particular religion, scripture is like music: the literary artistry of a text comes alive when it is spoken. Try reading aloud some of the passages that follow so you can *hear* them.

3. **Write.** As you read these passages, keep a pen or pencil in
your hand.
- <u>Underline</u> words you do not understand as a reminder to
look them up in a dictionary.
- Put a check mark (✓) in the margin next to a sentence,
phrase, or word that seems interesting or stands out for
any reason.
- Put a question mark (?) in the margin next to any part that
seems confusing.

Judaism, Christianity, Islam: The Abrahamic Faiths

The earliest stories of the Bible are foundational texts for
Judaism, Christianity, and Islam. These three religions are called
"Abrahamic" because they all trace their origins to Abraham in
the book of Genesis in the Hebrew Scriptures. It is a narrative that
begins in the Hebrew Scriptures for Jews and continues into the
New Testament for Christians and the Qur'an for Muslims.

God comes to Abraham in Genesis 12:1–3 and says, "Go from
your country and your kindred and your father's house to the land
that I will show you. I will make of you a great nation, and I will
bless you and make your name great, so that you will be a blessing. I will bless those who bless you, and the one who curses you
I will curse; and in you all the families of the earth shall be
blessed" (Genesis 12:1–3 NRSV). With this statement God initi-
ates a covenant with the people of Abraham, an agreement that
promises Abraham, his family, his people, and all of their descen-
dants a land of their own with divine protection. In return, they
agree to acknowledge and worship God as the one and only god in
a system that would eventually become known as monotheism
(belief in one God as opposed to the belief in multiple gods).

Abraham and his wife's servant, Hagar, have a son, Ishmael,
whom many Muslims revere as an ancestor. The second son of
Abraham and his wife Sarah is Isaac, who with his wife, Rebecca,
has a son named Jacob, who with his wife, Rachel, has a son
named Joseph. At the end of Genesis, Joseph is taken captive to
Egypt, setting the stage for the book of Exodus, in which Moses
leads the Hebrews out of their slavery in Egypt. Joshua leads
them into battle for the Promised Land, and once established
there, they are ruled first by judges until they ask God to establish
a monarchy. The rule by kings reaches its climax with David and
his son, Solomon, but several of the kings violate the covenant

with God, which leads to their being conquered by the empire of the Babylonians and later the Greek and Roman empires.

As the writers of the Hebrew Scriptures recount all of this history, they interpret events as being signs of God's approval or disapproval of how much the Hebrews are fulfilling their part of the covenant. Specifically, the writers strive to understand why God's chosen people were conquered and lost the land that was promised to them. The historical books of the Bible reflect the writers' struggle to understand the relationship between the Israelites and God, and this is a central question addressed in the books of the Prophets and the highly literary books of wisdom, known as the Writings.

For Christians the covenant between God and the Jewish people is reaffirmed as a "New Covenant" in the New Testament. Jesus is the messiah the Jews were waiting for; he is the culmination of a genealogy that goes all the way back to David and Abraham. Because God loves the world and all humanity, he sends Jesus as the savior of humanity who will lead the way toward the ultimate victory over all earthly empires and the victory over death itself into eternal life. The New Testament reorders Hebrew Scriptures, now thinking of them as an Old Testament full of events, people, prophesies, and themes that prefigure the coming of Christ.

For Muslims the narrative continues with Muhammad being called by an angel of God and directed to "recite" God's narratives and messages to the people of Arabia in their native language. The Qur'an (also spelled "Koran") affirms that "there is no god but God" for Muslims as well as for the "People of the Book" (Jews and Christians). It celebrates Abraham as the first Muslim, that is, the first person who showed full submission to God in an act of faith that serves as the ultimate model for all humankind. The Qur'an recounts many of the stories of the Bible, showing respect toward the Jewish and Christian prophets from Abraham and Moses to Jesus. On the other hand, for Muslims, Jesus is a great prophet and teacher rather than the Son of God, and he is not God's last prophet. Muhammad is the final and greatest of the prophets.

The following two stories from Genesis have had an enormous influence on the ideas, beliefs, and doctrines of all three Abrahamic religions. The temptation in the Garden of Eden recounts how the first human beings lived in a state of paradise but disobeyed God. The story has been interpreted as an explanation for the hardships of life, the existence of human suffering, the presence of evil in the world, the human will to act rightly or wrongly, the relationships between the sexes, and the relationship of God to the world. In the next story, God tests Abraham's faith by directing him to sacrifice his son, Isaac. Abraham goes through the steps to do what God has ordered, all the way up to raising his hand over Isaac to strike him dead, until an angel of God stops him.

Both narratives are about tests. In Eden it is a test to avoid committing a transgression against God, and in the story of Abraham it is a test to carry out a command from God. As you read these stories, consider how the tests are related and how they differ from each other. Consider what these tests tell us about human beings. Perhaps most fascinating of all, consider what these tests tell us about God.

Genesis 3: Temptation in the Garden of Eden

Now the serpent was more crafty than any other wild animal that the LORD God had made. He said to the woman, "Did God say, 'You shall not eat from any tree in the garden'?" ²The woman said to the serpent, "We may eat of the fruit of the trees in the garden; ³but God said, 'You shall not eat of the fruit of the tree that is in the middle of the garden, nor shall you touch it, or you shall die.'" ⁴But the serpent said to the woman, "You will not die; ⁵for God knows that when you eat of it your eyes will be opened, and you will be like God, knowing good and evil." ⁶So when the woman saw that the tree was good for food, and that it was a delight to the eyes, and that the tree was to be desired to make one wise, she took of its fruit and ate; and she also gave some to her husband, who was with her, and he ate. ⁷Then the eyes of both were opened, and they knew that they were naked; and they sewed fig leaves together and made loincloths for themselves.

⁸They heard the sound of the LORD God walking in the garden at the time of the evening breeze, and the man and his wife hid themselves from the presence of the LORD God among the trees of the garden. ⁹But the LORD God called to the man, and said to him, "Where are you?" ¹⁰He said. "I heard the sound of you in the garden, and I was afraid, because I was naked; and I hid myself." ¹¹He said, "Who told you that you were naked? Have you eaten from the tree of which I commanded you not to eat?" ¹²The man said, "The woman whom you gave to be with me, she gave me fruit from the tree, and I ate." ¹³Then the LORD God said to the woman, "What is this that you have done?" The woman said, "The serpent tricked me, and I ate." ¹⁴The LORD God said to the serpent,

"Because you have done this,
cursed are you among all
animals
and among all wild creatures;
upon your belly you shall go,
and dust you shall eat
all the days of your life.
15I will put enmity between you and
the woman,
and between your offspring and
hers;
he will strike your head,
and you will strike his heel."
16To the woman he said,
"I will greatly increase your pangs
in childbearing;
in pain you shall bring forth
children,
yet your desire shall be for your
husband,
and he shall rule over you."
17And to the man he said,
"Because you have listened to the
voice of your wife,
and have eaten of the tree
about which I commanded you,
'You shall not eat of it,'
cursed is the ground because of
you;
in toil you shall eat of it all the
days of your life;
18thorns and thistles it shall bring
forth for you;
and you shall eat the plants of
the field.
19By the sweat of your face
you shall eat bread
until you return to the ground,
for out of it you were taken;
you are dust,
and to dust you shall return."

20The man named his wife Eve, because she was the mother of all living. 21And the LORD God made garments of skins for the man and for his wife, and clothed them.

^{22}Then the LORD God said, "See, the man has become like one of us, knowing good and evil; and now, he might reach out his hand and take also from the tree of life, and eat, and live forever"—^{23}therefore the LORD God sent him forth from the garden of Eden, to till the ground from which he was taken. ^{24}He drove out the man; and at the east of the garden of Eden he placed the cherubim, and a sword flaming and turning to guard the way to the tree of life.

Questions about Content

1. The ancient tale of the garden describes the relationships of human beings to the land and its animals, to each other, and to God. What does the story say or imply about each of those relationships?
2. In this story, God is the Lord of Eden, a sort of landlord, who tells his tenants not to eat from the trees, but they disobey. Look at the sequence of events in the act of disobedience, and determine how much responsibility goes to each character in the story. The serpent was under no prohibition, so is he responsible? Eve never got the order directly, as God spoke only to Adam about the trees; is she responsible? Adam is in charge but didn't make the initial decision to eat the fruit; is he responsible? God created the serpent, the people, the garden, and the trees; is he responsible?

Questions about Rhetorical Analysis

1. Once God discovers that something is amiss, he asks Adam what happened, and Adam points to Eve. Next, God questions Eve, and she points to the serpent. Then God stops his interrogation. Why? Speculate for a moment: if God had asked the serpent what happened, what might the serpent have said? Is there anyone the serpent might point to? Why does the writer of Genesis not pursue this line of questioning?
2. The story has been interpreted in many ways: as an attempt to understand why suffering is an inescapable part of life, as a story identifying the origin of traditional gender roles, and as a fable describing the roles of humans and animals. What purposes do you think the writers of this story were trying to fulfill? Explain.
3. After Genesis, Adam and Eve are almost never mentioned again in the Hebrew Bible. Why do you think this is so?

Genesis 22: God Tests Abraham

After these things God tested Abraham. He said to him, "Abraham!" And he said, "Here I am." ^{2}He said, "Take your son, your only son Isaac, whom you love, and go to the land of

Moriah, and offer him there as a burnt offering on one of the mountains that I shall show you." [3]So Abraham rose early in the morning, saddled his donkey, and took two of his young men with him, and his son Isaac; he cut the wood for the burnt offering, and set out and went to the place in the distance that God had shown him. [4]On the third day Abraham looked up and saw the place far away. [5]Then Abraham said to his young men, "Stay here with the donkey; the boy and I will go over there; we will worship, and then we will come back to you." [6]Abraham took the wood of the burnt offering and laid it on his son Isaac, and he himself carried the fire and the knife. So the two of them walked on together. [7]Isaac said to his father Abraham, "Father!" And he said, "Here I am, my son." He said, "The fire and the wood are here, but where is the lamb for a burnt offering?" [8]Abraham said, "God himself will provide the lamb for a burnt offering, my son." So the two of them walked on together.

[9]When they came to the place that God had shown him, Abraham built an altar there and laid the wood in order. He bound his son Isaac, and laid him on the altar, on top of the wood. [10]Then Abraham reached out his hand and took the knife to kill his son. [11]But the angel of the Lord called to him from heaven, and said, "Abraham, Abraham!" And he said, "Here I am." [12]He said, "Do not lay your hand on the boy or do anything to him; for now I know that you fear God, since you have not withheld your son, your only son, from me." [13]And Abraham looked up and saw a ram, caught in a thicket by its horns. Abraham went and took the ram and offered it up as a burnt offering instead of his son. [14]So Abraham called that place "the Lord will provide"; as it is said to this day. "On the mount of the Lord it shall be provided."

[15]The angel of the Lord called to Abraham a second time from heaven, [16]and said, "By myself I have sworn, says the Lord: Because you have done this, and have not withheld your son, your only son, [17]I will indeed bless you, and I will make your offspring as numerous as the stars of heaven and as the sand that is on the seashore. And your offspring shall possess the gate of their enemies, [18]and by your offspring shall all the nations of the earth gain blessing for themselves, because you have obeyed my voice."

Questions about Content

1. Commentators and theologians have struggled for centuries to understand this compelling story of a test in which God orders a father to sacrifice his son. Does God actually intend for Abraham to kill Isaac? What evidence in this text supports your answer? What do God's intentions reveal about him as a character in the story?

2. Does Abraham actually intend to kill Isaac? At two points—when he speaks to his servants in line five and when he answers Isaac in line eight—Abraham keeps secret what he is about to do; what does this suggest about his intentions?

Questions about Rhetorical Analysis

1. The story of Abraham shows much emotion in the way the characters speak. Look at the quotations of the characters in the passage. How would you describe the way God talks to Abraham? The way Abraham talks to his servants? The way Isaac talks to his father? The way Abraham responds to his son?

2. In Genesis 22 and in later chapters, for the rest of his life Isaac never says anything about being bound and almost slain by his father. Nor does Isaac's mother, Sarah, ever say anything about the fact that her husband planned to kill their son. What might be the reason that no writer included reactions from Isaac or Sarah in the text?

Judaism: The Torah

Judaism holds that there is one God who created the world and judges the actions of human beings. Jews believe that God made a covenant with Abraham establishing a special relationship with the Hebrew people. God protects them and gives them the Promised Land, and they worship God and obey his laws in all they do. Jewish people emphasize constant devotion to God in regular ritual, daily practice, and ethical behavior.

The roots of Judaism began with the Hebrew people approximately 2000–2500 B.C.E. in the region now known as Israel. Modern Judaism began in the earliest centuries of the Roman Empire, known as the Common Era, when Jews, expelled from the Holy Land with their temple destroyed, developed texts, practices, and traditions that they could practice in the diaspora *(the dispersion from their homeland to other parts of the world). At this time, new* rabbis (scholars and teachers) *began to write the* Mishna *and later the* Talmud, important commentaries on scripture, law, and religious practice. *Although adherents of Judaism currently comprise a very small population worldwide, their scriptures and strict belief in* monotheism (one God) *have had a major influence on world history, religion, and culture.*

The foundational scripture of Judaism is the Hebrew Bible, known as the Tanakh, *consisting of the Torah, the Prophets, and the literary books of wisdom, the Writings. To Christians these scriptures are known as the Old Testament. These two terms represent different concepts, as Jews do not think of their scriptures as "old"* *or superceded, whereas Christians think of them as being the foundation for a new testament. While both Tanakh and Old Testament consist mostly of the same books, the order is different. <u>Most notably, the Tanakh concludes with Chronicles, which looks forward to the restoration of the Jews in Israel; the Old Testament concludes with the Prophets to emphasize the coming of Jesus</u>.*

The most important part of the Tanakh is the Torah, or the five books of Moses, beginning with the creation of the world and the initiation of the covenant, and continuing with the entire history of the Israelites. Two selections from Genesis, the temptation in the Garden of Eden and the binding of Isaac, have already appeared earlier. The following passage from Deuteronomy includes the central statement of Jewish faith in line four, called the **Shema.**

✦

DEUTERONOMY

Now this is the commandment—the statutes and the ordinances—that the LORD your God charged me to teach you to observe in the land that you are about to cross into and occupy, [2]so that you and your children and your children's children may fear the LORD your God all the days of your life, and keep all his decrees and his commandments that I am commanding you, so that your days may be long. [3]Hear therefore, O Israel, and observe them diligently, so that it may go well with you, and so that you may multiply greatly in a land flowing with milk and honey, as the LORD, the God of your ancestors, has promised you.

[4]Hear, O Israel: <u>The LORD is our God, the LORD alone</u>. [5]You shall love the LORD your God with all your heart, and with all your soul, and with all your might. [6]Keep these words that I am commanding you today in your heart. [7]Recite them to your children and talk about them when you are at home and when you are away, when you lie down and when you rise. [8]Bind them as a sign on your hand, fix them as an emblem on your forehead, [9]and write them on the doorposts of your house and on your gates.

[10]When the LORD your God has brought you into the land that he swore to your ancestors, to Abraham, to Isaac, and to Jacob, to give you—a land with fine, large cities that you did not build, [11]houses filled with all sorts of goods that you did not fill, hewn cisterns that you did not hew, vineyards and olive groves that you did not plant—and <u>when you have eaten your fill, [12]take care that you do not forget the LORD, who brought you out of the land of Egypt, out of the house of slavery.</u> [13]The LORD your God you shall fear; him you shall serve, and by his name alone you

shall swear. ¹⁴Do not follow other gods, any of the gods of the peoples who are all around you, ¹⁵because the LORD your God, who is present with you, is a jealous God. The anger of the LORD your God would be kindled against you and he would destroy you from the face of the earth.

¹⁶Do not put the LORD your God to the test, as you tested him at Massah. ¹⁷You must diligently keep the commandments of the LORD your God, and his decrees, and his statutes that he has commanded you. ¹⁸Do what is right and good in the sight of the LORD, so that it may go well with you, and so that you may go in and occupy the good land that the LORD swore to your ancestors to give you, ¹⁹thrusting out all your enemies from before you, as the LORD has promised.

²⁰When your children ask you in time to come, "What is the meaning of the decrees and the statutes and the ordinances that the LORD our God has commanded you?" ²¹then you shall say to your children. "We were Pharaoh's slaves in Egypt, but the LORD brought us out of Egypt with a mighty hand. ²²The LORD displayed before our eyes great and awesome signs and wonders against Egypt, against Pharaoh and all his household. ²³He brought us out from there in order to bring us in, to give us the land that he promised on oath to our ancestors. ²⁴Then the LORD commanded us to observe all these statutes, to fear the LORD our God, for our lasting good, so as to keep us alive, as is now the case. ²⁵If we diligently observe this entire commandment before the LORD our God, as he has commanded us, we will be in the right."

Questions about Content

1. Summarize what God is saying to the people of Israel in this passage. According to this passage, what should the people of Israel do?
2. What seems to be important to God in this passage? What would anger God or cause him to be displeased with the people? Does he indicate why these things are important to him?

Questions about Rhetorical Analysis

1. The verses in Deuteronomy promise great earthly rewards for obedience and worshipping only the one God, and they warn of the Lord's anger and destruction for failure. Commentators have debated whether God, in such passages, feels emotions. Does he? Is his tone in this passage a tone of love or fear?
2. God communicates to his people in lines 20–25 by telling them what they should communicate to their children. Specifically, God gives them a historical account to pass on to their children when the children ask them what the laws of God mean. Why does God frame those lines of history as a quotation

to give to the children? How would the effect of that passage different if God had just related the history and not mentioned the children?

Christianity: The New Testament

Christianity is based on the birth, life, teachings, death, and resurrection of Jesus of Nazareth. Christians believe Jesus is the Son of God and the Messiah, whose appearance in the world is prophesized in earlier scriptures and who brings salvation or liberation from sin and death, the main problem facing humanity. A central statement of Christian belief appears in the Gospel of John: "For God so loved the world, that He gave his only begotten Son, so that whoever believes in him should not perish but will have everlasting life" (John 3:16). The largest religion in the world and the majority religion of the United States, Christianity exists in three major forms: Roman Catholicism, Protestantism, and Eastern Orthodoxy.

Christians place great emphasis on the importance of faith and salvation, the sanctity of every human being as a creation of God, and the call to perform works of charity and compassion for the weak and oppressed.

The central text of Christianity is the Bible, which consists of the New Testament and the Old Testament. The New Testament consists of three main parts: (1) the four Gospels (Matthew, Mark, Luke, and John), which relate the history of Jesus, and the Acts of the Apostles, which relates the history of the spread of Christianity immediately following the death of Jesus; (2) the Epistles, letters that the apostle Paul wrote to new congregations with directions for proper behavior and interpretations of Jesus' life and teachings; and (3) Revelation, which presents visions of the end of the world and God's ultimate triumph over evil.

The three brief passages that follow are taken from the New Testament, and in each one Jesus teaches a lesson about ethical behavior. The first passage, from Matthew 5, is a selection from the Sermon on the Mount. In addition to his parables and other statements, Jesus' central teaching appears in the Sermon on the Mount, a poetic statement of faith and ethics and perhaps the most famous sermon that Jesus gave. It includes the Lord's Prayer and the Golden Rule. The following passage quoted from the Sermon is called the beatitudes, *or blessings. The second passage, from Matthew 25, is a statement of ethics central to the Christian values of charity and compassion. The final passage, from Luke 15, is the popular story, the parable of the prodigal son.*

◆

MATTHEW 5

[1]When Jesus saw the crowds, he went up the mountain; and after he sat down, his disciples came to him. [2]Then he began to speak, and taught them, saying:

[3]"Blessed are the poor in spirit, for theirs is the kingdom of heaven.

[4]"Blessed are those who mourn, for they will be comforted.

[5]"Blessed are the meek, for they will inherit the earth.

[6]"Blessed are those who hunger and thirst for righteousness, for they will be filled.

[7]"Blessed are the merciful, for they will receive mercy.

[8]"Blessed are the pure in heart, for they will see God.

[9]"Blessed art the peacemakers, for they will be called children of God.

[10]"Blessed are those who are persecuted for righteousness' sake, for theirs is the kingdom of heaven.

MATTHEW 25

[31]When the Son of Man comes in his glory, and all the angels with him, then he will sit on the throne of his glory. [32]All the nations will be gathered before him, and he will separate people one from another as a shepherd separates the sheep from the goats, [33]and he will put the sheep at his right hand and the goats at the left. [34]Then the king will say to those at his tight hand, 'Come, you that are blessed by my Father, inherit the kingdom prepared for you from the foundation of the world; [35]for I was hungry and you gave me food, I was thirsty and you gave me something to drink, I was a stranger and you welcomed me, [36]I was naked and you gave me clothing, I was sick and you took care of me, I was in prison and you visited me.' [37]Then the righteous will answer him, 'Lord, when was it that we saw you hungry and gave you food, or thirsty and gave you something to drink? [38]And when was it that we saw you a stranger and welcomed you, or naked and gave you clothing? [39]And when was it that we saw you sick or in prison and visited you?' [40]And the king will answer them, 'Truly I tell you, just as you did it to one of the least of these who are members of my family, you did to me.'

LUKE 15

Now all the tax collectors and sinners were coming near to listen to him. [2]And the Pharisees and the scribes were grumbling and saying. "This fellow welcomes sinners and eats with them."

[3]So he told them this parable: [4]"Which one of you, having a hundred sheep and losing one of them, does not leave the

ninety-nine in the wilderness and go after the one that is lost until he finds it? [5]When he has found it, he lays it on his shoulders and rejoices. [6]And when he comes home, he calls together his friends and neighbors, saying to them, 'Rejoice with me, for I have found my sheep that was lost.' [7]Just so, I tell you, there will be more joy in heaven over one sinner who repents than over ninety-nine righteous persons who need no repentance.

[8]"Or what woman having ten silver coins, if she loses one of them, does not light a lamp, sweep the house, and search carefully until she finds it? [9]When she has found it, she calls together her friends and neighbors, saying, 'Rejoice with me, for I have found the coin that I had lost.' [10]Just so, I tell you, there is joy in the presence of the angels of God over one sinner who repents."

[11]Then Jesus, said, "There was a man who had two sons. [12]The younger of them said to his father, 'Father, give me the share of the property that will belong to me.' So he divided his property between them.[13]A few days later the younger son gathered all he had and traveled to a distant country, and there he squandered his property in dissolute living. [14]When he had spent everything, a severe famine took place throughout that country, and he began to be in need. [15]So he went and hired himself out to one of the citizens of that country, who sent him to his fields to feed the pigs. [16]He would gladly have filled himself with the pods that the pigs were eating; and no one gave him anything. [17]But when he came to himself he said, 'How many of my father's hired hands have bread enough and to spare, but here I am dying of hunger! [18]I will get up and go to my father, and I will say to him, "Father, I have sinned against heaven and before you; [19]I am no longer worthy to be called your son; treat me like one of your hired hands." '[20]So he set off and went to his father. But while he was still far off, his father saw him and was filled with compassion; he ran and put his arms around him and kissed him. [21]Then the son said to him, 'Father, I have sinned against heaven and before you; I am no longer worthy to be called your son.' [22]But the father said to his slaves, 'Quickly, bring out a robe—the best one—and put it on him; put a ring on his finger and sandals on his feet. [23]And get the fatted calf and kill it, and let us eat and celebrate; [24]for this son of mine was dead and is alive again; he was lost and is found!' And they began to celebrate.

[25]"Now his elder son was in the field; and when he came and approached the house, he heard music and dancing. [26]He called one of the slaves and asked what was going on. [27]He replied, 'Your brother has come, and your father has killed the fatted calf, because he has got him back safe and sound.' [28]Then he became angry and refused to go in. His father came out and began to plead with him. [29]But he answered his father, 'Listen! For all these years

I have been working like a slave for you, and I have never disobeyed your command; yet you have never given me even a young goat so that I might celebrate with my friends. ³⁰But when this son of yours came back, who has devoured your property with prostitutes, you killed the fatted calf for him!' ³¹Then the father said to him, 'Son, you are always with me, and all that is mine is yours. ³²But we had to celebrate and rejoice, because this brother of yours was dead and has come to life; he was lost and has been found.'

Questions about Content

1. Matthew 5 presents part of a sermon rather than a story, but the first two verses do tell a story about how the sermon was given. Where does Jesus go, who follows, and what does this suggest about their relationship to him? Whom does Jesus say is blessed, and what does this tell you about what Jesus values?

2. In the passage from Matthew 25, Jesus implies that people are separated from each other by certain differences that must be overcome. What are those differences and what perspective does he suggest as a way to get past those differences?

3. As the story in Luke 15 begins, Jesus is seen sitting and eating with sinners. When someone complains about him doing this, Jesus responds by asking questions about a lost sheep and a lost coin and then telling the story of the lost son. How do the lost sheep, coin, and son answer those who criticize Jesus for associating with sinners?

Questions about Rhetorical Analysis

1. The passages from Matthew 5 and Matthew 25 use a type of repetition called *parallelism*, in which statements are constructed in a similar way but with different words. Select a couple of those sentences and describe how they are parallel. Why does the gospel writer portray Jesus speaking in this manner? What effect does parallelism have on the reader?

2. The passage from Luke is an example of a *parable*, a story intended to teach a lesson. Someone asks Jesus to explain or clarify a point, and he responds with a story. Why does the author of this gospel present Jesus composing a parable instead of offering an explanation or telling his listeners how to act toward others?

Islam: The Qur'an

Islam means "submission," and an adherent of Islam is a Muslim, one who submits to God. As one of the three "Abrahamic" religions, Muslims revere Abraham and believe that Muhammad is the latest prophet in a line of prophets extending from Jesus back to Moses. Islam was founded in the year 610 C.E. in the region now known as Saudi Arabia, when Muhammad was called by Allah (God) to bring his message to the Arab-speaking world. There are two major branches, Sunnis (the majority) and Shiites. Islam is the second largest religion in the world and is continually expanding with the largest populations being in Indonesia, Pakistan, Bangladesh, and India followed by nations in the Middle East.

Muslims believe in putting God's laws into constant practice in their daily lives through worship and ethical behavior. They define their practice by the five pillars: (1) faith, expressed in the Shahadah, *"There is no God but Allah, and Muhammad is his Prophet"; (2) prayer, five times daily, facing the direction of the holy city of Mecca; (3) charity by giving money and performing service for the poor, sick, elderly, and oppressed; (4) fasting during the holy month of Ramadan; and (5) pilgrimage to the holy city of Mecca, if one is physically and financially able to do so.*

The central scripture of Islam is the Qur'an, which is composed of 114 chapters called suras *and verses called* ayat. *Structured in a nonlinear, nonchronological order, the book is often recited aloud in parts rather than being read straight from beginning to end. Throughout the Qur'an, which means "recitation," God commands Muhammad to "recite" his word to the Arab people in their language. When the Qur'an is chanted in its original language, the text resonates with beauty and poetry.*

The following passage, Sura 12, is about Joseph, son of Jacob, descendant of Abraham. Like many other suras in the Qur'an, this one recounts and celebrates events and figures from the Hebrew and Christian Bibles. Notice that the narrator is actually God, using the word "We" as a self-reference. The person hearing the story is the Prophet, Muhammad.

---◆---

SURA 12: JOSEPH

In the name of God, the Lord of Mercy, the Giver of Mercy

[1]*Alif Lam Ra*

These are the verses of the Scripture that makes things clear— [2]We have sent it down as an Arabic Qur'an so that you [people] may understand.

[3]We tell you [Prophet] the best of stories in revealing this Qur'an to you. Before this you were one of those who knew nothing

about them. ⁴Joseph said to his father, "Father, I dreamed of eleven stars and the sun and the moon: I saw them all bow down before me" ⁵and the replied "My son, tell your brothers nothing of this dream, or they may plot to harm you—Satan is man's sworn enemy. ⁶This is about how your Lord will choose you, teach you to interpret dreams, and perfect His blessing on you and the House of Jacob, just as He perfected it earlier on your forefathers Abraham and Isaac: your Lord is all knowing and wise."

⁷There are lessons in the story of Joseph and his brothers for all who seek them. ⁸The brothers said [to each other] "Although we are many, Joseph and his brother are dearer to our father than we are— our father is clearly in the wrong" ⁹[One of them said], "Kill Joseph or banish him to another land, and your father's attention will be free to turn to you. After that you can be righteous." ¹⁰[Another of them] said, "Do not kill Joseph, but, if you must, throw him into the hidden depths of a well where some caravan may pick him up."

¹¹They said to their father, "Why do you not trust us with Joseph? We wish him well. ¹²Send him with us tomorrow and he will enjoy himself and play—we will take good care of him!" ¹³He replied, "The thought of you taking him away with you worries me: I am afraid a wolf may eat him when you are not paying attention." ¹⁴They said, "If a wolf were to eat him when there are so many of us, we would truly be losers!"

¹⁵Then they took him away with them, resolved upon throwing him into the hidden depths of a well—We inspired him, saying, "You will tell them of all this [at a time] when they do not realize [who you are]"—¹⁶and at nightfall they returned to their father weeping. ¹⁷They said, "We went off racing one another, leaving Joseph behind with our things, and a wolf ate him. You will not believe us, though we are telling the truth!" ¹⁸and they showed him his shirt, deceptively stained with blood. He cried, "No! Your souls have prompted you to do wrong! But it is best to be patient: from God alone I seek help to bear what you are saying."

¹⁹Some travellers came by. They sent someone to draw water and he let down his bucket. "Good news!" he exclaimed. "Here is a boy!" They hid him like a piece of merchandise—God was well aware of what they did—²⁰and then sold him for a small price, for a few pieces of silver: so little did they value him.

²¹The Egyptian who bought him said to his wife, "Look after him well! He may be useful to us, or we may adopt him as a son." In this way We settled Joseph in that land and later taught him how to interpret dreams: God always prevails in His purpose, though most people do not realize it.

²²When he reached maturity, We gave him judgement and knowledge: this is how We reward those who do good. ²³The

woman in whose house he was living tried to seduce him: she bolted the doors and said, "Come to me," and he replied, "God forbid! My master has been good to me; wrongdoers never prosper." ²⁴She made for him, and he would have succumbed to her if he had not seen evidence of his Lord—We did this in order to keep evil and indecency away from him, for he was truly one of Our chosen servants. ²⁵They raced for the door—she tore his shirt from behind—and at the door they met her husband. She said, "What, other than prison or painful punishment, should be the reward of someone who tried to dishonour your wife?" ²⁶but he said, "She tried to seduce me." A member of her household suggested, "If his shirt is torn at the front, then it is she who is telling the truth and he who is lying, ²⁷but if it is torn at the back, then she is lying and he is telling the truth." ²⁸When the husband saw that the shirt was torn at the back, he said, "This is another instance of women's treachery: your treachery is truly great. ²⁹Joseph, overlook this; but you [wife], ask forgiveness for your sin—you have done wrong."

³⁰Some women of the city said, "The governor's wife is trying to seduce her slave! Love for him consumes her heart! It is clear to us that she has gone astray." ³¹When she heard their malicious talk, she prepared a banquet and sent for them, giving each of them a knife. She said to Joseph, "Come out and show yourself to them!" and when the women saw him they were stunned by his beauty, and cut their hands exclaiming, "Great God! He cannot be mortal! He must be a precious angel!" ³²She said, "This is the one you blamed me for. I tried to seduce him and he wanted to remain chaste, but if he does not do what I command now, he will be put in prison and degraded." ³³Joseph said, 'My Lord! I would prefer prison to what these women are calling me to do. If You do not protect me from their treachery, I shall yield to them and do wrong," ³⁴and his Lord answered his prayer and protected him from their treachery—He is the All Hearing, the All Knowing.

³⁵In the end they thought it best, after seeing all the signs of his innocence, that they should imprison him for a while. ³⁶Two young men went into prison alongside him. One of them said, "I dreamed that I was pressing grapes"; the other said, "I dreamed that I was carrying bread on my head and that the birds were eating it." [They said], "Tell us what this means—we can see that you are a knowledgeable man."

³⁷He said, "I can tell you what this means before any meal arrives: this is part of what my Lord has taught me. I reject the faith of those who disbelieve in God and deny the life to come, ³⁸and I follow the faith of my forefathers Abraham, Isaac, and Jacob. Because of God's grace to us and to all mankind, we would never worship anything beside God, but most people are ungrateful.

39Fellow prisoners, would many diverse gods be better than God the One, the All Powerful? [No indeed!] 40All those you worship instead of Him are mere names you and your forefathers have invented, names for which God has sent down no sanction. Authority belongs to God alone, and He orders you to worship none but Him: this is the true faith, though most people do not realize it. 41Fellow prisoners, one of you will serve his master with wine; the other will be crucified and the birds will peck at his head. That is the end of the matter on which you asked my opinion. 42Joseph said to the one he knew would be saved, "Mention me to your master," but Satan made him forget to do this, and so Joseph remained in prison for a number of years.

43The king said, "I dreamed about seven fat cows being eaten by seven lean ones; seven green ears of corn and [seven] others withered. Counsellors, if you can interpret dreams, tell me the meaning of my dream." 44They said, "These are confusing dreams and we are not skilled at dream-interpretation," 45but the prisoner who had been freed at last remembered [Joseph] and said, "I shall tell you what this means. Give me leave to go."

46"Truthful Joseph! Tell us the meaning of seven fat cows being eaten by seven lean ones, seven green ears of corn and [seven] others withered, 47then I can return to the people to inform them." Joseph said, "You will sow for seven consecutive years as usual. Store all that you reap, left in the ear, apart from the little you eat. 48After that will come seven years of hardship which will consume all but a little of what you stored up for them; 49after that will come a year when the people will have abundant rain and will press grapes."

50The king said, "Bring him to me," but when the messenger came to fetch Joseph, he said, "Go back to your master and ask him about what happened to those women who cut their hands—my Lord knows all about their treachery." 51The king asked the women, "What happened when you tried to seduce Joseph?" They said, "God forbid! We know nothing bad of him!" and the governor's wife said, "Now the truth is out: it was I who tried to seduce him—he is an honest man." 52[Joseph said, "This was] for my master to know that I did not betray him behind his back: God does not guide the mischief of the treacherous. 53I do not pretend to be blameless, for man's very soul incites him to evil unless my Lord shows mercy: He is most forgiving, most merciful."

54The king said, "Bring him to me: I will have him serve me personally," and then, once he had spoken with him, "From now on you will have our trust and favour." 55Joseph said, "Put me in charge of the nation's storehouses: I shall manage them prudently and carefully." 56In this way We settled Joseph in that land to live wherever he wished: We grant Our mercy to whoever We will and do not fail to reward those who do good. [57]The reward of the Hereafter is best for those who believe and are mindful of God.

[58]Joseph's brothers came and presented themselves before him. He recognized them—though they did not recognize him—[59]and once he had given them their provisions, he said, "Bring me the brother [you left with] your father. Have you not seen me giving generous measure and being the best of hosts? [60]You will have no more corn from me if you do not bring him to me, and you will not be permitted to approach me." [61]They said, "We shall do all we can to persuade his father to send him with us, indeed we shall." [62]Joseph said to his servants, "Put their [traded] goods back into their saddlebags, so that they may recognize them when they go back to their family, and [be eager to] return."

[63]When they returned to their father, they said, "Father, we have been denied any more corn, but send our brother back with us and we shall be given another measure. We shall guard him carefully." [64]He said, "Am I to entrust him to you as I did his brother before? God is the best guardian and the Most Merciful of the merciful." [65]Then, when they opened their packs, they discovered that their goods had been returned to them and they said, "Father! We need no more [goods to barter] look, our goods have been returned to us. We shall get corn for our household; we shall keep our brother safe; we shall be entitled to another camel-load of grain—an extra measure so easily achieved!" [66]He said, "I will never send him with you, not unless you swear by God that you will bring him back to me if that is humanly possible." Then, when they had given him their pledge, he said, "Our words are entrusted to God." [67]He said, "My sons, do not enter all by one gate—use different gates. But I cannot help you against the will of God: all power is in God's hands. I trust in Him; let everyone put their trust in Him," [68]and, when they entered as their father had told them, it did not help them against the will of God, it merely satisfied a wish of Jacob's. He knew well what We had taught him, though most people do not.

[69]Then, when they presented themselves before Joseph, he drew his brother apart and said, "I am your brother, so do not be saddened by their past actions;" [70]and, once he had given them their provisions, he placed the drinking-cup in his brother's pack. A man called out, "People of the caravan! You are thieves!" [71]and they turned and said, "What have you lost?" [72]They replied, "The king's drinking-cup is missing," and, "Whoever returns it will get a camel-load [of grain]," and, "I give you my word." [73]They said, "By God! You must know that we did not come to make mischief in your land: we are no thieves." [74]They asked them, "And if we find

that you are lying, what penalty shall we apply to you?" [75]and they answered, "The penalty will be [the enslavement of] the person in whose bag the cup is found: this is how we punish wrongdoers." [76][Joseph] began by searching their bags, then his brother's, and he pulled it out from his brother's bag.

In this way We devised a plan for Joseph—if God had not willed it so, he could not have detained his brother as a penalty under the king's law—We raise the rank of whoever We will. Above everyone who has knowledge there is the One who is all knowing.

[77][His brothers] said, "If he is thief then his broth was a thief before him," but Joseph kept his secrets and did not reveal anything to them. He said, "You are in a far worse situation. God knows best the truth of what you claim." [78]They said, "Mighty governor, he has an elderly father. Take one of us in his place. We can see that you are a very good man." [79]He replied, "God forbid that we should take anyone other than the person on whom we found our property: that would be unjust of us." [80]When they lost hope of [persuading] him, they withdrew to confer with each other: the eldest of them said, "Do you not remember that your father took a solemn pledge from you in the name of God and before that you failed in your duty with regard to Joseph? I will not leave this land until my father gives me leave or God decides for me—He is the best decider—[81]so go back to your father and say, 'Your son stole. We can only tell you what we saw. How could we guard against the unforeseen? [82]Ask in the town where we have been; ask the people of the caravan we travelled with: we are telling the truth.'"

[83]Their father said, "No! Your souls have prompted you to do wrong! But it is best to be patient: may God bring all of them back to me—He alone is the All Knowing, the All Wise," [84]and he turned away from them, saying, "Alas for Joseph!" His eyes went white with grief and he was filled with sorrow. [85]They said, "By God! You will ruin your health if you do not stop thinking of Joseph, or even die." [86]He said, "I plead my grief and sorrow before God. I have knowledge from God that you do not have. [87]My sons, go and seek news of Joseph and his brother and do not despair of God's mercy—only disbelievers despair of God's mercy."

[88]Then, when they presented themselves before Joseph, they said, "Mighty governor, misfortune has afflicted us and our family. We have brought only a little merchandise, but give us full measure. Be charitable to us: God rewards the charitable." [89]He said, "Do you now realize what you did to Joseph and his brother when you were ignorant?" [90]and they cried, "Could it be that you are Joseph?" He said, "I am Joseph. This is my brother. God has been gracious to us: God does not deny anyone who is mindful of God and steadfast in

adversity the rewards of those who do good." ⁹¹They said, "By God! God really did favour you over all of us and we were in the wrong!" ⁹²but he said, "You will hear no reproaches today. May God forgive you: He is the Most Merciful of the merciful. ⁹³Take my shirt and lay it over my father's face: he will recover his sight. Then bring your whole family back to me."

⁹⁴Later, when the caravan departed, their father said, "You may think I am senile but I can smell Joseph," ⁹⁵but [people] said, "By God! You are still lost in that old illusion of yours!" ⁹⁶Then, when the bearer of good news came and placed the shirt on to Jacob's face, his eyesight returned and he said, "Did I not tell you that I have knowledge from God that you do not have?" ⁹⁷The [brothers] said, "Father, ask God to forgive our sins—we were truly in the wrong." ⁹⁸He replied, "I shall ask my Lord to forgive you: He is the Most Forgiving, the Most Merciful."

⁹⁹Later, when they presented themselves before Joseph, he drew his parents to him—he said, "Welcome to Egypt: you will all be safe here, God willing"—¹⁰⁰and took them up to [his] throne. They all bowed down before him and he said, "Father, this is the fulfillment of that dream I had long ago. My Lord has made it come true and has been gracious to me—He released me from prison and He brought you here from the desert—after Satan sowed discord between me and my brothers. My Lord is most subtle in achieving what He will; He is the All Knowing, the Truly Wise. ¹⁰¹My Lord! You have given me authority; You have taught me something about the interpretation of dreams; Creator of the heavens and the earth, You are my protector in this world and in the Hereafter. Let me die in true devotion to You. Join me with the righteous."

¹⁰²This account is part of what was beyond your knowledge [Muhammad]. We revealed it to you: you were not present with Joseph's brothers when they made their treacherous plans. ¹⁰³However eagerly you may want them to, most men will not believe. ¹⁰⁴You ask no reward from them for this: it is a reminder for all people ¹⁰⁵and there are many signs in the heavens and the earth that they pass by and give no heed to—¹⁰⁶most of them will only believe in God while also joining others with Him. ¹⁰⁷Are they so sure that an overwhelming punishment from God will not fall on them, or that the Last Hour will not come upon than suddenly when they least expect it? ¹⁰⁸Say. "This is my way: based on clear evidence, I, and all who follow me, call [people] to God—glory be to God!—I do not join others with Him."

¹⁰⁹All the messengers We sent before you [Muhammad] were men to whom We made revelations, men chosen from the people of their towns. Have the [disbelievers] not travelled through the land and seen the end of those who went before them? For those

who are mindful of God, the Home in the Hereafter is better. Do you [people] not use your reason? [110]When the messengers lost all hope and realized that they had been dismissed as liars, Our help came to them: We saved whoever We pleased, but Our punishment will not be turned away from guilty people. [111]There is a lesson in the stories of such people for those who understand. This revelation is no fabrication: it is a confirmation of the truth of what was sent before it; an explanation of everything, a guide and a blessing for those who believe.

Questions about Content

1. Consider Joseph's roles and personality throughout the story. How does he relate to his brothers at the beginning of the story, when they come to Egypt, and then at the end? What roles does Joseph assume once he is in Egypt?
2. In verses 102–111 at the conclusion of the story, God addresses Muhammad directly. Why does God make references to earlier prophets and messages in verses 109–110? In verse 111, God says the story offers a lesson. What is that lesson?

Questions about Rhetorical Analysis

1. In the first three verses, the angel of Allah speaks to Muhammad, commenting on the story that follows, assuring him of its value, and giving him directions for using the story. How do these introductory verses put the story into a Muslim context?
2. Consider God as a narrator throughout the story, and notice that he inserts comments about his reasons or purposes as an actor in the story. For example, in verse 22 he says, "We gave him [Joseph] judgment and knowledge: this is how We reward those who do good." The other characters also make comments about God. Find another couple of times when this kind of commentary appears. How do these statements affect the story or influence the way a reader might understand the story?
3. Turn to the final verse of the story where God tells the Prophet, "This revelation is no fabrication." Reread the whole verse. Why does God end with this verse?
4. Read the Joseph story in the Bible, Genesis chapters 37–50. Compare and contrast the version in the Qur'an with the version in the Bible. How does the Qur'an present the story in a unique way for a new audience?

Hinduism: The Bhagavad Gita

One of the oldest religions in existence, Hinduism is the third largest religion in the world, with most adherents located in India and neighboring countries. Hinduism embraces the idea that there is a single unified divine power, and many other gods as well as all living things are manifestations and representations of that power.

Hindus believe that life is samsara, an endless cycle of birth, death, and reincarnation that leaves one separate from the divine. Karma, the law of cause and effect, brings consequences to one's actions either in this life or the next. To seek liberation from samsara, one must create good karma through faith, devotion, and ethical thought and action. This liberation can be achieved through any one of various schools or practices of training, called yogas. A yoga may emphasize learning, work, service, meditation, or self-discipline.

The sacred texts of Hinduism include the Vedas and Upanishads, but one of the best known in the West is the Bhagavad Gita, a celebrated work of poetry that may be translated as, "song of the blessed one." Consisting of eighteen sections of seven hundred verses, the Gita is actually book six of a much larger work, the Indian national epic, Mahabharata. The main character is Krishna, the avatar or incarnation of Vishnu, who is God, the spirit who pervades and sustains all things in creation. Krishna appears to the warrior Arjuna, who is feeling conflicted about going into battle. The conversation with Krishna teaches him about life, death, love, the nature of God, and the purpose of existence.

The Gita may be considered one of the most beautiful poems ever written. Poet and translator Stephen Mitchell has called it "a love song to God." In the following passage, Krishna defines supreme wisdom and the essence of God and describes what a human being such as Arjuna must do to show true love to him. Krishna reveals that one must let go of material attachments and surrender oneself completely to God as the only means to true freedom and peace. As you read, notice how the language can be, at the same time, both sensuous and deeply spiritual.

———————— ✦ ————————

THE NINTH TEACHING: THE SUBLIME MYSTERY

Lord Krishna

I will teach the deepest mystery
to you since you find no fault;
realizing it with knowledge and judgment,

1   you will be free from misfortune.

This science and mystery of kings
is the supreme purifier,

intuitive, true to duty,
joyous to perform, unchanging.   2

Without faith in sacred duty,
men fail to reach me, Arjuna;
they return to the cycle
of death and rebirth.   3

The whole universe is pervaded
by my unmanifest form;
all creatures exist in me,
but I do not exist in them.   4

Behold the power of my discipline;
these creatures are really not in me;
my self quickens creatures,
sustaining them without being in them.   5

Just as the wide-moving wind
is constantly present in space,
so all creatures exist in me;
understand it to be so!   6

As an eon ends, all creatures
fold into my nature, Arjuna;
and I create them again
as a new eon begins.   7

Gathering in my own nature,
again and again I freely create
this whole throng of creatures,
helpless in the force of my nature.   8

These actions do not bind me,
since I remain detached
in all my actions, Arjuna,
as if I stood apart from them.   9

Nature, with me as her inner eye,
bears animate and inanimate beings;
and by reason of this, Arjuna,
the universe continues to turn.   10

Deluded men despise me
in the human form I have assumed,
ignorant of my higher existence
as the great lord of creatures.   11

Reason warped, hope, action,
and knowledge wasted,
they fall prey to a seductive
12   fiendish, demonic nature.

In single-minded dedication, great souls
devote themselves to my divine nature,
knowing me as unchanging,
13   the origin of creatures.

Always glorifying me,
striving, firm in their vows,
paying me homage with devotion,
14   they worship me, always disciplined.

Sacrificing through knowledge,
others worship my universal presence
in its unity
15   and in its many different aspects.

I am the rite, the sacrifice,
the libation for the dead, the healing herb,
the sacred hymn, the clarified butter,
16   the fire, the oblation.

I am the universal father,
Mother, granter of all, grandfather,
object of knowledge, purifier,
17   holy syllable OM, threefold sacred lore.

I am the way, sustainer, lord,
witness, shelter, refuge, friend,
source, dissolution, stability,
18   treasure, and unchanging seed.

I am heat that withholds
and sends down the rains;
I am immortality and death;
19   both being and nonbeing am I.

Men learned in sacred lore,
Soma drinkers, their sins absolved,
worship me with sacrifices,
seeking to win heaven.
Reaching the holy world of Indra,
king of the gods,

they savor the heavenly delights
of the gods in the celestial sphere.   20

When they have long enjoyed
the world of heaven
and their merit is exhausted,
they enter the mortal world;
following the duties
ordained in sacred lore,
desiring desires,
they obtain what is transient.   21

Men who worship me,
thinking solely of me,
always disciplined,
win the reward I secure.   22

When devoted men sacrifice
to other deities with faith,
they sacrifice to me, Arjuna,
however aberrant the rites.   23

I am the enjoyer
and the lord of all sacrifices;
they do not know me in reality,
and so they fail.   24

Votaries of the gods go to the gods,
ancestor-worshippers go to the ancestors,
those who propitiate ghosts go to them,
and my worshippers go to me.   25

The leaf or flower or fruit or water
that he offers with devotion,
I take from the man of self-restraint
in response to his devotion.   26

Whatever you do—what you take,
what you offer, what you give,
what penances you perform—
do as an offering to me, Arjuna!   27

You will be freed from the bonds of action,
from the fruit of fortune and misfortune;
armed with the discipline of renunciation,
your self liberated, you will join me.   28

I am impartial to all creatures,
and no one is hateful or dear to me;
but men devoted to me are in me,
29   and I am within them.

If he is devoted solely to me,
even a violent criminal
must be deemed a man of virtue,
30   for his resolve is right.

His spirit quickens to sacred duty,
and he finds eternal peace;
Arjuna, know that no one
31   devoted to me is lost.

If they rely on me, Arjuna,
women, commoners, men of low rank,
even men born in the womb of evil,
32   reach the highest way.

How easy it is then for holy priests
and devoted royal sages—
in this transient world of sorrow,
33   devote yourself to me!

Keep me in your mind and devotion,
sacrifice to me, bow to me,
discipline your self toward me,
34   and you will reach me!

Questions about Content

1. According to what Krishna says in verses 1 through 10, what is the relationship between God and all things in the universe?
2. Lord Krishna describes himself with a number of "I am" statements in verses 16 through 19 and again in verses 24 and 29. Read those verses carefully. Briefly summarize that description. What kind of relationship does he want human beings to have with him?
3. Reread verse 23. What does this statement tell Hindus about who or what God is?

Questions about Rhetorical Analysis

1. The writer uses a number of images. Select an image and analyze how it works. What does it mean, what is it intended to show, and how effective is it?

2. Which lines use repetition of words or phrases to create an almost musical rhythm throughout these verses? What is the effect of this kind of rhythm and repetition?

Buddhism: The Legend of the Buddha Shakyamuni

The Buddha was Siddhartha Gautama, a prince who lived a life of wealth and privilege sometime in the fourth, fifth, or sixth century B.C.E. Outside the palace one day, he witnessed people suffering, so he abandoned his life of comfort and sensual pleasures to meditate, seek enlightenment, and teach others. The word buddha *literally means one who is awake, and Buddhism is based primarily in direct experience, devoted practice, the application of reason, and persistent self-reflection rather than faith or theology or reliance on authority.*

Buddhists embrace the Four Noble Truths: (1) dukkah, discomfort, suffering, and pain are unavoidable, as they are the very condition of existing as a living creature; (2) tanha, desire or attachment to oneself, to others, and to anything in the material world causes suffering because change is inevitable and everything that exists is ephemeral or temporary and cannot be grasped indefinitely; (3) nirvana, the end of suffering is possible through achievement of a state of nonattachment; and (4) dharma, the path to nirvana lies in the teaching, the "Eightfold Path," which consists of serious meditation and mindfulness, pure work and effort, and moral thought and action.

There are various schools of Buddhism, located mostly in Asia, though branches such as Zen, which emphasizes meditation and mindfulness, have attracted adherents in the West. The exiled Tibetan monk, the Dalai Lama, has been popular with Americans and Europeans for his message of compassion and world peace.

Buddhist scriptures are a large and wide-ranging body of teachings, stories, commentaries, rules for practice, and philosophical arguments. No single, comprehensive history of the Buddha's life exists. The passage that follows is Buddhacarita, *"Acts of the Buddha," an account of his life by the Indian poet Ashvaghosha written in the Sanskrit and Tibetan languages. The term* Shakyamuni *refers to the historical Buddha, and the term* Bodhisattva *means one who has achieved enlightenment. As you read, notice how the earliest experiences of the prince seem to fall into place to prepare him to become the future Buddha.*

◆

THE BIRTH OF THE BODHISATTVA

There lived once upon a time a king of the Shakyas, a scion of the solar race, whose name was Shuddhodana. He was pure in conduct, and beloved of the Shakyas like the autumn-moon. He had a wife, splendid, beautiful, and steadfast, who was called the Great Maya, from her resemblance to Maya the Goddess. These two tasted of love's delights, and one day she conceived the fruit of her womb, but without any defilement, in the same way in which knowledge joined to trance bears fruit. Just before her conception she had a dream. A white king elephant seemed to enter her body, but without causing her any pain. So Maya, queen of that god-like king, bore in her womb the glory of his dynasty. But she remained free from the fatigues, depressions, and fancies which usually accompany pregnancies. Pure herself, she longed to withdraw into the pure forest, in the loneliness of which she could practice trance. She set her heart on going to Lumbini, a delightful grove, with trees of every kind, like the grove of Citraratha in Indra's Paradise. She asked the king to accompany her, and so they left the city, and went to that glorious grove.

When the queen noticed that the time of her delivery was approaching, she went to a couch overspread with an awning, thousands of waiting-women looking on with joy in their hearts. The propitious constellation of Pushya shone brightly when a son was born to the queen, for the weal of the world. He came out of his mother's side, without causing her pain or injury. His birth was as miraculous as that of Aurva, Prithu, Mandhatri, and Kakshivat, heroes of old who were born respectively from the thigh, from the hand, the head or the armpit. So he issued from the womb as befits a Buddha. He did not enter the world in the usual manner, and he appeared like one descended from the sky. And since he had for many aeons been engaged in the practice of meditation, he now was born in full awareness, and not thoughtless and bewildered as other people are. When born, he was so lustrous and steadfast that it appeared as if the young sun had come down to earth. And yet, when people gazed at his dazzling brilliance, he held their eyes like the moon. His limbs shone with the radiant hue of precious gold, and lit up the space all around. Instantly he walked seven steps, firmly and with long strides. In that he was like the constellation of the Seven Seers. With the bearing of a lion he surveyed the four quarters, and spoke these words full of meaning for the future: "For enlightenment I was born, for the good of all that lives. This is the last time that I have been born into this world of becoming."

THE BODHISATTVA'S YOUTH AND MARRIAGE

Queen Maya could not bear the joy which she felt at the sight of her son's majesty, which equalled that of the wisest seers. So she went to heaven, to dwell there. Her sister, his aunt, then brought up the prince as if he were her own son. And the prince grew up, and became more perfect every day.

His childhood passed without serious illness, and in due course he reached maturity. In a few days he acquired the knowledge appropriate to his station in life, which normally it takes years to learn. Since the king of the Shakyas had, however, heard from Asita, the great seer, that the supreme beatitude would be the prince's future goal, he tried to tie him down by sensual pleasures, so that he might not go away into the forest. He selected for him from a family of long-standing unblemished reputation a maiden, Yashodhara by name, chaste and outstanding for her beauty, modesty, and good breeding, a true Goddess of Fortune in the shape of a woman. And the prince, wondrous in his flashing beauty, took his delight with the bride chosen for him by his father, as it is told of Indra and Shaci in the Ramayana.

The monarch, however, decided that his son must never see anything that could perturb his mind, and he arranged for him to live in the upper storeys of the palace, without access to the ground. Thus he passed his time in the upper part of the palace, which was as brilliantly white as rain clouds in autumn, and which looked like a mansion of the Gods shifted to the earth. It contained rooms suited to each season, and the melodious music of the female attendants could be heard in them. This palace was as brilliant as that of Shiva on Mount Kailasa. Soft music came from the gold-edged tambourines which the women tapped with their finger-tips, and they danced as beautifully as the choicest heavenly nymphs. They entertained him with soft words, tremulous calls, wanton swayings, sweet laughter, butterfly kisses, and seductive glances. Thus he became a captive of these women who were well versed in the subject of sensuous enjoyment and indefatigable in sexual pleasure. And it did not occur to him to come down from the palace to the ground, just as people who in reward for their virtues live in a palace in heaven are content to remain there, and have no desire to descend to the earth.

In the course of time the fair-bosomed Yashodhara bore to the son of Shuddhodana a son, who was named Rahula. It must be remembered that all the Bodhisattvas, those beings of quite incomparable spirit, must first of all know the taste of the pleasures which the senses can give. Only then, after a son has been born to them, do they depart to the forest. Through the accumulated effects of his past deeds the Bodhisattva possessed in himself the root cause of enlightenment, but he could reach it only after first enjoying the pleasures of the senses.

THE AWAKENING

In the course of time the women told him how much they loved the groves near the city, and how delightful they were. So, feeling like an elephant locked up inside a house, he set his heart on making a journey outside the palace. The king heard of the plans of his dearly beloved son, and arranged a pleasure excursion which would be worthy of his own affection and royal dignity, as well as of his son's youth. But he gave orders that all the common folk with any kind of affection should be kept away from the royal road, because he feared that they might agitate the prince's sensitive mind. Very gently all cripples were driven away, and all those who were crazy, aged, ailing, and the like, and also all wretched beggars. So the royal highway became supremely magnificent.

The citizens jubilantly acclaimed the prince. But the Gods of the Pure Abode, when they saw that everyone was happy as if in Paradise, conjured up the illusion of an *old man*, so as to induce the king's son to leave his home. The prince's charioteer explained to him the meaning of old age. The prince reacted to this news like a bull when a lightning-flash crashes down near him. For his understanding was purified by the noble intentions he had formed in his past lives and by the good deeds he had accumulated over countless aeons. In consequence his lofty soul was shocked to hear of old age. He sighed deeply, shook his head, fixed his gaze on the old man, surveyed the festive multitude, and, deeply perturbed, said to the charioteer: "So that is how old age destroys indiscriminately the memory, beauty, and strength of all! And yet with such a sight before it the world goes on quite unperturbed. This being so, my son, turn round the horses, and travel back quickly to our palace! How can I delight to walk about in parks when my heart is full of fear of ageing?" So at the bidding of his master's son the charioteer reversed the chariot. And the prince went back into his palace, which now seemed empty to him, as a result of his anxious reflections.

On a second pleasure excursion the same gods created a *man with a diseased body*. When this fact was explained to him, the son of Shuddhodana was dismayed, trembled like the reflection of the moon on rippling water, and in his compassion he uttered these words in a low voice: "This then is the calamity of disease, which afflicts people! The world sees it, and yet does not lose its confident ways. Greatly lacking in insight it remains gay under the constant threat of disease. We will not continue this excursion, but go straight back to the palace! Since I have learnt of the danger of illness, my heart is repelled by pleasures and seems to shrink into itself."

On a third excursion the same gods displayed a *corpse*, which only the prince and his charioteer could see being borne along the road. The charioteer again explained the meaning of this sight to the prince. Courageous though he was, the king's son, on hearing of death, was suddenly filled with dismay. Leaning his, shoulder against the top of the chariot rail, he spoke these words in a forceful voice: "This is the end which has been fixed for all, and yet the world forgets its fears and takes no head! The hearts of men are surely hardened to fears, for they feel quite at ease even while traveling along the road to the next life. Turn back the chariot! This is no time or place for pleasure excursions. How could an intelligent person pay no heed at a time of disaster, when he knows of his impending destruction?"

WITHDRAWAL FROM THE WOMEN

From then onwards the prince withdrew from contact with the women in the palace, and in answer to the reproaches of Udayin, the king's counsellor, he explained his new attitude in the following words: "It is not that I despise the objects of sense, and I know full well that they make up what we call the 'world', But when I consider the impermanence of everything in this world, then I can find no delight in it. Yes, if this triad of old age, illness, and death did not exist, then all this loveliness would surely give me great pleasure. If only this beauty of women were imperishable, then my mind would certainly indulge in the passions, though, of course, they have their faults. But since even women attach no more value to their bodies after old age has drunk them up, to delight in them would clearly be a sign of delusion. If people, doomed to undergo old age, illness, and death, are carefree in their enjoyment with others who are in the same position, they behave like birds and beasts. And when you say that our holy books tell us of gods, sages, and heroes who, though high-minded, were addicted to sensuous passions, then that by itself should give rise to agitation, since they also are now extinct. Successful high-mindedness seems to me incompatible with both extinction and attachment to sensory concerns, and appears to require that one is in full control of oneself. This being so, you will not prevail upon me to devote myself to ignoble sense pleasures, for I am afflicted by ill and it is my lot to become old and to die. How strong and powerful must be your own mind, that in the fleeting pleasures of the senses you find substance! You cling to sense-objects among the most frightful dangers, even while you cannot help seeing all creation on the way to death. By contrast I become frightened and greatly alarmed when I reflect on the dangers of old age, death, and disease. I find neither peace nor contentment, and enjoyment is quite out of the question, for the world looks to me as if ablaze with an all-consuming fire. If a man has once grasped that death is quite inevitable, and if nevertheless greed arises in his heart, then he must surely have an iron will not to weep in this great danger, but to enjoy it." This discourse indicated that the prince had come to a final decision and had combated the very foundations of sensuous passion. And it was the time of sunset.

Questions about Content

1. The narrator says the prince "issued from the womb as befits a Buddha," indicating that his birth was miraculous and not in the usual manner. How does the story of his birth set the stage for his life as an extraordinary human being who will influence world history? Compare this story to others you might be familiar with, such as the birth of Moses or the birth of Jesus. What similarities can you identify?

2. Describe the prince's relationship with his father. Why does his father try to shield him from the world? In what ways is the prince similar to the Prodigal Son of the New Testament or Joseph of the Qur'an or Arjuna of the Gita?

Questions about Rhetorical Analysis

1. How would you describe the tone that the translator gives the story from the first line, "There lived once upon a time," to the last line, "And it was the time of sunset"? How does this tone shift? What effect do you think the writer was trying to achieve in shifting the tone?

2. Various mystical figures play roles in this narrative: the king elephant, the seer, and the gods. Consider why the narrative makes these references to such figures. What do these references give the narrative that the narrative would lack without them?

Taoism: The Tao Te Ching

"Tao" means the source of reality and life, the central principle and power of the world. As a basis for living, "Tao" means the way, the path, and the fundamental nature of every thing, which must be discovered for true knowledge to be attained.

Founded by Lao Tzu in China in the sixth century B.C.E., Taoism teaches harmony or conformity with the life force or Tao by means of simplicity, spontaneity, intuition, and wu-wei, or "nonaction." Not to be confused with inaction, nonaction is efficient action in harmony with the flow of things, action that is not forced or wasted. As one verse says, "True mastery can be gained/by letting things go their own way. It can't be gained by interfering." Taoists accept the world as consisting of forces in harmony and balance, the yin (the feminine) and the yang (the masculine), which are in opposition but not in conflict because each needs the other and each completes or complements the other. Some Taoists practice diets, movements, exercises, martial arts, or meditation to conserve and nurture the flow of energy, known as ch'i, in various parts of the body.

The central scripture is the Tao Te Ching, *which is translated in various ways such as* The Way and its Power *or* The Book of the Way. *Many poets have felt drawn to translate this book because its poetry is so resonant with possible meanings. Different from some of the other selections in this chapter, the verses of the Tao Te Ching do not form a narrative. Rather they present observations, situations, contradictions, riddles, and mysteries for the reader to ponder. As you read the following verses, look for these qualities.*

———————————— ✦ ————————————

Verse 1

The tao that can be told
is not the eternal Tao.
The name that can be named
is not the eternal Name.

The unnamable is the eternally real.
Naming is the origin
of all particular things.

Free from desire, you realize the mystery.
Caught in desire, you see only the manifestations.

Yet mystery and manifestations
arise from the same source.
This source is called darkness.

Darkness within darkness.
The gateway to all understanding.

Verse 13

Success is as dangerous as failure.
Hope is as hollow as fear.

What does it mean that success is as dangerous as failure?
Whether you go up the ladder or down it,
your position is shaky.
When you stand with your two feet on the ground,
you will always keep your balance.

What does it mean that hope is as hollow as fear?
Hope and fear are both phantoms
that arise from thinking of the self.
When we don't see the self as self,
what do we have to fear?

See the world as your self.
Have faith in the way things are.
Love the world as your self;
then you can care for all things.

Questions about Content

1. Verse 1 contrasts several abstract terms: "mystery" and "manifestation," the "nameable" and the "unnameable," "free from desire" and "caught in desire." What do you think those abstract contrasts are referring to?
2. Verse 13 says, "success is as dangerous as failure" and then asks, "what does it mean?" According to the writer of this verse, what is the answer to that question?
3. Both verses seem intended for the reader to learn something: the first verse concludes by mentioning "the gateway to all understanding" and the other verse ends by telling the reader to do three things and "then you can care for all things." Ultimately, what does the writer want the reader to do?

Questions about Rhetorical Analysis

1. The Tao Te Ching contains many contradictions, the joining of opposites, which act almost as riddles. For example, some verses say that empty things are full. Another verse asks, when two armies meet, which one will win the battle? The answer is, the army with no enemy. Look at the two verses mentioned earlier and notice these kinds of riddles. Can these contradictions be resolved, or can they only be contemplated?
2. What might be the writer's reasons for using these contradictions? What effect might he want this device to have on the reader?

Connecting the Readings

1. As you have read these scriptural passages, what have you discovered? Has anything surprised you? Did you learn something about an unfamiliar faith?
2. Trace a theme that appears in several of these passages. For example, the theme of relationships between fathers and sons, or between mentors and less experienced individuals, appears in several of the passages. How do the different religious traditions use that theme to draw different lessons or achieve different effects?
3. What roles does the genre or form of the writing play in the lesson each text teaches? For example, could the Tao Te Ching passages be written in narrative form like the Genesis passages? Could the parables in the New Testament passages be written in poetic form such as the Bhagavad Gita passage? Is it possible to separate the message of a passage from the form in which it is written, or is there something about the form itself that makes the message possible?

Writing Projects

1. Read more of the scripture of one of the religions examined in this chapter. You can learn about a religion that is not your own or explore an aspect of your religion that you are not familiar with. Then, use that research to write your own analysis or comparison of faith and values. Write an analysis of that religion's scriptures, thoughts, and ethics. How do people in that religion write about their faith?
2. Compare and contrast the scriptures of two different religions. What similarities do they have? What ethical principles do they have in common? Do they have perspectives that are incompatible, or can some of their differences be reconciled?
3. Choose one of these topics and find out what the scriptures of several world religions say about the topic you have selected:
    *   Nature and the environment
    *   The "Golden Rule"
    *   Wealth and poverty
    *   War and peace
    *   Crime, punishment, and forgiveness
    *   Family
    *   Community
    *   Love
    *   Why human beings suffer
    *   Human relationship to God

    Write an essay comparing and contrasting how the scriptures of various religions address your topic.

Sources

Prothero, Stephen. "A Dictionary of Religious Literacy" in *Religious Literacy*. New York: Harper Collins, 2007.

"Religion" in the *World Almanac*. New York: World Almanac Books, 2007: pages 711–722.

Smith, Huston. *The Illustrated World's Religions: A Guide to Our Wisdom Traditions*. New York: Harper Collins, 1994.

CHAPTER 3

Religion in Academic Writing

How do academic disciplines write about matters of religion?

BACKGROUND

When you register for courses every semester, you are presented with choices of classes in various departments at your college or university. Where did those choices come from? Who invented the subjects of history, calculus, marketing, and psychology? How did it become possible to take a course in chemistry or writing or accounting? Where did "literature" and "biology" and "music appreciation" come from? And why does your school consider it important for you to study these different areas even though you are not going to major in them?

Every area of study, or discipline, has its own history and can tell its own story of how it came into existence, but if there is a common thread among all of them, it is this: each discipline comes into being because it offers a way of looking at the world. That is why college students are required to take such courses. Being college-educated means having some familiarity with the many ways one can think about situations and issues in the world.

Consider this example: In the eastern United States there is a region called Appalachia, which is mostly identified with the states of West Virginia, Kentucky, and Tennessee. A long-term industry in this region has been coal. Recently, controversy has surrounded a new coal mining process called *mountaintop removal*, a type of strip-mining that uses explosives to blast away the top of a mountain to reach the coal inside, and then dumps the debris into the valleys below. Many residents of Appalachia are opposed to this practice because, they argue, it is damaging their homes, communities, environment, and health. Others support this practice because, according to their arguments, the damage is overstated, mining brings jobs to the region, and mining has long been part of their heritage and culture.

If you wanted to study this issue to arrive at your own opinion, the various disciplines you encounter in school could guide your exploration. An economics class could teach you about the business practices of coal mining and its positive or negative effects on the economies of Appalachia. The science disciplines, such as biology, geology, and ecology, could help you understand the effects of mountaintop removal on the ecosystems of Appalachia, and they could help you judge how effective efforts by the mining industry have been to minimize damage. In a political science course, you could learn about state and federal laws and agencies that regulate the mining industry. In your arts and humanities courses, you could study the history, literature, music, crafts, and religions of the region. Different disciplines offer various perspectives for looking at the topic, and the result is a fuller understanding of the complexities of this controversial issue.

An educated person is one who appreciates that knowledge is created, produced, and developed, and that it continually changes. That appreciation helps one make more nuanced decisions and take more informed action as a citizen. Faith and religion are phenomena that can be studied, understood, and appreciated more when approached from a large number of perspectives.

AS YOU READ

Notice how the academic disciplines represented in these readings offer unique perspectives on faith and religion.

- *Literary Studies scholars* read the scriptures of a religion to learn about how those writings were written, edited, translated, and selected for inclusion in a holy book, and to interpret the plots and characters in the narratives of those scriptures.
- *Psychologists* explore how human beings are emotionally affected by faith and how faith shapes the ways in which they interpret the world and their own lives. More recently, psychology is joining neuroscience and evolutionary biology to explore how the human mind is structured to develop faith.
- *Sociologists* examine the roles faith plays in forming societies, how faith and religions shape interactions among individuals within societies, and how institutions of religion function as societies in themselves.
- *Economists* consider how economic forces have shaped religious beliefs, how all religions together constitute a "religious marketplace," and how a religious institution operates

similarly to a business, offering adherents a spiritual "product" or service.

These disciplines are interrelated because each one uses information the others provide. For example, scholars in literary studies depend upon the discoveries of archaeologists and historians to put written texts into the context of the times and places they come from. At the same time, each perspective offers a distinct point of entry into the subject of faith.

Because each discipline offers a unique path to knowledge, each one has developed a unique way of communicating its knowledge in writing. As you read, notice how each writer thinks and writes about faith in his or her discipline.

1. **Notice what question each writer is asking.** Each writer defines the problem he or she wants to answer. A sociologist, for example, defines faith as a social phenomenon, whereas a psychologist defines faith as an individual phenomenon.
2. **Notice the methods each writer uses to answer his or her question.** Again, the sociologist studies groups of people to identify ways in which their faiths impact the structures and functions of those groups. The psychologist studies large numbers of people to make generalizations about the relationship between an individual's faith and mental processes.

Literary Studies

To consider faith from a literary perspective, we read the stories, poems, histories, legends, and other forms that writers have used to establish and represent faith. Whether or not the stories these texts tell correspond to actual historical events is a matter for other disciplines, such as archaeology or history, to figure out. The literary perspective appreciates the texts as works of art and cultural influences that have been open to interpretation for many centuries. Whether an ancient or sacred story is a work of fiction or nonfiction, the literary scholar wants to know who the author of the story is, how the author's social context affected the way she or he wrote it, and how the story has been changed through editing and translating. Literary studies seek what the sources of the story are, that is, how the story may not actually be original but may have borrowed characters or plots or themes from previous stories. The literary perspective identifies the elements of the narrative—its settings, characters, and plot actions—and how they all function together to construct the narrative.

What Makes God Godlike?

JACK MILES

Jack Miles has compared reading the Bible as a work of literature to looking at a stained glass window: it is not looked through, *like other windows; instead, it is looked* at, *so the viewer can appreciate the story it tells and the artistry that went into creating it. Miles makes this argument in his book,* Christ: A Crisis in the Life of God, *the sequel to his first book,* God: A Biography, *which won the Pulitzer Prize. Miles received his Ph.D. in Near Eastern languages from Harvard University. A former Jesuit priest, his writings about religion have appeared in prominent newspapers and magazines, and he maintains an active web site of new writings about contemporary events as well as biblical interpretation. His web site, www.jackmiles.com, offers biographical information, access to many of his publications and interviews, descriptions of his books, and a question-answer section.*

Miles finds much meaning in the Bible by trying to understand the characters in its stories. In the following selection from God: A Biography, *Miles explores the character of God in the Garden of Eden, both as an individual and in relationship to the other characters of the story, Adam and Eve. As you read, notice how the literary perspective opens up new questions about God.*

◆

God—and in this brief interlude we intend the word *God* to mean not *elohim* but the protagonist of the Tanakh in as much complexity as has appeared by the end of the Book of Genesis—is in the most basic sense of the word the protagonist, the *protos agonistes* or "first actor," of the Bible. He does not enter the human scene. He *creates* the human scene that he then enters. He creates the human antagonist whose interaction with him shapes all the subsequent action. This is his first and most obvious distinguishing feature.

If God's priority makes his human antagonist uniquely dependent on him, it is nonetheless also true that God is uniquely dependent on his human antagonist and that this dependence complicates the attempt to do what we are doing—namely, to read the Bible as God's story. For though human dependence on God is never denied in the Bible, in practice much of what humans are seen doing in it has a "natural" autonomy that is unmatched by anything that God is seen doing. By no means all the human action reported in the Bible joins mankind to God as antagonist to protagonist, but the reverse is not true: None of the divine action reported in the Bible is unlinked to human beings none of it is, in that sense, purely divine. God takes no action that does not have man as its object. There are no "adventures of God."

This is, up to a point, the inevitable result of monotheism. Polytheistic Greek mythology includes some stories that tell of intervention by Zeus in human affairs but others that tell of Zeus's life among his fellow gods. In the Bible, God, being the only god, does not have that second kind of action through which to present himself. But the peculiarity of God's character does not end there. God could conceivably engage in some kind of demonstrative action that would serve his own self-presentation apart from any interaction with man: miraculous displays, cosmic disruptions, the creation of other worlds. But in fact he refrains from all such activity. Not only does he lack any social life among other gods *but* he also lacks what we might call a private life. His only way of pursuing an interest in himself is through mankind.

God's words show the same symbiotic character as his deeds. Even lacking, as he does, all divine companionship (he is, to begin with, without a consort), why does God never talk to himself? Surely the divine mind could open itself in discursive soliloquy. But it does not. In the opening scenes of the Book of Genesis—the creation and the flood—something close to soliloquy is heard. From that point on, however, all of God's speech is directed at man, and, in most cases, it is also directive *of* man. God is like a novelist who is literally incapable of autobiography or criticism and can *only* tell his own story through his characters. Moreover, he can only deal with his characters creatively; his only creative tactic with them is direction. He tells them what to do so that they will be what he wants them to be. He is not interested in them in their own right. He does not deal with them analytically. He is always directive, never appreciative.

As for the concrete particulars of what God wants mankind to be, this he only discovers as he goes along. His manner is always supremely confident, but he does not announce or seem even to know all his plans in detail or in advance. Again and again, God is displeased with man, but often enough it seems that he discovers only in and through his anger just what pleases him. To change the analogy slightly, he is like a director whose actors never seem to get it right and who is, as a result, often angry but who doesn't, himself, always know beforehand what getting it right will be. When the actors get it wrong, he too gets it wrong until, finally, they get it more or less right, and he calms down enough to admit it. Getting it right is, in the Bible, not just a matter of mankind's observing the law of God (at this point in the story, the law has not even been given). It is rather, and much more broadly, a matter of mankind's becoming the image of God. That quest, arising from the protagonist's sole stated motive, drives the only real plot that the Bible can be said to have. But that plot, God's attempt to shape mankind in his image, would be far more comprehensible if God had a richer subjective life, one more clearly separate from, more clearly prior to, the human object of his shaping.

As it is, the plot of the Bible is difficult and elusive in a way that is intimately related to the difficulty and elusiveness of God as its protagonist. Experience shapes character, and character determines action. A character totally without experience is all but a contradiction in terms. If such a character could exist at all, we would scarcely know what to expect of him or what it would mean to be shaped in his image. True, we are well enough accustomed—in life and in literature—to see an innocent character living through new, sometimes painful experiences and so undergoing a character development. But that innocence, that lack of experience, is always only a relative lack. A country boy come to the big city does, when all is said and done, have eighteen or so years of history behind him. It is that history that makes him comprehensible to us. How would we understand him if chronologically he were eighteen but characterologically, a parentless newborn babe? His character would then necessarily lie entirely in his future rather than in his past. He could only be what he would become, and so at the outset he could only be a kind of living question mark.

God, though we have managed to say a good deal about him in the Book of Genesis, is this kind of living question mark, a wholly prospective character. He has no history, no genealogy, no past that in the usual way of literature might be progressively introduced into his story to explain his behavior and induce some kind of catharsis in the reader. No human character could be so fully without a past and still be human, yet we may see that by giving this inhuman character words to speak in human language and deeds to do in interaction with human beings, the writers of the Bible have created a new literary possibility. God frustrates our ordinary literary expectations, shaped as they are by the expectations that we have of other human beings when we meet them. We expect to learn who they are by learning how their past has led to their present. This is, almost by definition, what makes any human character interesting and coherent.

God is not interesting or coherent in this way. That the Greek gods had recognizably human bodies was ultimately less important to their anthropomorphism than that they had genealogies and desires, pasts and futures. God has neither, and the stray anthropomorphisms of detail that appear in the Book of Genesis are dwarfed by that overwhelming fact. We must think of God as newborn and yet not a babe, his possibilities not confined within the boundaries of human experience and yet, paradoxically, not to be realized unless in relationship with human beings. His manner in the Book of Genesis is, very roughly, that of a man of unreflective self-confidence, intrusive-to-aggressive habits, and unpredictable eloquence but, above all, a man who discloses nothing about his past and next to nothing about his needs or desires. When the adjective *godlike* refers implicitly to this God—Adam's maker and Abraham's partner—rather than, say, to the youthful, physically beautiful, and brilliant Apollo, it signifies a set of qualities like those just mentioned; and if the type in question is a familiar one in the West, biblical influence must be presumed. What is most compelling about the type is an air of power coupled with the absence of any of the usual clues as to how the power might be used.

In the case of absolutely every human character, we know that, though he may disclose nothing about his past, he has had one, nonetheless, one that included a mother, a birth, and a mewling and puking infancy. As for his future, though he may disclose no intentions, we do not believe him to be without desires. A powerful manner can intimidate, but adults know that godlikeness resting on a denial of the past and the future can be nothing more than a pose. Just here, however, the analogy breaks down: God is not posing. He is not the Wizard of Oz. He is portrayed, with apparent sincerity and unwavering consistency, as truly without a past and, though not without intentions, as truly without desires except the desire that mankind should be his self-image. Otherwise, though his intentions, rudimentary at first, grow more complex, and though he is surprised by their effects and inclined to repudiate them, they are not the product of desire until very late in his story. At the start, and for a long while after the start, God relies on man even for the working out of his own intentions and is, to this extent, almost parasitic on human desire. If man wanted nothing, it is difficult to imagine how God would discover what God wanted.

Once we recognize God as dependent on human beings in this way, we may appreciate why, for him, the quest for a self-image is not an idle and optional indulgence but the sole and indispensable tool of his self-understanding. If no one has painted your portrait, you, as a human being, still know who you are. Even if you have never seen yourself in a mirror, the same will be true. The person in the portrait, the person reflected in the mirror, is already in existence, and you know that person. Your history has both made you and made you a fact evident to yourself. God, as the Bible begins, is as yet unmade by any history and is therefore less than evident to himself. Though he is, uniquely, a protagonist who gives life itself to his antagonist, he is also, uniquely again, a protagonist who receives his life story from his antagonist.

Questions about Content

1. According to theology, God is unlike humans because God is eternal, omniscient, and omnipotent. However, according to this passage, especially the sixth and seventh paragraphs, how is the character of God unlike the other characters in the Bible?
2. According to the third and eighth paragraphs, how is the character of God in the Bible similar to or different from the Greek gods?
3. From a theological perspective, we would say that human beings are dependent upon God. But from the literary perspective, Miles says the opposite. What does Miles mean by saying that God is dependent upon human beings? Explain how that is possible in a literary interpretation of the story.

Questions about Rhetorical Analysis

1. One of Miles' talents is his ability to think "outside the box" and offer a different point of view. Find one statement that strikes you as unique or especially creative or surprising. How does that statement provoke you to think in a new way?
2. Imagine that Miles wrote this description of God to answer a question he was struggling with. What might that question have been? Describe his method for arriving at an answer to that question.
3. Occasionally, Miles uses a comparison to make his point: the country boy in paragraph six, the living question mark in paragraph seven, the Wizard of Oz in paragraph nine, and the portrait and mirror in the final paragraph. Select one of these analogies or a different one, and describe how Miles uses it. What is he attempting to prove with this comparison?

Psychology

By applying the tools of scientific inquiry to the human mind and emotions, the field of psychology studies how human beings believe and what the effects of belief are on the human mind. Several fields have been converging to explore how human beings, as a species, have evolved to adopt beliefs. Biological studies of the human brain and genetic makeup are now seeking to discover how human beings are biologically structured or equipped to have faith. Scientists ask questions such as, is there a "faith gene," something in human DNA that makes faith possible?

Is there a "faith center" in the brain, a part of the nervous system that is "wired" for belief? The fields of genetics, neuroscience (studying brains and nervous systems), cognitive psychology (studying how the brain learns), and evolutionary psychology (studying how the functions of the mind may have evolved) are asking how the minds of human beings are structured to believe. These scientists are also asking why these structures developed or how faith might be the result of certain developments that contributed to the survival of the species.

The Evolutionary Psychology of Religion
STEVEN PINKER

A professor in the Department of Psychology at Harvard University, Steven Pinker does research on language and cognition. He has taught in the Department of Brain and Cognitive Sciences at MIT, and has published several books, including The Language Instinct, How the Mind Works, *and most recently,* The Stuff of Thought: Language as a Window into Human Nature. *His articles have appeared in many publications including* the New York Times, Time *magazine, and* Slate. *He teaches courses in the human mind, language and human nature, cognitive and behavioral genetics, and evolutionary psychology. For access to many of Pinker's publications, lectures, interviews, and course descriptions, check his web site at http://pinker.wjh.harvard.edu.*

The following reading selection is a speech that Dr. Pinker gave upon being honored at the annual meeting of the Freedom from Religion Foundation. Pinker begins by defining his objective: to explain religious belief as a phenomenon of the human mind because the mind is where the act of believing occurs. As a psychologist following the theory of evolution, he then poses his question: how and why did the human mind evolve to hold beliefs? The first explanation is that religion could be a biological adaptation, a trait that evolved to help the species survive. Pinker lists and refutes several reasons to support the "adaptation" claim and then shifts to another possibility: that belief is a by-product, a trait that results from an adaptation but is not innate or necessary for survival. He gives several examples of by-products and explains how religion might have evolved as beneficial to producers and consumers, two

₁ biology. His essay concludes with a summary of his
As you read, notice how Pinker relates a complex argu-
₁ader by offering examples, illustrations, or small stories.

———————— ◆ ————————

PRESENTED AT THE ANNUAL MEETING OF THE FREEDOM FROM RELIGION FOUNDATION, MADISON, WISCONSIN, OCTOBER 29, 2004, ON RECEIPT OF "THE EMPEROR'S NEW CLOTHES AWARD."

Thank you very much; this is a tremendous honor. I look forward to displaying the Emperor proudly in my office at Harvard. It's a special honor to be here on the occasion that is recognizing the accomplishments of Anne Gaylor and I'd like to express my appreciation for the wonderful work that she has done in this Foundation.

Do we have a "God gene," or a "God module"? I'm referring to claims that a number of you may have noticed. Just last week, a cover story of *Time* magazine was called "The God Gene: Does our deity compel us to seek a higher power?" Believe it or not, some scientists say yes. And a number of years earlier, there were claims that the human brain is equipped with a "God module," a subsystem of the brain shaped by evolution to cause us to have a religious belief. "Brain's God module may affect religious intensity," according to the headline of the *Los Angeles Times*. In this evening's talk, I want to evaluate those claims.

There certainly is a phenomenon that needs to be explained, namely religious beliefs. According to surveys by ethnographers, religion is a human universal. In all human cultures, people believe that the soul lives on after death, that ritual can change the physical world and divine the truth, and that illness and misfortune are caused and alleviated by a variety of invisible person-like entities: spirits, ghosts, saints, evils, demons, cherubim or Jesus, devils and gods.

All cultures, you might ask? Yes, all cultures. I give you an example of a culture we're well familiar with, that of the contemporary United States. The last time I checked the figures, 25% of Americans believe in witches, 50% in ghosts, 50% in the devil, 50% believe that the Book of Genesis is literally true, 69% believe in angels, 87% believe Jesus was raised from the dead, and 96% believe in a god or a universal spirit. You've got your work cut out for you!

So what's going on? In many regards, the human mind appears to be well-engineered. Not literally well engineered, but it has the *signs* or appearance of engineering in the biologist's sense.

That is, we can see, think move, talk, understand, and attain goals better than any robot or computer. You can't go to Circuit City and buy Rosie the Maid from "The Jetsons" and expect to it to put away the dishes or run simple errands. These feats are too difficult for human-made creations, though they're things that a five-year-old child could do effortlessly. The explanation for signs of engineering in the natural world is Darwin's theory of natural selection, the only theory we've come up with so far that can explain the illusion of design in causal terms.

The question is, how can a powerful taste for apparently irrational beliefs evolve? H. L Mencken said that "the most common of all follies is to believe passionately in the palpably not true. It's the chief occupation of humankind." This poses an enigma to the psychologist.

There is one way in which religious belief could be an adaptation. Many of our faculties are adaptations to enduring properties of the real world. We have depth perception, because the world really is three-dimensional. We apparently have an innate fear of snakes, because the world has snakes and they are venomous. Perhaps there really is a personal, attentive, invisible, miracle-producing, reward-giving, retributive deity, and we have a God module in order to commune with him. As a scientist, I like to interpret claims as testable hypotheses, and this certainly is one. It predicts, for example, that miracles should be observable, that success in life should be proportional to virtue, and that suffering should be proportional to sin. I don't know anyone who has done the necessary studies, but I would say there is good reason to believe that these hypotheses have not been confirmed. There's a Yiddish expression: "If God lived on earth, people would break his windows."

There have been other, more plausible attempts to explain religion as a biological adaptation. Even though I'm far more sympathetic to Darwinian explanations of mental life than most psychologists, I don't find any of these convincing.

The first is that religion gives comfort. The concepts of a benevolent shepherd, a universal plan, an afterlife, or just deserts, ease the pain of being a human; these comforting thoughts make us feel better. There's an element of truth to this, but it is not a legitimate adaptationist explanation, because it begs the question of *why* the mind should find comfort in beliefs that are false. Saying that something is so doesn't make it so, and there's no reason why it should be comforting to *think* it so, when we have reason to believe it is *not so*. Compare: if you're freezing, being told that you're warm is not terribly soothing. If you're being threatened by a menacing predator, being told that it's just a rabbit is not particularly comforting. In general, we are not that easily deluded. Why should we be in the case of religion? It simply begs the question.

The second hypothesis is that religion brings a community together. Those of you who read the cover story of *Time* might be familiar with this hypothesis because the geneticist Dean Hamer, whose new book *The God Gene* inspired the cover story, offered this as his Darwinian explanation of religion. Again I think again there's an element of truth in this. Religion certainly does bring a community together. But again it simply begs the question as to *why*. Why, if there is a subgoal in evolution to have people stand together to face off common enemies, would a belief in spirits, or a belief that ritual could change the future, be necessary to cement a community together? Why not just emotions like trust and loyalty and friendship and solidarity? There's no a priori reason you would expect a belief in a soul or a ritual would be a solution to the problem of how you get a bunch of organisms to cooperate.

The third spurious explanation is that religion is the source of our higher ethical yearnings. Those of you who read the book *Rock of Ages* by Steven Jay Gould, who argued that religion and science could co-exist comfortably, are familiar with his argument: since science can't tell us what our moral values should be, that's what religion is for, and each "magisterium" should respect the other. A big problem for this hypothesis is apparent to anyone who has read the Bible, which is a manual for rape and genocide and destruction. God tells the Israelites invading all Midianite villages, "Kill all the men, kill all the kids, kill all the old women. The young women that you find attractive, bring them back to your compound, lock them up, shave their heads, lock them in a room for 30 days till they stop crying their eyes out because you've killed their mom and dad, and then take her as a second or third or fourth or fifth wife." So the Bible, contrary to what a majority of Americans apparently believe, is far from a source of higher moral values. Religions have given us stonings, witch-burnings, crusades, inquisitions, jihads, fatwas, suicide bombers, gay-bashers, abortion-clinic gunmen, and mothers who drown their sons so they can happily be united in heaven.

To understand the source of moral values, we don't have to look to religion. Psychologists have identified universal moral sentiments such as love, compassion, generosity, guilt, shame, and righteous indignation. A belief in spirits and angels need have anything to do with it. And moral philosophers such as Peter Singer who scrutinize the concept of morality have shown that it is logically rooted in the interchangeability of one's own interests and others. The world's enduring moral systems capture in some way the notion of the interchangeability of perspectives and interests, the idea that "I am one guy among many": the golden rule;

the categorical imperative; Singer's own notion of "the expanding circle," John Rawls' "veil of ignorance," and so on. A retributive, human-like deity meting out justice doesn't have a role in our best explanations of the logic of morality.

To answer the "why is *Homo sapiens* so prone to religious belief?" you first have to distinguish between traits that are *adaptations*, that is, product of Darwinian natural selection, and traits that are *byproducts* of adaptations, also called spandrels or exaptations. An example: Why is our blood red? Is there some adaptive advantage to having red blood, maybe as camouflage against autumn leaves? Well, that's unlikely, and we don't need any other adaptive explanation, either. The explanation for why our blood is red is that it is adaptive to have a molecule that can carry oxygen, mainly hemoglobin. Hemoglobin happens to be red when it's oxygenated, so the redness of our blood is a byproduct of the chemistry of carrying oxygen. The color per se was not selected for. Another non-adaptive explanation for a biological trait is genetic drift. Random stuff happens in evolution. Certain traits can become fixed through sheer luck of the draw.

To distinguish an adaptation from a byproduct, first of all you have to establish that the trait is in some sense innate, for example, that it develops reliably across range of environments and is universal across the species. That helps rule out reading, for example, as a biological adaptation. Kids don't spontaneously read unless they are taught, as opposed to spoken language, which *is* a plausible adaptation, because it does emerge spontaneously in all normal children in all societies.

The second criterion is the causal effects of the trait would, on average, have improved the survival or reproduction of the bearer of that trait in an ancestral environment—the one in which our species spent most of its evolutionary history, mainly the foraging or hunter-gatherer lifestyle that predated the relatively recent invention of agriculture and civilization.

Crucially, the advantage must be demonstrable by some independently motivated causal consequences of the putative adaptation. That is, the laws of physics or chemistry or engineering have to be sufficient to establish that the trait would be useful. The usefulness of the trait can't be invented ad hoc; if it is, you have not a legitimate evolutionary explanation but a "just-so story" or fairy tale. The way to tell them apart is to independently motivate the usefulness of the trait. An example: Via projective geometry, one can show that by combining images from two cameras or optical devices, it is possible to calculate the depth of an object from the disparity of the projections. If you write out the specs for what you need in order to compute stereoscopic depth, you find that humans and other primates seem to have exactly those specs in our sense of stereoscopic depth perception. It's exactly what engineers would design if they were building a robot that had to see in depth. That similarity is a good reason to believe that human stereoscopic depth perception is an adaptation.

Likewise for fear of snakes. In all societies people have a wariness of snakes; one sees it even in laboratory-raised monkeys who had never seen a snake. We know from herpetology that snakes were prevalent in Africa during the time of our evolution, and that getting bitten by a snake is not good for you because of the chemistry of snake venom. Crucially, that itself is not a fact of psychology, but it helps to establish that what is a fact of psychology, namely the fear of snakes, is a plausible adaptation.

Our sweet tooth is yet another example. It's not terribly adaptive now, but biochemistry has established that sugar is packed with calories, and therefore could have prevented starvation in an era which food sources were unpredictable. That makes a sweet tooth a plausible adaptation.

In contrast, it's not clear what the adaptive function of humor is, or of music. I think the explanations of religion that I've reviewed have the same problem, namely not having an independent rationale, given an engineering analysis of why that trait should, *in principle*, be useful.

The alternative, then, is that just as the redness of blood is a byproduct of other adaptations, so may our predisposition to religious belief. A crucial corollary of the theory of evolution is that conflicts of interests among organisms, of different species or of the same species, lead to the biological equivalent of an arms race. An organism evolves more clever or lethal weapons, another organism evolves even more ingenious defenses, and soon, spiraling the process spiral. At any given stage in an arms race, a feature can be adaptive for one organism but not for its adversaries, as long as the first is overcoming the defenses of the second. That's another reason why not everything in biology is adaptive, at least not for every organism. What's adaptive for the lion is not so adaptive for the lamb.

So a way of rephrasing the question "Why is religious belief so pervasive?" is to ask, Who benefits? Another way of putting it is that one must distinguish the possible benefits of religion to the *producers* of religious belief—the religious establishment of shamans and priests and so on—from the benefits to the *consumers* of religion—the parishioners, the flock, the believers. The answer might be different for the two cases. One must distinguish the question "What good is an inculcation of religious belief by priests, shaman, and so on?" from the question "What good is a acceptance of religious belief by believers?"

A number of anthropologists have pointed out the benefits of religion to those causing *other* people to have religious beliefs. One ubiquitous component of religion is ancestor worship. And ancestor worship must sound pretty good if you're getting on in years and can foresee the day when you're going to become an ancestor. Among the indignities of growing old is that you know that you're not going to be around forever. If you plausibly convince other people that you'll continue to oversee their affairs even when you're dead and gone, that gives them an incentive to treat you nicely up to the last day.

Food taboos are also common in religious belief, and might be explained by the psychology of food preference and dispreference, in particular, disgust. If you withhold a food, especially a food of animal origin, from children during a critical period, they'll grow up grossed out at the thought of eating that food. That's why most of us would not eat dog meat, monkey brains, or maggots, things that are palatable in other societies. There are often ecological reasons why food taboos develop, but there are probably also reasons of control. Since neighboring groups have different favored foods, if you keep your own kids from having a taste for the foods favored by your neighbors, it can keep them inside the coalition, preventing them from defecting to other coalitions, because to break bread with their neighbors they'd have to eat revolting stuff.

Rites of passage are another intelligible feature of religion. Many social decision have to be made in categorical, yes-or-no, all-or-none fashion. But a lot of our biology is fuzzy and continuous. A child doesn't go to bed one night and wake up an adult the next morning. But we do have to make decisions such as whether they can vote or drive or buy a gun. There's nothing magical about the age of 13 or the age of 18 or any other age. But it's more convenient to arbitrarily anoint a person as an adult on a particular, arbitrarily chosen day, than to haggle over how mature every individual is every time he wants a beer. Religious rites of passage demarcate stages of life, serving the function that we have given over to driver's licenses and other forms of ID. Another fuzzy continuum is whether someone is available as a potential romantic partner or are committed to someone else. Marriage is a useful way of demarcating that continuum with a sharp line.

Costly initiations or sacrifices are also present in almost all the world's religions. A general problem in the maintenance of cooperation is how to distinguish people who are altruistically committed to a coalition from hangers-on and parasites and free-riders One way to test who's genuinely committed is to see who is willing to undertake a costly sacrifice. To take an example close to home: To see whether someone is committed to an ethnic group

I am familiar with, you can say, "You've just had a baby. Please hand over your son so I can cut some skin off his penis." That's not the kind of thing that anyone would do unless they took their affiliation with the groups seriously. And there are far more gruesome examples from the rest of the world.

Yet another explicable feature of religion is signs of expertise in occult knowledge. If you're the one who knows mysterious but important arcane knowledge, then other people will defer to you. Even in non-religious contexts, most societies have some division of labor inexpertise, where we accord prestige and perquisites to people who know useful stuff. So a good strategy for providers of religion is to mix some genuine expertise—and indeed, anthropologists have shown that the tribal shaman or witch doctor really is an expert in herbal medicine and folk remedies—with a certain amount of hocus-pocus, trance-inducing drugs, stage magic, sumptuous robes and cathedrals, and so on, reinforcing the claim that there are worlds of incomprehensible wonder, power, and mystery that are reachable only through one's services.

These practical benefits take some of the mystery over why people like to encourage religious belief in others, without committing oneself to a specific biological adaptation for religion. The inculcation of religious belief would be a byproduct of these other, baser, motives.

What about the other side of these transactions, namely the consumers? Why do they buy it? One reason is that in most cases we *should* defer to experts. That's in the very nature of expertise. If I have a toothache, I open my mouth and let a guy drill my teeth. If I have a bellyache, I let him cut me open. That involves a certain amount of faith. Of course, in these cases the faith is rational, but that deference could, if manipulated, lead to *irrational* deference, even if the larger complex of deference can be adaptive on the whole.

There are also emotional predispositions which evolved for various reasons and make us prone to religious belief as a byproduct. The anthropologist Ruth Benedict summed up much of prayer when she said, "Religion is universally a technique for success." Ethnographic surveys suggest that when people try to communicate with God, it's not to share gossip or know-how it's to ask him for stuff: recovery from illness, recovery of a child from illness, success in enterprises, success in the battlefield. (And of course, the Red Sox winning the World Series, which almost made me into a believer.) This idea was summed up by Ambrose Bierce in *The Devil's Dictionary*, which defines "to pray" as "to ask that the laws of the universe be annulled in behalf of a single petitioner, confessedly unworthy." This aspect of religious belief is thus a desperate measure that people resort to when the stakes are high and they've exhausted the usual techniques for the causation of success.

Those are some of the emotional predispositions that make people fertile ground for religious belief. But there also are cognitive predispositions, ways in which we intellectually analyze the world, which have been very skillfully explored by the anthropologists Dan Sperber, Pascal Boyer, and Scott Atran. Anyone who is interested in the evolutionary psychology of religion would enjoy Pascal Boyer's *Religion Explained* and Scott Atran called *In Gods We Trust*. Hamer's *The God Gene* is also good, but I am more sympathetic to Boyer and Atran.

The starting point is a faculty of human reason that psychologists call intuitive psychology or the "theory of mind module"— "theory" here not referring to a theory of the scientist but rather to the *intuitive* theory that people unconsciously deploy in making sense of other people's behavior. When I try to figure out what someone is going to do, I don't treat them as just a robot or a wind-up doll responding to physical stimuli in the world. Rather, I impute *minds* to those people. I can't literally know what someone else is thinking or feeling, but I assume that they're thinking or feeling something, that they have a mind, and I explain their behavior in terms of their beliefs and their desires. That's intuitive psychology. There is evidence that intuitive psychology is a distinct part of our psychological make-up. It seems to be knocked out in a condition called autism: autistic people can be prodigious in mathematics, art, language, and music, but they have a terrible time attributing minds to other people. They really do treat other people as if they were robots and wind-up dolls. There's also a concerted effort underway to see where intuitive psychology is computed in the brain. Parts of it seems to be concentrated in the ventromedial and orbital frontal cortex, the parts of the brain that kind of sit above the eyeballs, as well as the superior temporal sulcus farther back.

Perhaps the ubiquitous belief in spirits, souls, gods, angels, and so on, consists of our intuitive psychology running amok. If you are prune to attributing an invisible entity called "the mind" to other people's bodies, it's a short step to imagining minds that exist *independently* of bodies. After all, it's not as if you could reach out and touch someone else's mind; you are always making an inferential leap. It's just one extra inferential step to say that a mind is not invariably housed in a body.

In fact the 19th-century anthropologist Edward Tyler pointed out that in some ways, there is good empirical support for the existence of the soul, or at least there used to be, until the fairly recent advent of neuroscience, which provides an alternative explanation for how minds work. Think about dreams. When you dream, your body is in bed the whole time, but some part of you seems to be up and about in the world. The same thing happens when you're in a trance from a fever, a hallucinogenic drug, sleep deprivation, or food poisoning.

Shadows and reflections ate rather mysterious, or were until the development of the physics of light with its explanation of those phenomena. But they appear to have the form and essence of the person but without any of their actual matter.

Death, of course, is the ultimate apparent evidence for the existence of the soul. A person may be walking around and seeing and hearing one minute, and the next minute be an inert and lifeless body, perhaps without any visible change. It would seem that some animating entity that was housed in the body has suddenly escaped from it.

So before the advent of modern physics, biology and especially neuroscience, a plausible explanation of these phenomena is that the soul wanders off when we sleep, lurks in the shadows, looks back at us from a surface of a pond, an leaves the body when we die.

To sum up. The universal propensity toward religious belief is a genuine scientific puzzle. But many adaptationist explanations for religion, such as the one featured in *Time* last week, don't, I think, meet the criteria for adaptations. There is an alternative explanation, namely that religious psychology is a byproduct of many parts of the mind that evolved for other purposes. Among those purposes one has to distinguish the benefits to the producer and the benefits to the consumer. Religion has obvious practical effects for producers. When it comes to the consumers, there are possible emotional adaptations in our desire for health, love and success, possible cognitive adaptations in our intuitive psychology, and many aspects of our experience that seem to provide evidence for souls. Put these together and you get an appeal to a mysterious world of souls to bring about our fondest wishes.

Questions about Content

1. Specifically, what question are evolutionary psychologists such as Pinker seeking to answer about religious belief? Do you think they might eventually be able to answer this question? If they do, could the answer have positive effects or negative effects on belief, or ultimately will the answer be irrelevant for people's faith?

2. What is the difference between an adaptation and a by-product? Pinker offers several examples of each. Why does he ultimately think the by-product theory is more convincing than the adaptation theory?

3. On the surface, belief seems very different from humor and music and the red color of blood, yet Pinker suggests that they share a similar characteristic. What makes these traits similar to each other?

4. Proving or disproving the existence of gods is not Pinker's purpose; his objective is only to prove a claim about how the mind functions. If Pinker's claim about the mind is valid or true, would it affirm, negate, or have no effect on proving the existence of a God?

Questions about Rhetorical Analysis

1. Pinker offers analogies, stories, or examples to illustrate a point. Which of these are most effective in challenging you to think about his argument? Are there any claims in his essay that would be more convincing if he presented additional experiments or illustrations?

2. What is Pinker's attitude or tone toward his subject and his audience? How does he use tone to guide his audience through his argument? Locate a specific statement and explain how it communicates his tone and how it affects his audience.

Sociology

Sociologists consider faith as a force that shapes society and society as a force that shapes faith. According to sociologist Joan Ferrante in her popular textbook, *Sociology: A Global Perspective*, a sociologist studies how faith and religious institutions affect relationships within a society and relationships between societies; the sociologist also studies how an institution of religion functions as a society in itself.

Sociology has two main schools of thought toward the study of religion. Ferrante provides a useful description of these approaches. The *functional perspective* explores how religion helps to shape and provide unity, order, and stability to a society. The functionalist sociologist asks what functions religion serves in a society and how religion contributes to the goals of a society. The *conflict perspective* in sociology studies conflict as an inevitable part of every society. Conflict occurs among individuals within a society as well as between societies. In terms of the sociology of religion, the conflict perspective explores how religious institutions, with their establishment of order and stability, reinforce the hierarchy or power structure of a society; religion can be useful to those who dominate others in a society. One criticism of the functional perspective is that it ignores how religious institutions consolidate power. A criticism of the conflict perspective is that it ignores the important role religion has played in giving hope to the oppressed and supporting the efforts of reform movements to secure human rights.

The following selection is taken from a much longer article in *Sociology of Religion*, a peer-reviewed journal in the field of sociology. "Peer-reviewed" means that a panel of the authors' peers, other experts in the authors' field, review articles submitted to the journal to determine whether the articles should be published. Those readers evaluate the validity and reliability of the research as well as the quality of the writing according to accepted standards and conventions in the discipline.

Mapping American Adolescent Subjective Religiosity and Attitudes of Alienation toward Religion: A Research Report

CHRISTIAN SMITH, ROBERT FARIS, MELINDA LUNDQUIST DENTON, MARK REGNERUS

The authors of the following reading are researchers who have completed a study to determine what attitudes high school and traditional college-aged students have toward religion. Christian Smith is professor of sociology and director of the Center for the Study of Religion and Society at the University of Notre Dame. He and his co-authors (Robert Faris and Melinda Lundquist Denton from the University of North Carolina at Chapel Hill and Mark Regnerus from the University of Texas at Austin) have published numerous books and peer reviewed articles in their fields. As scientific researchers, the authors present their questions, define their terms, survey the work of other researchers, describe how they set up a systematic study, present the results of their study, and interpret their findings. As you read, notice what question these researchers want to answer, and notice the method that they use to go about answering that question.

◆

We know relatively little about the religious lives of American adolescents. The vast majority of studies in the sociology of fields pay close attention to youth's religious lives. As a result, our scientific knowledge of the religious affiliations, practices, beliefs, experiences, and attitudes of American youth is lacking.

To be sure, there exist vast literatures that address religion in the lives of American youth. However, much of this literature is riddled with serious problems. First, much of the existing literature on American youth and religion is not systematically empirical, but consists largely of theoretical works on moral formation and faith development, proposals for ministry models, unsystematic case studies, etc. Second, most existing empirical research on youth is out of date. While some subjects of study change relatively slowly, American youth pass through time in culturally-shaped generations which can change significantly from decade to decade. We do know from the literature a fair amount about Baby Boomers in their youth, but this is a generation now passing through middle age and toward retirement, with teenage and adult children of their own. Furthermore, members of the much discussed "Generation X" are typically defined as those born between the years 1965 and 1980, a generation that has passed into adult hood; GenXers are now about 22–37 years old—many with children of their own. We cannot claim to understand youth today by referencing existing research conducted on GenX teens (the age-median of whom were getting their driver's licences before the fall of the Berlin Wall) or older. Third, many works in the literature involve analyses that do contain a religion variable, but do not make religion a focus of analysis or explanation. Many studies exist which control for religion by adding a religion variable in an analytical model, but are not particularly concerned to understand that religious effect; they are interested instead in some other independent variable and use religion only as a non-explicated control variable to bolster the main argument. Fourth, the vast majority of published empirical studies-on American youth and religion employ samples of subjects and respondents that are methodologically problematic. While some studies are based on strong research designs, many rely on samples that are quite small, that are not randomly selected, and/or that represent a very narrow segment of a population. As a result, it is difficult to assess about whom findings can be generalized as representing; and it is difficult to piece together the findings collectively into a coherent picture of American youth. For example, our review of empirical studies published in 1999 and 2000 related to religious beliefs, practices, and commitment are based on the following samples: participants in a Protestant youth conference; 300 Iowa children; 3 Muslim teenagers; 1,500 teenagers from Seventh-Day Adventist churches; 86 youth attending alternative music concerts; 276 high school parochial school juniors; 125 eleventh graders from West Virginia; 77 college students; 273 Jewish teenagers from the Philadelphia area; an unspecified number of participants in Buddhist and Catholic retreats; and 2,358 black youth from poverty areas of three cities; only two other of the studies during these years were based on large, nationally representative samples of youth.

This is a problem, for many reasons. American adolescents between the ages of 10–19 represent about 14 percent of all Americans (adolescents ages 10–24 represent 21 percent), an age-minority population deserving scholarly attention as much as any other group. Indeed, American adolescents may deserve extra scholarly attention by sociologists of religion. Adolescence represents a crucial developmental transition from childhood to adulthood, and so can disclose a tremendous amount of knowledge about religious socialization and change in the life course. Adolescents are a population that many religious organizations, both congregations and para-church ministries, particularly target in order to exert influence in their lives. Adolescence and young adulthood is also the life stage when religious conversion is most likely to take place. Adolescence furthermore provides a unique opportunity to study religious influences on family relationships and dynamics, peer interactions, risk behaviors, and many other outcome variables. Finally, adolescence provides an ideal baseline stage for longitudinal research on religious influences in people's lives.

Gaining a solid understanding of the religion of American adolescents can also enable sociologists of religion to make useful contributions to a variety of non-academic audiences for whom our findings might have relevance. A series of high-profile events—including multiple school shootings and local epidemic outbreaks of sexually-transmitted diseases among youth—have heightened broad public concern about problems in youth culture. There appears to be a growing awareness of and interest in religious, spiritual, and moral influences in the lives of youth among not only religious leaders, but also educators, social service providers, public policy makers, philanthropists, and journalists. Unfortunately, although impressionistic and journalistic works on youth religion abound (for example, Lewis, Dodd, and Tippens 1995; McAllister 1999; Mahedy and Bernardi 1994; Zoba 1999; Beaudoin 2000; Rabey 2001) and a few suggestive opinion-poll-based studies on American youth religion exist (Gallup n.d.; Barna 1995, 1999, 2001), sociologists of religion currently have relatively little solidly dependable, nationally representative, empirical knowledge about adolescent religiosity to contribute to these public discussions. Some good qualitative studies of American youth religion do make helpful contributions to our knowledge (for example, Lytch 2000; Flory and Miller 2000; Davis 2001; Myers 1991), yet these are not designed to make nationally representative claims about the religiosity of American youth. Of the best works on adolescent religiosity, most focus specifically on inter-generational religious transmission (Wuthnow 1976; Sherkat 1998; Nelson 1981; Hoge, Petrillo, and Smith 1982; Meyers 1996; Ozorak 1989; Parker and Gaier 1980; Cornwall 1988; Erickson 1992; Keysar, Kosmin, and Scheckner 2000). But, in general, much of the existing social science literature on youth and religion is simply out of date. For instance, one important, older synthesis of the literature is Hyde's (1990) 529-page Religion in Childhood and Adolescence, which digested roughly 1,760 pieces of literature. But only 16 of the 119 references in his chapter on "Religion and Morality in Adolescence," for example, were published after 1985—meaning almost everything that we know from Hyde about adolescent religion and morality (when accounting for the data-publication lag time) is based on studies of people who were teenagers before Ronald Reagan had become President (also see Bensen, Donahue, and Erickson 1989).

The problem is, to some degree, a simple lack of interest and attention among sociologists. But the problem also stems from failing to put useful religion questions on many good surveys of youth, which typically understand and measure religion in narrow and deficient terms. Of 18 of the best national surveys of youth that we investigated in our research, for example, fully 12 contain a mere three religion questions or less; only three high-quality, nationally-representative surveys of adolescents include 6 or more questions about religion (www.youthandreligion.org/resources/surveys.html). Moreover, it appears that few studies have analyzed these few religion questions systematically—which is what we intend to do here. Sociologists of religion who get involved in this research need to advise other scholars in family and adolescence on the importance of measuring religion well. We also need to conduct our own surveys of adolescent religion.

Meanwhile, however, we can move in the right direction in redressing our lack of knowledge about youth religion by analyzing and compiling available survey data, as inadequate in some respects as they may be, to provide a big-picture view of adolescent religiosity. It is possible to scour reputable existing survey data on youth to learn about some religious aspects of their lives. Even simple descriptive work can serve to heighten broader understanding of and to help lay down a baseline of essential information about American adolescent religion. That is the goal of this article. Here we analyze existing data from two of the best, recent national surveys of American youth to present descriptive statistics on three fundamental aspects of youth subjective religiosity (importance of religion, frequency of prayer, born again status) and four measures of youth attitudes about religion (agreement with parents, approval of churches, desired influence of churches, financial donations to churches). We also examine the influences of age, race, gender, and region on most of these religious outcomes, as the survey data allow.

We believe that since our collective substantive knowledge of American youth religion is so relatively thin, and since available datasets do contain a great deal of interesting and important descriptive information on the religiosity of American adolescents, a purely descriptive article mapping the contours and correlates of youth religiosity using frequencies and crosstabs is more than warranted. In a separate analysis, we have examined three variables concerning youth religious participation (affiliation, attendance, and participation in religious youth groups) (Smith, Denton, Fans, Regnerus 2002). Having mapped the religious terrain descriptively in this article, we intend in subsequent work to conduct multivariate analyses to predict factors explaining variance in youth religiosity and religious participation. But first, in this article, we concentrate on one of the crucial tasks of sociological work: describing the configurations of (religious) social life.

• • •

What, in review, have we found about American adolescent religiosity? We believe the following eight summary observations are most important to note:

1. Religious faith is important for the majority of American youth. Nearly one-third of youth each say that their faith is "very important" and "pretty important." Available data also suggest that the importance of religious faith to American adolescents has not declined (or increased) during the two decades from 1976 to 1996. While youth for whom faith is very important are spread across all religious traditions and denominations, they tend to cluster in more among theologically conservative, Pentecostal, and sectarian traditions.

2. On the other hand, religious faith is not really important for a large minority of American youth. Four out of ten American youth do not find their religious faith to be even somewhat important in their lives. Historical trend data, however, do not show this group of American youth to be growing remarkably over time (at least since the mid-1970s). The highest proportion of these youth for whom their religion is less important appear to be from Jewish, mainline Protestant, and Catholic backgrounds.

3. The vast majority of American youth pray regularly. Nearly two-thirds of American youth pray daily or weekly. These youth also tend to be the same for whom religious faith is important, meaning that those youth who have high religiosity tend to express this through multiple forms of subjective religiosity.

4. Only a minority of American adolescents think of themselves as being "born again." Our findings suggest that about one-quarter of Protestant youth report that they are born again; we unfortunately do not have data on born again Catholic youth, or youth from other non-Protestant religious traditions. Even the highest estimates by other surveys suggest that no more than one-third of all American teenagers say they are born again.

5. Adolescent girls exhibit somewhat higher levels of subjective religiosity than boys. Girls are more likely than boys to report that their faith is important to them, to pray more frequently, and (among Protestants) to be born again.

6. The subjective religiosity of American adolescents does not appear to decline much with age. Older teens do not appear to have declined in subjective religiosity as measured here, compared younger teens. Frequency of prayer may be one minor exception. Elsewhere (Smith et al. 2002), we have found that increased age among adolescents is associated with declining participation in organized religious activities. But decline in participation do not appear to affect adolescent subjective religiosity. This may reflect the apparently growing emphasis on subjective religiousness reported among youth (Rabey 2001; Beaudoin 2000).

7. The subjective religiosity of American adolescents is somewhat differentiated by race. Black youth exhibit the highest levels of importance of faith, pray the most, and (among Protestants) are most likely to be born again. On these three measures, American white, Hispanic, and Asian youth appear rather similar, with slight variations on importance of faith, born again status, and prayer.

8. The subjective religiosity of American adolescents varies somewhat by region of residence. Southern youth have the highest levels of subjective religiosity as measured by importance of faith, frequency of prayer, and born again status. That Southern culture is generally more friendly to religion than non-Southern cultures in the United States shows in teenage religiosity. Youth from the North Central and Western states exhibit lower levels of subjective religiosity, followed by the lowest levels in Northeastern teenagers. Northeast culture tends to be relatively more secular than many other regions of the country, and its dominant religion is Catholicism, which is associated among youth with lower levels of importance of faith and frequency of prayer.

9. The vast majority of older adolescents in America—about two thirds—are not alienated from or hostile toward organized religion in America. Two-thirds of them closely agree with the religious ideas of their parents. One-half believe churches and religious organizations are doing a good job for the country, and another one-quarter believe they are doing a fair job. Seven in ten 12th graders would like to see religion exert the same, more, or much more influence in society. And two-thirds say that they either already contribute money to churches or religious organizations or that they plan to in the future. In sum, the vast majority of older American adolescents display positive regard, not negative hostility toward or disaffection from organized religion.

10. Yet a significant minority of older American adolescents—about fifteen percent—does appear to be alienated from organized religion. Ten percent each have religious ideas that are very different from those of their parents, and believe churches and religious organizations are doing a poor job for the country. Nineteen percent would like to see churches and religious organizations exert less influence in society. And 19 percent do not now nor plan in the future to contribute money to church or religious organizations. It appears that it is mostly the same respondent who are giving the more alienated answers to all four of our questions, that alienation tends to cluster among the same respondents.

11. Another significant minority of older adolescents in America—about fifteen percent—appear to be simply disengaged in attitudes toward religion, being neither warm nor cold toward organized religion. Between 12 and 17 percent do not know how their religious ideas compare to their parents' have no opinion about whether churches are doing a good or bad job for the country; have no opinion about whether the social influence of churches and religious organizations should increase or decrease; and do not know whether or not they expect to contribute money to churches or religious organizations. It appears that it is mostly the same respondents who are giving the "Don't Know" answers to our four questions, that is, indifference to or disengagement from religion tends to cluster among the same respondents.

12. The minority of older adolescents in America who do appear to be hostile to or estranged from organized religion has not grown (or declined) in recent decades. The percentage of American 12th graders who disagree with their parents about religion, who think churches are doing a bad job for society, who would like to see organized religion's influence reduced, and who do not plan to give to organized religion in the future did not increase in any major way between 1976 and 1996. Youth evaluative attitudes about organized religion appear to have been stable over time.

Future multivariate analyses beyond the scope of this article will help to sort out the relative importance of alternative factors in predicting variance in subjective religiosity and alienation from religion

among American youth. Also including more useful religion questions on otherwise good adolescent surveys—which the forthcoming
third wave of the National Longitudinal Study of Adolescent Health
is actually doing—will be important for improving future research.
We suggest that all adolescent surveys include questions on religious
service attendance, importance of faith, religious youth group participation, views of God, and born-again status.

CONCLUSION

Current social scientific knowledge about the religious lives of
American adolescents is inadequate. Given the increasing interest in
many sectors of society in the religious and spiritual lives of
American youth, and an apparently growing interest in "spirituality"
among American youth themselves, sociologists of religion need to
invest more resources into research on adolescent religion and its
social effects. This article is a modest step in that direction. We have
employed existing data from two high-quality national surveys of
American youth, however wanting on some points they may be. We
have focused our analysis on adolescents' importance of religious
faith, frequency of prayer, and born again status; have examined
gender, race, age, and regional effects; and have investigated four
measures of possible youth alienation from religion. We hope that
our findings help to raise broader awareness about the religious lives
of American youth, and perhaps help to establish some core body of
available knowledge about the extent of adolescent religiosity in the
United States. Further survey research of American youth needs to
develop much better and more extensive measures of adolescent
religious practices, experiences, beliefs, and interests; to combine
quantitative survey methods with qualitative interviews and ethno-
graphies; to use multivariate analysis to identify the most important
variables predicting religiosity; and ideally to conduct a longitudinal
design that will track the same respondents over time, in order to
strengthen our ability to assess causal religious influences.

References

Barna, G. 1995. Generation next. Ventura, CA: Regal Books.
———. 1999. Third millennium teens. Ventura, CA: The Barna Research
    Group.
———. 2001. Real teens. Ventura, CA: Regal Books.
Beaudoin, T. 2000. Virtual faith: The irreverent spiritual quest of genera-
    tion X. San Francisco: Jossey-Bass.
Bensen, P., M. Donahue, and J. Erickson. 1989. Adolescence and Religion:
    A review of the literature from 1970 to 1986. In Research in the social

scientific study of religion. Vol. 1. edited by M. Lyunn and D. Moberg, 153–81. Greenwich, CT: JAI Press.

Cornwall, M. 1988. The influence of three agents of socialization. In The religion and family connection, Vol. 16, edited by D.L. Thomas, 207–31. Provo, UT: Brigham Young University Press.

Davis, P. 2001. Beyond nice: The spiritual wisdom of adolescent girls. Minneapolis: Fortress Press.

Erickson, J. 1992. Adolescent religious development and commitment. Journal for the Scientific Study of Religion 31(2):131–152.

Gallup, n.d. The spiritual life of young Americans: Approaching the year 2000. Princeton: The George H. Gallup International Institute.

Hoge, D., G. Petrillo, and E. Smith. 1982. Transmission of religious and social values from parents to teenage children. Journal of Marriage and the Family 44(3):569–579.

Hyde, K. 1990. Religion in childhood and adolescence. Birmingham: Religious Education Press.

Keysar, A., B. Kosmin, and J. Scheckner. 2000. The next generation: Jewish children and adolescents. Albany: State University of New York Press.

Lewis, D., C. Dodd, and D. Tippens. 1995. The gospel according to generation X. Abilene, TX: ACU Press.

Lytch, C. 2000. Choosing faith across generations. Unpublished Ph.D. dissertation. Emory University.

Mahedy, W., and J. Bernardi. 1994. A generation alone. Downers Grove: InterVarsity.

McAllister, D. 1999. Saving the millennial generation. Nashville: Thomas Nelson.

Meyers, 5. 1996. An interactive model of religious inheritance. American Sociological Review 61:858–66.

Myers, W. 1991. Black and white styles of youth ministry. New York: The Pilgrim Press.

Nelson, H. 1981. Religions conformity in an age of disbelief. American Sociological Review 46:632–40.

Ozorak, E. W. 1989. Social and cognitive influences on the development of religious beliefs and commitments in adolescence. Journal for the Scientific Study of Religion 28(4):448–463.

Parker, M., and E. Gaier. 1980. Religion, religious beliefs, and religious practices among Conservative Jewish adolescents. Adolescence XVI: 361–374.

Rabey, 5. 2001. In search of authentic faith: How emerging generations are transforming the church. Colorado Springs: Waterbrook Press.

Sherkat, D. 1998. Counterculture or continuity? Social Forces 76(3): 1087–1115.

Smith, C., M. L. Denton, R. Fans, and M. Regnerus. 2002. Mapping American adolescent religious participation. Journal for the Scientific Study of Religion December 41(4):597–612.

Wuthnow, R. 1976. Recent patterns of secularization. American Sociological Review 41:850–67.

Zoba, W. 1999. Generation 2K: What parents need to know about the millennials. Downers Grove, II: InterVarsity Press.

Questions about Content

1. According to this research study, what are the main problems with current research into the religious attitudes of teenagers and people in their 20s?

2. What is the authors' reason for doing this research? In other words, why is it valuable to determine how young people feel about religion? What do the writers say this research will enable sociologists to do?

3. What conclusions do the writers reach? In your experience, do these conclusions sound reasonable, or do they challenge what you know from your own observations of high school and college students?

Questions about Rhetorical Analysis

1. Every field has certain conventions or expectations for writing. An article in sociology is expected to have certain sections, each serving a particular function for presenting the authors' research methods and findings. Notice that the authors use the first three paragraphs to present a list of problems. Why do they do that? Notice that the authors survey previous research in the fifth paragraph. What is the purpose of that paragraph? What are the purposes of other sections in this article?

2. Based upon this selection, what is the question that motivated these authors to do research and to write this article? What methods or steps did they take to answer that question?

Economics

The field of economics is largely about how human beings make choices and set up markets as frameworks for those decisions to be made. Economists study how we decide which goods and services to produce and consume, and what costs we are willing to pay for certain benefits. In the context of religion, economists may take several perspectives.

- Economists study how people choose religious beliefs, behaviors, and institutions. As the writer says, the economist begins by "viewing religious behavior as an instance of rational choice, rather than an exception to it." Since this article was written, some economists are also examining how nonrational factors, namely emotion, influence decisions in all market-places, including religion. Whatever the approach, economists explore how people make decisions about what to believe and which institutions of religion to support and join.

- Economists study how institutions such as churches function as agents in the "marketplace" of religious institutions. Just as businesses work to attract customers, earn profits, and grow, institutions of religion, such as churches, also try to attract adherents and become larger. Religious institutions, like businesses, "compete" for a share of a "market."
- Economists study the impact that institutions of religion have on the economy and society of a country as a whole. For example, they may ask, do certain religious beliefs affect the choices of products or services that producers or consumers make? By supporting or opposing progress in science and technology, are religious beliefs positive or negative factors in the growth of economies?
- Some economists might take a faith-based approach, evaluating economic choices on the basis of religious scriptures, doctrines, and beliefs. Thus, a "Catholic economist" might observe and report the choices Catholics make, and she might also make recommendations about the choices she thinks Catholics ought to make.

You can find more information about these and other approaches on the Economics of Religion Gateway, a web site of the Center for the Economic Study of Religion (CESR) and the Association for the Study of Religion, Economics and Culture (ASREC), at www.religionomics.com.

Progress in the Economics of Religion

LAURENCE R. IANNACCONE

The director of CESR is Larry Iannaccone, a professor at George Mason University, who has published many articles in journals such as American Economic Review, *the* Journal of Political Economy, *the* American Journal of Sociology, *and the* Journal for the Scientific Study of Religion. *In addition to being a founder of the organizations CESR and ASREC, he has also established an annual national conference on religion, economics, and culture, and in support of all of these endeavors, he was awarded a grant by the Templeton Foundation, one of the most prestigious foundations, which recognizes the best researchers and thinkers around the world. For more information about Dr. Iannaccone and access to many of his publications, you can find a link to his web site on the CESR web page noted earlier.*

In the following article, Iannaccone provides an overview of the economics of religion. He begins by explaining why the study of religion is an important area of research for economists. Then he describes theories or models of religious behavior to explain how religious markets work. In the third section he combines the concepts from the previous sections to consider how the economic study of religion has implications for the policies or positions government takes toward religion. The final section briefly mentions other areas of study into how religion influences personal behavior, and the writer concludes by stating how we can all benefit from the discoveries about religion that economists can make. As you read, consider how the theories mentioned in the article create an entirely new way for you to think about religion.

As you read, you might come across some unfamiliar terms. Club theory *is the study of how groups make decisions, which involves the process of individuals coming together to make a collective choice on behalf of an organization. When the writer uses the word* firm, *he is referring to a business or corporation, which is the kind of group an economist might apply "club theory" to. The term* laissez-faire *is a policy dictating that the government should not interfere in the economy, instead limiting its role and giving individuals full freedom to choose and act according to their own interests.*

◆

---

1. INTRODUCTION

The past few decades have witnessed dramatic growth in the domain of economics. Once limited largely to the study of commerce, economists now routinely analyze such diverse subjects as heath, crime, education, fertility, discrimination, voting, marriage, and addiction.

A number of researchers are working to add religion to this list. Armed with the tools of economic theory and a growing body of data, they are exploring the determinants of religious behavior, the nature of religious institutions, and the social and economic impact of religion. Viewing religious behavior as an instance of rational choice rather than en exception to it, their work parallels other attempts to expand the domain of economics. Hence, the research is quite unlike "Islamic economics,"

"Christian economics," or any other faith-based approach to economic theory and policy.

To date, the economics of religion has had its greatest impact in sociology, since it directly addresses concerns central to the sociology of religion. Sociologists have thus begun speaking of market models and rational choice theory as the "new paradigm" for religious research (Warner [1993], Young [1995]). This new paradigm explains and integrates a wealth of existing data, generates new predictions that suggest new avenues for empirical research, and yields policy implications about the welfare effects of government intervention in the religions marketplace.

Since most work in the economics of religion is new and scattered over a variety of journals, a brief overview would seem to be in order. An overview serves also to dispel the popular but increasingly untenable view of religion as a fading vestige pre-scientific times.

2. THE CONTINUING IMPORTANCE OF RELIGION

Throughout the middle of this century, the social-scientific study of religion languished for lack of interest. In disciplines like sociology and anthropology, whose founders had devoted much of their attention to religion, religion receded to backward status. In economics, which had never said much about beliefs, norms, and culture, the subject was ignored altogether. Though no one denied religion's *historic* importance—it was, after all, one the most fundamental, durable, and pervasive features of human culture—most scholars came to view *contemporary* religion as little more than a fossil, and an uninteresting one at that. Without always realizing it, academics had come to accept (and perhaps even relish) the "secularization thesis," a doctrine predicting the rapid decline and eventual extinction of religion in the modern world.

But these days, the secularization thesis has fallen on hard times. The political resurgence of conservative Christianity in the U.S., the rise of Islamic fundamentalism in the Middle East, the explosive growth of Protestantism in Latin America, the religious ferment in Eastern Europe and the former Soviet Union, and the influence of religion in ethnic conflicts world-wide confirm religion's persistence. Throughout the world, religion remains more vital than the pundits proclaimed (and one is reminded of Mark Twain's quip that "rumors of my death are exaggerated"). Western European trends, once viewed as the bellweather of worldwide secularization, look increasingly exceptional (more the consequence of state regulation than underlying social change). Finally, a growing body of empirical research finds no evidence of religious decline in

America. These findings bear emphasis, since the secularization thesis remains entrenched in the minds of many academics not familiar with contemporary religious research.

- Rates of church membership in America have risen steadily in the past two centuries: from 17% of the population at the time of the Revolution, to 34% by the mid-1800's, to more than 60% today (Finke and Stark [1992]). These data come from a variety of reliable sources, including the U.S. government's decennial Census of Religious Bodies conducted from 1850 through 1936.
- More than 40% of Americans claim to attend church in a typical week, and this figure has remained largely unchanged since the advent of Gallup Polis in the late-1930's (Greeley [1989]).
- Surveyed religious beliefs have proved nearly as stable as church attendance. The fraction of American's professing atheism remains well below 10%, and the fraction claiming belief in the Bible, heaven, and hell remains high and nearly constant (Greeley [1989]).
- Religion is *not* an inferior good. Rates of religions belief and religious activity do not decline with increased income *or education*, a finding that holds in both cross-sections and aggregate time series.
- Styles of religion *do* vary with income and education. Fundamentalist, pentecostal, and other sectarian denominations are mush more likely to draw their members from among the poor, less educated, and minority members of society (Iannaccone [1992]).
- Church contributions make up more than half of all charitable giving in the U.S. (approximately 60 billion dollars per year), and the majority of nonprofit institutions are or were religiously based.

Economic theory has much to say about all these facts, but the facts themselves refute the outmoded notion that religion is "unimportant" and therefore "uninteresting". Religion remains a force in the personal, institutional, and political life of most people throughout the world. Social scientists have little choice but to take account of religion, since religion shows no sign of going away.

3. MODELING RELIGIOUS BEHAVIOR

Contemporary research on the economics of religion began with Azzi and Ehrenberg's [1975] household production model of church attendance and contributions. Within this model, individuals allocate their resources so as to maximize the overall utility derived from religious and secular commodities. Although Azzi and Ehrenberg emphasized the hope of "afterlife consumption" as the motive for religious behavior, subsequent work tends to be less explicit about why people value religious commodities. Iannaccone [1984], [1990] extended Azzi and Ehrenberg's model to incorporate the accumulation of "religious human capital." The extended model explains age-increasing patterns of religious participation as a consequence of experience effects and rational habit formation. The model also generates predictions concerning denominational mobility, religious intermarriage, and conversion ages, all of which receive strong empirical support. Greeley and Durkin [1991] have presented a related model that incorporates "faith" as a type of human capital and views religious choice as the consequence of expected utility maximization.

Although household production provides a convenient starting point for the study of religious behavior, recent work pays more attention to religious groups. Simple models of isolated utility maximizers, constrained only by personal income and commodity prices, have given way to others that emphasize the role of specialized firms or clubs in the production of religious commodities.

Some papers in this category build on standard theories of the firm. Viewing the clergy as the producers of religious products and the laity as consumers, these papers seek to explain the development of religious doctrine, the organizational structure of religious institutions, and the evolution of religions practices. For example, Exelund, Hebert and Tollison [1989] use the model of a rent-seeking monopoly to explain the medieval Catholic church's usury doctrine. According to this argument highly placed church officials manipulated usury doctrine so as to maximize rents from downstream producers (the clergy) and from input suppliers (banks) by controlling the borrowing and lending interest rates.

Other papers take club theory as their starting point. These emphasize that although religious institutions manifest many firm-like characteristics, the standard distinction between producer and consumer is only partially applicable.

Congregations, like families, combine the functions of production and consumption. Except for a few full-time religious professionals and a handful of benchwarmers, most church members act as both producers and consumers of religious commodities. Moreover, many religious activities such as public worship and charity generate collective benefits.

Iannaccone [1992] addresses these issues in a club-theoretic model that turns the standard "swimming pool" story on its head.

Rather than emphasize problems of congestion, the model emphasizes the *positive* externalities associated with religious participation. In congregational settings, an active member (who attends
regularly, sings wholeheartedly, and greets others enthusiastically)
increases the utility of other members. Free riders (who participate
less frequently and less energetically) thus threaten to undermine
the viability of most religions—a problem well-documented by sociologists of religion. The theory and data show that apparently gratu-
itous costs ("sacrifice and stigma") can function to mitigate free
rider problems by screening out half-hearted members and induc-
ing higher levels of participation among those who remain. Perfectly
rational individuals may thus find it in their interest to join so-called
"sects" and "cults" that demand stigma, self-sacrifice, and bizarre
behavioral standards. At the same time, other people (particularly
those with higher market opportunities) will find it optimal to form
less demanding groups, such as mainstream churches.

The club-theoretic model of high-cost "sects" and easy-going
"churches" explains and integrates a large body of empirical findings that have fascinated sociologists of religion for more than a
century. The predicted correlates of sectarian religion include strict
behavioral standards, dramatic conversions, high rates of church
attendance and giving, resistance to social change, small congregations, and lower-class and minority appeal. A dynamic version of
the model (Montgomery [1994]) explains the well-documented tendency for sects to moderate their demands over time and to thereby
transform themselves into mainstream denominations (which
eventually become so lax that they lose members). For a somewhat
different view of sacrifice and stigma, see Schlicht [1995].

4. RELIGIOUS MARKETS

If individual denominations function as religious firms, then they
collectively constitute a religious market. This insight dates to none
other than Adam Smith. In a largely ignored chapter of *The Wealth
of Nations*, Smith argued that established religions face the same
incentive problems that plague other state sponsored monopolies,
and he advocated religious *laissez-faire* as the best way to satisfy the
demand for religious instruction, reduce religious conflict, and promote "pure and rational religion, free from every mixture of absurdity, imposture, or fanaticism" (Smith [1776/1965, 745]).

Anderson [1988] has reviewed Smith's arguments in some
detail, and McConnell and Posner [1989] use Smith's argument to
interpret the First Amendment's impact on religion in America.
Iannaccone [1991] uses contemporary theories of regulation to
extend Smith's analysis and test the prediction that competition

stimulates religious activity. Data from eighteen Western countries show that church attendance, belief in God, and the perceived importance of religion are all greater in countries with numerous competing churches than in countries dominated by a single Protestant church. Finke and Stark [1992] draw similar conclusions based on the analysis of historical data from turn-of-the-century American cities, and Hamberg and Pettersson [1994] observe a similar pattern across the provinces of contemporary Sweden. Finke [1990] reviews the impact of religious "deregulation" in post-colonial American religious history, showing that rates of church membership rose as the colonial pattern of established churches and *de facto* religious monopoly gave way to a free religious market. Olds [1994] provides econometric evidence that the number and wages of preachers in colonial New England rose in response to the disestablishment and privatization of religion. In Post-WWII Japan, the abolition of state Shinto and the advent of religious freedom inaugurated a period known as "the Rush Hour of the Gods." All these findings run counter to the long-standing sociological assumption that religious pluralism undermines religiosity and facilitates secularization.

5. POLICY IMPLICATIONS

As the preceding examples illustrate, economics has much to say about the determinants of individual religious behavior, the characteristics of different religious groups, and even the causes of cross-national variation in religiosity. Although these insights have value in their own right, they also concern public policy issues.

One issue concerns government regulation of deviant religious groups—extremist "cults" and "sects"—often viewed as a threat to individual and social welfare. Such groups, though small in actual numbers of members, have been highly visible in the media, public debate, and legal disputes. Indeed, virtually all court cases (and hence all legal precedents) regarding religion center on the practices of deviant minority religions. A recurrent issue has been whether participation in such groups constitutes the exercise of religious freedom or enslavement to organizations bent on "brainwashing" and exploitation. Thus, many media accounts, psychological articles, and legal decisions treat cult membership as a *priori* proof of pathology or coercion.

The club-theoretic view of sectarian religion challenges these interpretations. Within the club model, bizarre and apparently pathological practices of deviant groups arise as rational, utility-maximizing attempts to limit free-riding. This argument is bolstered by a growing body of empirical research that totally discredits most media accounts of "brainwashing" and coercion. Theory and data thus suggest that most attempts to protect the populace from deviant religions will actually reduce social welfare.

A related set of policy issues concerns the overall consequences of regulating religion. The research cited above indicate that competition yields the same benefits in religious markets as elsewhere. It ensures the availability of a variety of different religious products, stimulates innovation, and forces organizations to be responsive to their members and to make efficient use of their resources. In contrast, religious monopolies tend to be less diverse, innovative, efficient, and responsive. Efficiency and welfare are thus fostered by governmental policies that maintain free and competitive religious markets. Conversely, governmental attempts to establish, regulate, or monopolize religion tend to reduce social welfare. These arguments deserve serious attention at a time when court rulings and the expanding welfare state threaten to erode the freedoms previously enjoyed by deviant religions.

6. CONCLUSIONS

One might say much more about religion and economics. Though I emphasized the insights that economics brings to religion, one might easily turn the tables and focus on the ways in which religion affects economic outcomes. Empirical studies invariably show that the members of some religions (such as Jews in America) earn significantly higher wages and incomes than average. Religion also affects individual rates of saving, occupational choice, levels of education, and numerous other economically important behaviors, such as voting, fertility, divorce, criminal activity, and drug and alcohol consumption.

Rather than pursue these issues, however, I will conclude with two examples illustrating the *indirect* benefits that flow from the study of religion. The benefits arise because religion provides an ideal testing ground for many theories of "non-market" behavior. No other non-market activity places so much emphasis on beliefs and norms, and few are as fully documented. Numerous surveys, government censuses, and church records provide regional, cross-national, and historical information on rates of church membership, church attendance, contributions, religious beliefs, and the like. Religion thus makes it relatively easy to develop and test theories of preference formation, normative constraints, cultural change, and the like.

Consider, for example, the concept of religious human capital (which models the way in which people get "hooked" on a particular religion and its beliefs). When I began studying religious behavior, it became apparent that upbringing and past religious involvement exerted major influence on a person's current religious practices. As a student of Gary Becker, it was only natural that I try to model this tendency as the consequence of national choice and the accumulation of human capital. The resulting model (Iannaccone [1984], [1986]) formalized Stigler and Becker's [1977] treatment of addiction. Subsequently, Becker and Murphy [1988] greatly extended this model in their theory of rational addiction. The economics of religion thus benefitted from and contributed to a very different line of research.

For a very different example of the synergies that arise when studying religion, consider the club-theoretic explanation for sacrifice and stigma. The model accounts for the continuing appeal of sectarian religion, and its predictions fit much of what is known about deviant religious groups. But the underlying argument applies also to non-religious "clubs" in which participation generates collective benefits and individual inputs are difficult to monitor. As the model predicts, many such collectives do demand apparently non-productive sacrifices: fraternities employ embarrassing initiations; secular communes separate members from family, friends, and society; primitive tribes employ painful and disfiguring rights of passage; and "boot camp" is notoriously demeaning. In principle, one might model any of these activities directly, but the data on religion prove more accessible.

In sum, religion remains a fundamental feature of human life and culture, a fact that social scientists ignore at their peril. Economics has much to say about religious behavior at the individual, group, and market levels; and economic theory tends to justify government policies that foster competitive religious markets. Religion also provides an ideal testing ground for extensions to traditional economic models.

References

Anderson, Gary M. [1988], "Mr. Smith and the Preachers: The Economics of Religion in the *Wealth of Nations*, " *Journal of Political Economy, 96(5)*, 1066–1088.

Azzi, Corry and Ehrenberg, Ronald [1975], "Household Allocation of Time and Church Attendance," *Journal of Political Economy, 83(1)*, 27–56.

Becker, Gary S. and Murphy, Kevin M. [1988], "A Theory of Rational Addiction," *Journal of Political Economy*, 96(4), 675–700.

Ekelund, Robert B. JR., Hebert, Robert F. and Tollison, Robert D. [1989], "An Economic Model of the Medieval Church: Usury as a Form of

Rent Seeking," *Journal of Law, Economics, and Organization*, 5(2), 307–331.

Finke, Roger [1990], "Religious Deregulation: Origins and Consequences," *Journal of Church and State*, 32, 609–626.

—— and Stark, Rodney [1992], *The Churching of America 1776–1990: Winners and Losers in our Religious Economy*, Rutgers University Press: New Brunswick, NI.

Greeley, Andrew M. [1989], *Religious Change in America*, Harvard University Press, Cambridge, MA.

—— and Durkin, John T. Jr. [1991], "A Model of Religious Choice Under Uncertainty," *Rationality and Society*, 3(2), 178–196.

Hamberg, Eve M. And Pettersson, Thorleif [1994], "The Religious Market: Denominational Competition and Religious Participation in Contemporary Sweden," *Journal for the Scientific Study of Religion*, 33(3), 205–216.

Iannaccone, Laurence R. [1984], "Consumption Capital and Habit Formation With an Application to Religious Participation," Ph.D. dissertation, University of Chicago.

—— [1986], "Addiction and Satiation," *Economics Letters*, 21, 95–99.

—— [1990], "Religious Participation: A Human Capital Approach," *Journal for the Scientific Study of Religion*, 29(3), 297–314.

—— [1991], "The Consequences of Religious Market Structure: Adam Smith and the Economics of Religion," *Rationality and Society*, 3(2), 156–177.

—— [1992], "Sacrifice and Stigma: Reducing Free-Riding in Cults, Communes, and Other Collectives," *Journal of Political Economy*, 100(2), 271–291.

McConnell, Michael W. and Posner, Richard A. [1989], "An Economic Approach to Issues of Religious Freedom," *University of Chicago Law Review*, 56(1), 1–60.

Montgomery, James [1994], "The Dynamics of the Religious Economy: Exit, Voice, and Denominational Secularization," Unpublished paper, Northwestern University, Evansion, IL.

Olds, Kelly [1994], "Privatizing the Church: Disestablishment in Connectient and Massachusetts," *Journal of Political Economy*, 102(2), 277–297.

Schlight, Ekkebart [1995], "Economic Analysis and Organized Religion," in: E. L. Jones and V. Reynolds (eds.), *Survival and Religion: Biological Evolution and Cultural Change*, Wiley: Chichester.

Smith, Adam [1776/1965], *An inquiry Into Nature and Causes of the Wealth of Nations*, Modern Library: New York.

Stigler, George J. and Becker, Gary S. [1977], "De Gustibus non est Disputandum," *American Economic Review*, 67, 76–90.

Warner, R. Stephen [1993], "Work in Progress Toward a new Paradigm in the Sociology of Religion," *American Journal of Sociology*, 98(5), 1044–1093.

Young, Lawrence (ed.) [1995], *Assessing Rational Choice Theories of Religion*.

Questions about Content

1. What is the "secularization thesis" and why, according to the writer, is it not valid?
2. By the end of the article, the writer has summarized many direct and indirect benefits that can be gained by studying religion from an economics perspective. What are some of those benefits?
3. An individual is deciding whether to adopt one religion or another. According to this article, that individual's decision-making process is influenced by factors that he or she might not even be aware of. What are some of those factors?
4. How does the word *market* create a new perspective in talking about religions and religious institutions? Does the term make you feel uneasy, and if so, why? On the other hand, how might a religious group or institution, such as a church, embrace that term and use the concept of *market* to gain more members?

Questions about Rhetorical Analysis

1. Just as the field of economics examines how individuals make decisions by weighing costs and benefits, the field of rhetoric examines the decisions writers make. A writer chooses to work for a goal, and to do that, the writer chooses to employ certain strategies in his writing. What is Iannaccone's goal in this article? To achieve that goal, how does he decide to organize the article?
2. The writer starts his conclusion by briefly surveying other issues, and then he states, "Rather than pursue these issues, however, I will conclude with two examples illustrating the *indirect* benefits that flow from the study of religion." Why does the writer decide to end the article this way? Does the choice to conclude this way help him accomplish his goal in the article?

Connecting the Readings

1. You have just encountered several approaches to thinking, researching, and writing about religion. Assess the writing style of each approach that you have encountered: literary studies, psychology, sociology, and economics. Do some of the approaches seem to be more useful for understanding faith than others?
2. Choose one of these words: *belief* or *religion*. Go to *Merriam-Webster's Collegiate Dictionary* (Tenth edition) and look up the definition of the word you selected. Now consider how each academic discipline represented in this chapter defines the term. Create a chart listing the dictionary definition at the top and then listing the definition for each of the disciplines. Step back and assess the differences in definitions. Do any of them contradict each other? Do they complement one another?

Writing Projects

1. Consider a research topic from one of the fields represented in this chapter. To get a sense of what kinds of topics a field has addressed, you could visit relevant web sites and search for articles in your library's databases. Select one article, and then locate another article from a different disciplinary perspective. Write an essay that compares, contrasts, and evaluates the usefulness of the two approaches toward that issue. You could argue for or against the way the two disciplines define faith or belief.

2. Interview a professional in your major field or another field of interest (such as a professor or someone working in the private, nonprofit, or government sectors) to discover how religion is perceived in that field of study, and write a profile or report of your findings. What kinds of religious issues does that field address? How does that area of study define faith, belief, and religion? What methods, materials, conventions, and assumptions does that field use in studying religion?

Religion in Public Issues

How are issues of religion written about in a pluralistic society?

BACKGROUND

Religion is often an implicit if not explicit factor in public debates. Because individuals take positions on controversial issues according to their values, their religious beliefs often play a role in the development of their opinions. Within a government that has established one official religion, the debate may be about how to interpret and apply the scriptures and doctrines of that religion to a particular situation. Voices of dissent may attempt to assert themselves, and given certain conditions they may even be successful in doing so, but they are forced to overcome their marginal status as a minority. In a democratic and pluralistic society—a society consisting of multiple cultures, ethnicities, traditions, religions, and beliefs—the voices of many faiths may participate in such debates.

Discussions that involve religion in American public life tend to circle back to the foundational argument about what role, if any, religion should take in those discussions. For the answer to that question, we consult the founding documents. The Declaration of Independence contains several explicit references to religious faith. The opening paragraph states that "the Laws of Nature and of Nature's God" entitles a collection of people such as the American colonies to assume a "separate and equal station" among other nations on earth. The second paragraph articulates the primary founding principle of the nation: "We hold these truths to be self-evident, that all men are created equal, that they are endowed by their Creator with certain unalienable Rights, that among these are Life, Liberty and the pursuit of Happiness." In the final sentence the signers state, "With a firm reliance on the protection of Divine Providence, we mutually pledge to each other our Lives, our Fortunes and our sacred Honor."

For over two hundred years, historians and scholars of political science have researched and argued what these phrases meant to those who wrote and signed the document and what these phrases should signify to present-day Americans. The term *Divine Providence*, for example, seems influenced by the Puritans, who believed that God was intimately involved in directing human history and intervening in the workings of nature. The term *Nature's God* is influenced by the eighteenth-century philosophy, Deism, which held that the world is like a huge mechanism set in motion by a creator who put the rules in place and let the machine run without intervention. The Deist concept of God stands in contrast with the Puritans' idea, and while traces of both can still be discerned in today's faiths, contemporary American concepts of the divine have diverged. Many Americans today hold individualistic beliefs in a God with whom they can establish a personal, one-to-one relationship. While they may pray for God's direct intervention in human affairs, they primarily rely upon faith and prayer for personal strength to overcome difficulties and accomplish life goals. Still others believe in a transcendent deity, one who is more of an unknowable presence infused throughout nature and in every human being. As much as they contrast with each other, all of these conceptions of God may even be found within the same religion.

Given the different interpretations of terms in the Declaration of Independence and the great variety of beliefs in the United States today, how are we to understand the meaning of this document's references to God? Even if we can come to some agreement on that question, another question remains: to what extent should the Declaration's eighteenth century-references to faith be applied in the very different America of today?

These questions become more pressing when we examine the Constitution. Whereas the Declaration provides statements of principles about government, the Constitution actually sets up a working government, and this document is the one we use to understand the functions of each major unit of government. This document lacks any reference to God with the exception of the phrase "year of our Lord one thousand seven hundred and eighty seven" in the conventional dating system of the time.

The Constitution does include references to religion, but rather than principles such as *Nature's God*, they are references intended to define the roles that institutions of government and institutions of religion may have in each other's operations. For example, Article II-Section One states that to assume the office of the presidency, the president-elect must make this *oath or affirmation*: "I do solemnly swear (or affirm) that I will faithfully execute the office of President of the United States, and will to the best of my ability, preserve, protect and defend the Constitution of the United States." Article VI further states that all senators and representatives in Congress must make "oath or affirmation" to support the Constitution, and it goes further, stating, "No religious test shall ever be required as a qualification to any office or public trust under the United States." The writers of the Constitution specified that a president and members of Congress have a choice to take an *"oath"* and *"swear"* (terms with religious connotations) or to make an *"affirmation"* and *"affirm"* (terms that carry no religious connotations). Article VI also states that religion cannot be used either to qualify or to disqualify someone from serving in a public office. The most complex mention of religion appears in the First Amendment, which declares: "Congress shall make no law respecting an establishment of religion, or prohibiting the free exercise thereof."

It is not our intent here to summarize, much less resolve, the conflicting interpretations of these clauses. Rather we must be aware, when we write about social issues, that the nature and extent of religion in government remains a topic in dispute. This unsettled question often lies behind the ways writers address issues of religion in the United States.

AS YOU READ

The following selections present arguments from different religious perspectives. Notice that some take pro or con positions. Notice that others explore all sides of an issue, seeking compromise and exploring ways to frame issues in new ways. The point of these readings is to invite you to think about how religious belief affects public debate.

You can find out more about these and other issues by checking the Internet for the web sites of organizations that advocate for one position or the other. You can also check your library's databases for books and articles in newspapers, magazines, and journals that argue about the issue.

Topic 1: What Should the Role of Religion be in American Society?

Is there a "conservative" view or a "liberal" view about the role of religion in American public debate? Going back to the seventeenth century, the earliest Puritan colonial governments made no distinction between religious life and public life; their roles were intertwined. For example, the right to vote or hold public office would require a religious loyalty oath or church membership, and taxes would support the churches. Such practices continued well through the eighteenth century, even past the American Revolution. At the same time, a few of the earliest Puritan colonists broke away to form new colonies that would allow full freedom of conscience, and that concept of religious freedom would gradually supplant laws and statutes throughout the states that formed the new nation.

Historically, conservative congregations in America advocated keeping their churches out of the mundane concerns of politics and free from government interference. Yet many of them would come to advocate involvement in politics, especially in issues of moral and social conduct. Progressive congregations have advocated separation to keep government free from religious interference. Yet, historically, progressive religious groups have also been involved in social movements such as the abolition of slavery, the civil rights movement, and advocacy for the poor. For both conservatives and liberals, the line separating religion and government can be difficult to define; its position can shift depending on the issue at hand.

The following selections feature two people of faith who hold different political perspectives: one is a progressive evangelical minister and one is a conservative political journalist. While these two writers disagree about particular public policies, they both believe that religious faith can and should play a positive role in the public square. As you read, notice not only what separates them, but also what might bring them together.

Take Back the Faith
The best contribution of religion is precisely *not* to be a loyal partisan
JIM WALLIS

Jim Wallis is a minister and the president and executive director of Sojourners, an evangelical Christian organization working for social justice and an end to poverty and war. His columns regularly appear in Sojourners *magazine, and he is the author of several books including the highly popular national bestseller,* God's Politics: Why the Right Gets It Wrong and the Left Doesn't Get It. *He has written articles for* the New York Times, Washington Post, Los Angeles Times, *and* Time *and* Newsweek *magazines. He gives speeches and lectures throughout the nation and appears regularly on radio and television programs such as* Meet the Press, The Daily Show, The O'Reilly Factor, *and news programs of CBS, NBC, ABC, CNN, MSNBC, Fox, and National Public Radio. You can learn more on the Sojourner's web site at* www.sojo.net *and Wallis's blog at* http://blog.beliefnet.com/godspolitics. *As you read his article, notice how he redefines the role of religion in politics.*

———————————— ◆ ————————————

Many of us feel that our faith has been stolen, and it's time to take it back. An enormous public misrepresentation of Christianity has taken place. Many people around the world now think Christian faith stands for political commitments that are almost the opposite of its true meaning. How did the faith of Jesus come to be known as pro-rich, pro-war, and pro-American? And how do we get back to a historic, biblical, and *genuinely* evangelical faith rescued from its contemporary distortions?

That rescue operation is even more crucial today, in the face of a social crisis that cries out for prophetic religion. The problem is clear in the political arena, where strident voices claim to represent Christians, when they clearly don't speak for *most* of us. We hear politicians who love to say how religious they are but utterly fail to apply the values of faith to their public leadership and political policies. It's time to take back our faith in the public square, especially in a time when a more authentic social witness is desperately needed.

When we do, we discover that faith challenges the powers that be to do justice for the poor, instead of preaching a "prosperity gospel" and supporting politicians that further enrich the wealthy. We remember that faith hates violence and tries to reduce it, and exerts a fundamental presumption against war, instead of justifying it in God's name. We see that faith creates community from racial, class, and gender divisions and prefers international community over nationalist religion, and we see that "God bless America" is found nowhere in the Bible. And we are reminded that faith regards matters such as the sacredness of life and family bonds as so important that they should never be used as ideological symbols or mere political pawns in partisan warfare.

The media likes to say, "Oh, then you must be the Religious Left." No, and the very question is the problem. Just because a Religious Right has fashioned itself in one predictable ideological guise does not mean that those who question this political seduction must be their opposite political counterpart. The best public contribution of religion is precisely *not to* be ideologically predictable nor a loyal partisan. To raise the moral issues of human rights, for example, will challenge both left- and right-wing governments who put power above principles. And religious action is rooted in a much deeper place than "rights"—that being the image of God in every human being.

Similarly, when the poor are defended on moral or religious grounds, it is not "class warfare" but rather a direct response to the overwhelming focus in the scriptures that claims the poor are regularly neglected, exploited, and oppressed by wealthy elites, political rulers, and indifferent affluent populations. Those scriptures don't simply endorse the social programs of liberals or conservatives, but make clear that poverty is indeed a religious issue and that the failure of political leaders to help uplift those in poverty will be judged a moral failing.

It is precisely because religion takes the problem of evil so seriously that it must always be suspicious of concentrated power—politically *and* economically—either in totalitarian regimes or in huge multinational corporations, which now have more wealth and power than many governments. It is indeed our theology of evil that makes us strong proponents of both political and economic democracy—not because people are so good, but because they often are not and need clear safeguards and strong systems of checks and balances to avoid the dangerous accumulations of power and wealth.

It's why we doubt the goodness of all superpowers and the righteousness of empires in any era, *especially* when their claims of inspiration and success invoke theology and the name of God. Given human tendencies for self-delusion and deception, is it any wonder that hardly a religious body in the world regards unilateral and pre-emptive war as "just?" Religious wisdom suggests that the more overwhelming the military might, the more dangerous its capacity for self and public deception.

The loss of religion's prophetic vocation is terribly dangerous for any society. Who will uphold the dignity of economic and political outcasts? Who will question the self-righteousness of nations and their leaders? Who will question the recourse to violence and the rush to wars long before any last resort has been unequivocally proven? Who will not allow God's name to be used to simply justify ourselves, instead of calling us to accountability?

In an election year, the particular religiosity of a candidate, or even how devout they might be, is less important than how their religious and/or moral commitments and values shape their political vision and their policy commitments. Understanding the moral compass they bring to their public lives and how their convictions shape their political priorities is the true litmus test.

Questions about Content

1. Throughout this article, the writer describes aspects of a larger problem with religion in America. What, according to his overall description, is the core of that problem?
2. Wallis envisions positive, productive contributions that people of faith can make in government and society, contributions that get beyond the labels of "conservative vs. liberal." Describe what those contributions are, according to Wallis.
3. The writer uses the terms *prophetic religion* and *religion's prophetic vocation* to describe the role religion should take. Look up the word *prophetic* in a collegiate dictionary. Explain what the word means and describe what the role of a prophetic religion would be.
4. "Poverty is indeed a religious issue." What does the writer mean by this statement?

Questions about Rhetorical Analysis

1. What words or phrases does Wallis use to appeal to his readers' values?
2. In the third and fourth paragraphs from the end, Wallis uses the words *we* and *us*. Whom do those words refer to?
3. In the second-to-last paragraph, Wallis presents several questions, called "rhetorical questions" because they are intended to prove a point. Why does he use rhetorical questions rather than make his points with direct statements?

Atheists' Bleak Alternative

Jeff Jacoby

Jeff Jacoby, formerly an editorial writer for the Boston Herald, *is a conservative columnist for the* Boston Globe. *An honors graduate from George Washington University and Boston University Law School, he has worked for the president of Boston University, practiced law, and worked in national politics. He is a political commentator on television and radio and received the Breindel Award for Excellence in Opinion Journalism. You can read his* Boston Globe *columns at www.boston.com/bostonglobe. As you read his article, notice how he raises concerns about what the loss of religious faith could mean for American society.*

---- ◆ ----

From the land that produced "A Christmas Carol" and Handel's "Messiah," more evidence that Christianity is fading in Western Europe: Nearly 99 percent of Christmas cards sold in Great Britain contain no religious message or imagery.

"Traditional pictures such as angels blowing trumpets over a stable, Jesus in his manger, the shepherds and three wise men following the star to Bethlehem are dying out," the Daily Mail reports. A review of some 5,500 Christmas cards turns up fewer than 70 that make any reference to the birth of Jesus. "Hundreds . . . avoided any image linked to Christmas at all"— even those with no spiritual significance, such as Christmas trees or Santa Claus.

Presumably the greeting-card industry is only supplying what the market demands; if Christian belief and practice weren't vanishing from the British scene, Christian-themed cards wouldn't be, either. But some Britons, not all of them devout, are resisting the tide. Writing in the Telegraph, editor-at-large Jeff Randall—who describes himself as "somewhere between an agnostic and a mild believer"—announces that any Christmas card he receives that doesn't at least mention the word "Christmas" goes straight into the trash. "Jettisoning Christmas-less cards is my tiny, almost certainly futile, gesture against the dark forces of political correctness," he writes. "It's a swipe at those who would prefer to abolish Christmas altogether, in case it offends 'minorities.' Someone should tell them that, with only one in 15 Britons going to church on Sundays, Christians are a minority."

Meanwhile, the employment law firm Peninsula says that 75 percent of British companies have banned Christmas decorations for fear of being sued by someone who finds the holiday offensive. And it isn't only in December that this anti-Christian animus rears its head. British Airways triggered a furor when it ordered an employee to hide the tiny cross she wears around her neck. At the BBC, senior executives agreed that they would not air a program showing a Koran being thrown in the garbage—but that the trashing of a Bible would be acceptable.

"It's extraordinary," remarks Randall. "In an increasingly godless age, there is a rising tide of hatred against those who adhere to biblical values." A "tyrannical minority" of intolerant secularists is openly contemptuous of traditional moral norms. "The teachings and guidance of old-fashioned Christianity offend them, so they seek to remove all traces of it from public life."

You don't have to be especially pious to find this atheist zealotry alarming. Nor do you have to live in Europe. Though religion remains important in American life, antireligious passion is surging here, too.

Examples abound: In two recent best sellers, Sam Harris heaps scorn on religious believers, whose faith he derides as "a few products of ancient ignorance and derangement." A study in the Journal of Religion and Society claims that belief in God correlates with higher rates of homicide, sexual promiscuity, and other social ills, and that when compared with relatively secular democracies, the churchgoing United States "is almost always the most dysfunctional." Secular absolutists demand that schools and government venues be cleansed of any hint of religious expression—be it a cross on the Los Angeles County seal, a courthouse display of the Ten Commandments, or the words "under God" in the Pledge of Allegiance.

What is at stake in all this isn't just angels on Christmas cards. What society loses when it discards Judeo-Christian faith and belief in God is something far-more difficult to replace: the value system most likely to promote ethical behavior and sustain a decent society. That is because without God, the difference between good and evil becomes purely subjective. What makes murder inherently wrong is not that it feels wrong, but that a transcendent Creator to whom we are answerable commands: "Thou shalt not murder." What makes kindness to others inherently right is not that human reason says so, but that God does: "Love thy neighbor as thyself; I am the Lord."

Obviously this doesn't mean that religious people are always good, or that religion itself cannot lead to cruelty. Nor does it mean that atheists cannot be beautiful, ethical human beings. Belief in God alone does not guarantee goodness. But belief tethered to clear ethical values—Judeo-Christian monotheism—is society's best bet for restraining our worst moral impulses and encouraging our best ones.

The atheist alternative is a world in which right and wrong are ultimately matters of opinion, and in which we are finally accountable to no one but ourselves. That is anything but a tiding of comfort and joy.

Questions about Content

1. Similar to the Wallis article, throughout this article, Jacoby describes aspects of a larger problem with religion in America. What, according to his overall argument, is that central problem?

2. Jacoby, like Wallis, envisions a positive, productive contribution that people of faith can make to American society. Describe that role according to Jacoby's article.

3. The article says, "What is at stake in all this isn't just angels on Christmas cards." What is the writer implying: what is at stake?

4. What, according to Jacoby, is the "atheist alternative" and what does he identify as its greatest danger? Do you think this fear is justified?

Questions about Rhetorical Analysis

1. The writer begins the article by employing several brief stories or examples. What function do they serve for his argument?
2. In the second-to-last paragraph, Jacoby makes statements that might be agreeable to readers who oppose his thesis. Why does he use those statements?

Connecting the Readings

1. Compare the concerns that Wallis and Jacoby voice. How might their values be similar? What problems would they agree exist?
2. Contrast their concerns. Does Wallis identify any problems or solutions that Jacoby might not identify? Does Jacoby identify any problems or solutions that Wallis might not identify?

Topic 2: Is the United States a Religious Nation?

On the 9th of March, 1790, Benjamin Franklin sat down to write a letter to his colleague, Ezra Stiles, who shared Franklin's passion for science. A pastor in the Congregational church and president of Yale University, Stiles had asked Franklin to explain his religious beliefs. Writing just a few weeks before his death, Franklin explained that he was a monotheist whose God created and governed the universe and judged the actions of human beings. Then Franklin explained his views of Jesus of Nazareth. Jesus's articulation of morals was among the best Franklin had ever seen, but Franklin went on to explain that he felt that the system Jesus set forth had been changed and corrupted by Christians themselves. Franklin stated that he doubted that Jesus was divine but also doubted that God would be displeased with those who did not believe. According to Franklin in this letter and others, there was no harm in believing or disbelieving one way or another, and he found little use in speculating about such things, preferring to steer his attention to more practical worldly matters.

So if you wanted to argue that Franklin was a man of deep religious faith, could you use this letter to support your opinion?

Or if you wanted to argue that faith was not very important to Franklin, could you use this letter for support? The answer to these questions is, respectively, yes, and yes. The founders of the United States of America were not unlike many people today; they held a variety of beliefs that developed throughout their lives. As a result, when we read the writings of just one of these extraordinary individuals, we find a range of statements on the topic of faith.

Writers who wish to argue that the United States is or is not a religious nation can use quotations from historical figures to prove different points of view. The writers in this section refer to history to answer the question of whether this is a religious nation. As you read, consider: Are there any areas of agreement between them? Is it even possible to write an ultimate set of "rules" for selecting and employing quotations to determine whether the historical appeal is a valid type of argument?

Fighting Words for a Secular America

ROBIN MORGAN

Robin Morgan, one of the founders of contemporary feminism in the United States, emerged as a prominent activist in the 1960s and 1970s and continues as a leader in the movement today. An editor at Ms. *magazine, she is also the editor of several major books in the women's movement—*Sisterhood Is Powerful, Sisterhood Is Global, *and* Sisterhood Is Forever—*and other books including* Fighting Words: A Toolkit for Combating the Religious Right. *You can learn more at the Ms. web site,* www.msmagazine.com *and Morgan's web site,* www.robinmorgan.us. *As you read her article, notice how she uses American history to support her thesis.*

---- ◆ ----

Alert: Americans who honor the U.S. Constitution's strict separation of church and state are now genuinely alarmed. Agnostics and atheists, as well as observant people of every faith, fear—sensibly—that the religious right is gaining historic political power, via an ultraconservative movement with highly placed friends.

But many of us feel helpless. We haven't read the Founding Documents since school (if then). We lack arguing tools, "verbal karate" evidence we can cite in defending a secular United States.

For instance, such extremists claim—and, too often, we ourselves assume—that U.S. law has religious roots. Yet the Constitution contains no reference to a deity.

The Declaration of Independence contains not one word on religion, basing its authority on the shocking idea that power is derived from ordinary people, which challenged European traditions of rule by divine right and/or heavenly authority. (Remember, George III was king of England *and* anointed head of its church.)

The words "Nature's God," the "Creator" and "divine Providence" do appear in the Declaration. But in its context—an era, and author, Thomas Jefferson, that celebrated science and the Enlightenment—these words are analogous to our contemporary phrase "life force."

Jerry Falwell notoriously blamed 9/11 on "pagans, abortionists, feminists, gays and lesbians ... [and other groups] who have tried to secularize America." He's a bit late: In 1798, Alexander Hamilton accused Jefferson of a "conspiracy to establish atheism on the ruins of Christianity" in the new republic. Deputy Undersecretary of Defense for Intelligence William Boykin thunders, "We're a Christian nation."

But the 1796 Treaty of Tripoli—initiated by George Washington and signed into law by John Adams—proclaims: *"The Government of the United States of America is not, in any sense, founded on the Christian Religion."*

Offices for "Faith-Based Initiatives" with nearly $20 billion in grants have been established (by executive order, circumventing Congress) in 10 federal agencies, as well as *inside* the White House. This fails "the Lemon Test," violating a 1971 Supreme Court decision (*Lemon v. Kurtzman*): "first, a statute [or public policy] must have a secular legislative purpose; second, its principal or primary effect must be one that neither advances nor inhibits religion; finally, the statute [or policy] must not foster 'excessive government entanglement with religion.'"

When Attorney General John Ashcroft repeatedly invokes religion, the Founders must be picketing in their graves. They were a mix of freethinkers, atheists, Christians, agnostics, Freemasons and Deists (professing belief in powers scientifically evinced in the natural universe). They surely were imperfect. Some were slaveholders.

Female citizens were invisible to them—though Abigail Adams warned her husband John, "If particular care and attention is not paid to the Ladies, we are determined to foment a Rebellion, and will not hold ourselves bound by any Laws in which we have no voice, or Representation."

But the Founders were, after all, *revolutionaries*. Their passion—especially regarding secularism—glows in the documents they forged and in their personal words.

THOMAS PAINE

Paine's writings heavily influenced the other Founders. A freethinker who opposed all organized religion, he reserved particular vituperation for Christianity. "My country is the world and my religion is to do good" (*The Rights of Man*, 1791).

"I do not believe in the creed professed by the Jewish church, by the Roman church, by the Greek church, by the Turkish church, by the Protestant church, nor by any church that I know of. My own mind is my own church" (*The Age of Reason*, 1794).

"Of all the systems of religion that ever were invented, there is no more derogatory to the Almighty, more unedifying to man, more repugnant to reason, and more contradictory in itself than this thing called Christianity" (Ibid.).

BENJAMIN FRANKLIN

Raised a Calvinist, Franklin rebelled—and spread that rebellion, affecting Adams and Jefferson. His friend, Dr. Priestley, wrote in his own *Autobiography*. "It is much to be lamented that a man of Franklin's general good character and great influence should have been an unbeliever in Christianity, and also have done as much as he did to make others unbelievers."

A scientist, Franklin rejected churches, rituals, and all "supernatural superstitions."

"Scarcely was I arrived at fifteen years of age, when, after having doubted in turn of different tenets, according as I found them combated in the different books that I read, I began to doubt of Revelation itself"
(Franklin's *Autobiography*, 1817–18).

"Some volumes against Deism fell into my hands ... they produced an effect precisely the reverse to what was intended by the writers; for the arguments of the Deists, which were cited in order to be refuted, appeared to me much more forcibly than the refutation itself; in a word, I soon became a thorough Deist" (Ibid.).

GEORGE WASHINGTON

The false image of Washington as a devout Christian was fabricated by Mason Locke Weems, a clergyman who also invented the cherry-tree fable and in 1800 published his *Life of George Washington*. Washington, a Deist and a Freemason, never once mentioned the name of Jesus Christ in any of his thousands of letters, and pointedly referred to divinity as "It."

Whenever he (rarely) attended church, Washington always deliberately left before communion, demonstrating disbelief in Christianity's central ceremony.

JOHN ADAMS

Adams, a Unitarian inspired by the Enlightenment, fiercely opposed doctrines of supernaturalism or damnation, writing to Jefferson: "I almost shudder at the thought of alluding to the most fatal example of the abuses of grief which the history of mankind has preserved—the Cross. Consider what calamities that engine of grief has produced!"

Adams realized how politically crucial—and imperiled—a secular state would be: "The United States of America have exhibited, perhaps, the first example of governments erected on the simple principles of nature; and if men are now sufficiently enlightened to disabuse themselves of artifice, imposture, hypocrisy, and superstition, they will consider this event as an era in their history. . . . It will never be pretended that any persons employed in that service [forming the U.S. government] had interviews with the gods, or were in any degree under the influence of Heaven, more than those at work upon ships or houses, or laboring in merchandise or agriculture; it will forever be acknowledged that these governments were contrived merely by the use of reason and the senses. . . . Thirteen governments [of the original states] thus founded on the natural authority of the people alone, without a pretence of miracle or mystery . . . are a great point gained in favor of the rights of mankind" (*A Defence of the Constitutions of Government of the United States of America*, 1787–88).

THOMAS JEFFERSON

It's a commonly stated error that U.S. law, based on English common law, is thus grounded in Judeo-Christian tradition.

Yet Jefferson (writing to Dr. Thomas Cooper, February 10, 1814) noted that common law "is that system of law which was introduced by the Saxons on their settlement in England . . . about the middle of the fifth century. But Christianity was not introduced til) the seventh century. . . . *We may safely affirm (though contradicted by all the judges and writers on earth) that Christianity neither is, nor ever was a part of the common law."*

Jefferson professed disbelief in the Trinity and the divinity of Jesus Christ, while respecting moral teachings by whomever might have been a historical Jesus. He cut up a Bible, assembling his own version: "The whole history of these books [the Gospels] is so defective and doubtful," he wrote Adams (January 24, 1814), "evidence that parts have proceeded from an extraordinary man; and that other parts are of the fabric of very inferior minds."

Scorning miracles, saints, salvation, damnation, and angelic presences, Jefferson embraced reason, materialism, and science. He challenged Patrick Henry, who wanted a Christian theocracy: "[A]n amendment was proposed by inserting 'Jesus Christ,' so that [the preamble] should read 'A departure from the plan of Jesus Christ, the holy author of our religion'; the insertion was rejected by a great majority, in proof that they meant to comprehend, within the mantle of its protection, the Jew and the Gentile, the Christian and Mohammedan, the Hindoo and Infidel of every denomination" (from Jefferson's *Autobiography*, referring to the Statute of Virginia for Religious Freedom).

The theme is consistent throughout Jefferson's prolific correspondence: "Question with boldness even the existence of a God" (letter to Peter Carr, August 10, 1787).

"[The clergy] believe that any portion of power confided to me, will be exerted in opposition to their schemes. And they believe rightly: for I have sworn upon the altar of God, eternal hostility against every form of tyranny over the mind of man" (letter to Dr. Benjamin Rush, September 23, 1800).

"I contemplate with sovereign reverence that act of the whole American people which . . . thus[built] a wall of separation between church and state" (letter to the Danbury [Connecticut] Baptist Association, January 1, 1802).

"History, I believe, furnishes no example of a priest-ridden people maintaining a free civil government" (letter to Alexander von Humboldt, December 6, 1813).

"In every country and in every age, the priest has been hostile to liberty. He is always in alliance with the despot, abetting his abuses in return for protection to his own" (letter to Horatio G. Spafford, March 17, 1814).

"[W]hence arises the morality of the Atheist? . . . Their virtue, then, must have had some other foundation than the love of God" (letter to Thomas Law, June 13, 1814).

"I am of a sect by myself, as far as I know" (letter to Ezra Stiles, June 25, 1819).

"The day will come when the mystical generation of Jesus . . . will be classed with the fable of the generation of Minerva in the brain of Jupiter" (letter to John Adams, April 11, 1823).

JAMES MADISON

Although prayer groups proliferate in today's Congress, James Madison, "father of the Constitution," denounced even the presence of *chaplains* in Congress—*and* in the armed forces—as unconstitutional. He opposed all use of "religion as an engine of civil policy," and accurately prophesied the threat of "ecclesiastical corporations."

"Religious bondage shackles and debilitates the mind and unfits it for every noble enterprise" (letter to William Bradford, April 1, 1774).

"During almost fifteen centuries has the legal establishment of Christianity been on trial. What have been its fruits? More or less in all places, pride and indolence in the Clergy, ignorance and servility in the laity; in both, superstition, bigotry and persecution" (*Memorial and Remonstrance Against Religious Assessments*, Section 7, 1785).

"What influence in fact have ecclesiastical establishments had on Civil Society? In some instances they have been seen to erect a spiritual tyranny on the ruins of the Civil authority; in many instances they have been seen upholding the thrones of political tyranny: in no instance have they been seen as the guardians of the liberties of the people. Rulers who wished to subvert the public liberty, may have found an established Clergy convenient auxiliaries" (Ibid., Section 8).

"Besides the danger of a direct mixture of Religion & civil Government, there is an evil which ought to be guarded agst. in the indefinite accumulation of property from the capacity of holding it in perpetuity by ecclesiastical corporations. The power of all corporations ought to be limited in this respect. . . . The establishment of the chaplainship to Congs. is a palpable violation of equal rights, as well as of Constitutional principles. . . . Better also to disarm in the same way, the precedent of Chaplainships for the army and navy. . . . Religious proclamations by the Executive [branch] recommending thanksgivings & fasts are shoots from the same root. . . . Altho' recommendations only, they imply a religious agency, making no part of the trust delegated to political rulers" (*Monopolies, Perpetuities, Corporations, Ecclesiastical Endowments*, circa 1819).

That's only a sampling, quotes that blast cobwebs off the tamed images we have of the Founders. Their own statements—not dead rhetoric but alive with ringing, still radical, ideas—can reconnect us to our proud, secular roots, and should inspire us to honor and defend them.

The Founders minced no words—and they acted on them. Dare we do less?

Questions about Content

1. Morgan presents much evidence, in the form of quotations, to advance her thesis. Select a couple of quotations that give the article its strongest evidence. What makes them strong? Select a couple of quotations that give the article its weakest evidence. What makes them weak?

2. The following statements appear in the article's introduction. Consider how you could research these statements. What additional information might lead you to find these statements more convincing? What information might lead you to find them less convincing? (You might need to look at the documents she is referring to.)
   - "The Constitution contains no reference to a deity."
   - "The Declaration of Independence . . . [bases] its authority on the shocking idea that power is derived from ordinary people."
   - "The words 'Nature's God,' the 'Creator' and 'divine Providence' . . . are analogous to our contemporary phrase 'life force.'"

Questions about Rhetorical Analysis

1. What is the writer's purpose in this article? What strategy for presenting evidence does the writer use to achieve that purpose? Does that strategy work? Explain your answer.

2. Describe the writer's tone and identify who her intended readers are. What words or phrases make the argument more, or less, effective in establishing trust with her intended readers?

Is America a Religious Country?
STUDENT ESSAY

A Student Essay offers a conservative voice in the historical role of religion in American politics. The student makes use of her own research as well as information that she has gathered from other college courses in history and literature. The writer's argument runs directly counter to Robin Morgan's article. As you read, notice how she has done research on American history to support her point that America was founded upon religious principles.

---◆---

America is a great nation, and part of our greatness stems from the amazing progress we have made in the area of individual rights. Over the past two hundred plus years of our existence, the rights and privileges of citizenship have been gradually extended to many who were originally excluded on the basis of race, gender, ethnicity, and other factors. We still have a way to go, but for the most part, when we hear about discrimination against an African American citizen or other citizen, most of us are outraged.

However, a form of discrimination still exists. Residents of a town are fighting just to be able to display the Ten Commandments outside the courthouse that their taxes pay for. Employees in the work place and students in schools are being told that they cannot put up Christmas decorations. A teacher in Virginia who put up posters with a Christian theme is now in court fighting for his right to free expression because the school took his posters down. Navy chaplains are being told what they can and cannot say in their prayers. These and many other cases are documented by the Rutherford Institute, a legal defense organization dedicated to the civil liberties of religious people.

Should towns and cities be permitted to display the Ten Commandments on government property? Should schools be allowed to display Christmas decorations? Is it acceptable for the people to ask candidates for public office if they believe in God? Is it fair for churches and religious groups to organize and speak out on social issues such as stem cell research and gay marriage? Secularists would answer "no" to all of these questions. They are those who want to keep religion and government separate.

The secularists are probably acting out of a fear of religion because the history of the world does show numerous instances of the damage that religious intolerance can do, from the Crusades to the Inquisition to acts of violence by religious extremists today. However secularists should acknowledge that world history also shows numerous instances of charity, compassion, love, forgiveness, and kindness motivated by the desire to serve God and humanity. Many of the leaders of the civil rights movement, such as Martin Luther King, were ministers, and churches were actively involved in that movement. According to a report published by the Heritage Foundation, religious people donate their money and time to charity much more than secular people. Without regard to income or any other factor, 90% of religious people give money as opposed to only 66% of secular people, and 67% of religious people volunteer their time versus 44% of secular people (Brooks). There is definitely something about faith that encourages people to be caring.

Secularists could acknowledge these positive aspects. They could also acknowledge that the feelings of religious people, who are after all the majority, deserve to be taken into consideration. Many people of faith in this country feel that they are being discriminated against because they are told that they should not practice their faith publicly. They are criticized for applying the most important aspects of their lives, their faith, to issues they care about in their society.

One way we can resolve these religious debates in America is to answer the basic question: Is America a religious country or not? The problem with answering this question is that there are many ways to come up with a definition of *religious country*. Looking at Christianity in America, Hugh Helco says there are many ways to approach the question. He says that we can look at surveys showing how many Americans say they are Christian. We can look at the everyday lives of Americans to see if they apply Christian morals in their lives. We can look at Americans' beliefs and behaviors and government institutions. Helco puts the question in seven ways, and his answer ends up being "yes—no—no—no—sort of—sort of—and no way" (64). I agree that the issue is complex, and Helco helps us think through it, but complexity is not going to end the debate. We need a more clear answer.

To do this, we could break the question down into two parts: America's past and America's present. Does our history show that we were founded on religious principles? Does our present situation show that we still value religion? The answer to both of these questions is "yes."

To start with history, we can see that religion played a huge role in the way the nation was founded. If you take a course in early American history or literature, you will see that the Puritans who came here made many references to God. They were doing God's work by coming to America and forming settlements. They even compared themselves to the Israelites escaping slavery and going to the Promised Land with the help of God, just like in the book of Exodus in the Bible. One Puritan minister, John Winthrop, who was a leader in settling the area of Salem, Massachusetts, said this to his people: "We shall be as a City upon a hill. The eyes of all people are upon us" (Winthrop 42). This statement comes directly out of the New Testament, and it definitely describes what America became.

We can also see the role of religion in the founding of our government. Samuel Huntington of the American Enterprise Institute says, "The Declaration of Independence appealed to 'Nature's God,' the 'Creator,' 'the Supreme Judge of the World,' and 'divine Providence' for approval, legitimacy, and protection." God is also in the Constitution. The last sentence in the Constitution states, "Done in Conversion by the Unanimous Consent of the States present the Seventeenth Day of September in the Year of our Lord one thousand seven hundred and Eighty seven." As Jeff Jacoby says, if the Framers wanted to create a government "sanitized of any hint of God, surely they would have found a different way to date their document."

Religion was definitely important to the founders of our nation. According to a web site that collects statistics on religion (Adherents. com), almost all of the signers of all of our founding documents were religious or affiliated with churches. Many statements by our Founders show that they believed a nation could not be peaceful and stable and long lasting unless the people were self-disciplined by morality and faith. They believed that churches were necessary to create this kind of environment. In his Farewell Address, George Washington said, "Of all the dispositions and habits which lead to political prosperity, Religion and morality are indispensable supports" (Kirkpatrick). John Adams wrote in a letter, "Our Constitution was made only for a moral and religious people. It is wholly inadequate to the government of any other" (Beliefnet). These are just two of many statements that can be found in the writings of the Founders listed on web sites such as beliefnet.com.

Religion was so important to our Founders that they created the First Amendment to protect religious freedom. There is a misconception that the purpose of that amendment was to separate church and state. Samuel Huntington makes a good point: "The words 'separation of church and state' do not appear in the Constitution." What the Founders opposed was the establishment of a national church; the First Amendment prevents the government from supporting one religion over others, and it prevents any one religion from having exclusive power in government. But the Founders did not intend for government to ignore religion or for people of faith to have no influence on their government. A paper published for the Heritage Foundation states, "The Founders did favor government encouragement and support of religion in public laws, official speeches and ceremonies, on public property and in public buildings, and even in public schools. . . . On the day after it approved the Bill of Rights, Congress called upon the president to 'recommend to the people of the United States a day of public thanksgiving and prayer, to be observed by acknowledging, with grateful hearts, the many signal favors of Almighty God" (Spalding). We could list many more of those instances (see Spalding).

Religion is at the core of the Declaration of Independence and the Constitution. The Judeo-Christian tradition places great value on the importance of community and the rights of the individual. In the Old Testament, God gave the Israelites many rules and regulations to live by to make sure they would be a peaceful community.

Those laws made sure that every individual was protected, which is necessary for a community to exist. For example, the "eye for an eye" law said that if one person wrongs another, then that person must compensate the other. If person A steals an ox from person B, then person A must give a healthy ox to person B along with some grain to pay for the inconvenience. Person B is not allowed to demand anything more. Our current laws are based upon these principles of fairness that are found in the Bible.

The principles of freedom and personal rights are basically religious. Christianity believes that each and every person is a creation of God. Jesus preached that the way we treat each other shows the way we feel about him and God. To serve God, we have to treat others in a respectful manner. Our Founding Fathers believed this, so as mentioned above, in the Declaration of Independence, they made sure to give God credit for being the source of our freedom. They gave us the Bill of Rights to guarantee each one of us certain rights that the government cannot infringe upon. The Constitution may not say it outright, but the principle behind every right in the Constitution is that the government cannot take away from the people what God has given.

Does any of this history matter? Well, if 100% or 90% or even 80% of the people in our country no longer believed in these principles, then I guess we would have to say it doesn't matter. But the fact is, almost all Americans hold to these ideals. This brings us to the second way we can define a religious nation: we can look at the present. A major survey shows that 86% of Americans identify themselves as belonging to a religion. About 75%–80% of Americans regularly call themselves Christian in these polls, and the rest identify with other religious groups. Of those who do not identify with a religion, most of them still have some kind of belief, and only 1% or less call themselves atheists or agnostics (American Religious Identity Survey).

Considering this reality of America today along with America's history, is it too much to ask for our public life to show some respect to our religious beliefs? The Ten Commandments are part of our history, and they are pretty good rules to live by, so there is no harm in displaying them on public property. The vast majority of Americans celebrate Christmas, even non-Christians, who can enjoy the company of friends, the good cheer, and the festivities of the season. People of faith can and should question candidates about their beliefs and speak out on social issues. Because our beliefs are so central to who we are and how we want to live, it is not reasonable or fair to ask religious people not to do that.

We can also do this with tolerance toward all faiths. A former Republican senator from Missouri who is also an

Episcopalian minister asks religious people to keep this in mind: "Religion should be inclusive, and it should seek to bridge the differences that separate people. We do not exclude from worship those who opinions differ from ours. . . . Following a Lord who cited love of God and love of neighbor as encompassing all the commandments, we reject a political agenda that displaces that love" (Danforth). We need to stop fighting so much and start sitting down and actually talking and finding out what we can agree on. The best way to start is for everyone to be tolerant. Religion definitely does have a central role in America's founding and in who we are today. America was founded on religious ideals. Today it is overwhelmingly a nation of religious people. To respect the rights of everyone, we should respect people of faith.

Works Cited

Adherents.com. "Religious Affiliation of the Founding Fathers of the United States of America." 7 December 2005. 6 February 2008. http://www.adherents.com/gov/Founding_Fathers_Religion.html

Beliefnet. "Founding Faith Archive." 10 April 2008. http://www.beliefnet.com/foundingfaith/default.aspx

Brooks, Arthur. "'Tis the Season: Who's Giving?" Heritage Lecture Number 1010. The Heritage Foundation. 18 December 2006. 15 March 2008. www.heritage.org/research/religion/hl1010.cfm.

City University of New York. *American Religious Identity Survey*. 2001. 13 June 2006. http://www.gc.cuny.edu.

Danforth, John C. "Onward, Moderate Christian Soldiers." *New York Times* 17 June 2005. 16 September 2007. http://www.nytimes.com.

Helco, Hugh. "Is America a Christian Nation?" *Political Science Quarterly* 122.1 (2007): 59–87.

Huntington, Samuel P. "Are We a Nation 'Under God'?" American Enterprise Institute 26 May 2007. 14 January 2008. http://www.taemag.com.

Jacoby, Jeff. "God Wasn't Optional to the Founders." *Boston Globe* 4 July 2002. 11 April 2008. http://www.bostonglobe.com.

Kirkpatrick, David D. "Putting God Back Into American History." *New York Times* 27 February 2005: WK1+.

Rutherford Institute. "Religious Freedom" and "Church Rights." 14 April 2008. http://www.rutherford.org.

Spalding, Matthew. "The Meaning of Religious Liberty." Web Memo No. 1722. The Heritage Foundation. 5 December 2007. 6 March 2008. www.heritage.org/Research/Thought/wm1722.cfm.

Winthrop, John. "A Model of Christian Charity." *The American Tradition in Literature*. Ed. George Perkins and Barbara Perkins. Boston: McGraw-Hill, 2002. 35–43.

Questions about Content

1. The student presents historical evidence to advance her thesis. What is her strongest evidence, and what makes it strong? What is the weakest evidence, and why is it weak?
2. How might someone who agrees with this student find additional evidence that would support the thesis?
3. How might someone who disagrees with this student argue against some of the statements in the essay?

Questions about Rhetorical Analysis

1. To answer the question, "Is America a religious country?" this writer takes a systematic approach. She analyzes the question itself, breaking it down into parts that can be addressed individually and in sequence. How did the student organize her paragraphs? Create a general paragraph-by-paragraph outline of this essay. Indicate not only what each paragraph is about but also what each paragraph is doing, what purpose it serves for the argument.
2. Describe the writer's tone, especially in her introductory paragraphs and in her concluding paragraphs. What strategies does the writer use to establish trust with readers?

Connecting the Readings

1. Compare, contrast, and ultimately assess the effectiveness of these essays. Notice the choices the writers make in evidence, organization, word choice, and tone. Regardless of whether you agree or disagree with the writers, does one of them seem to do a better job of putting forth her argument?
2. Select one of the quotations that appears in these articles. Do a little Internet search to learn about that quotation and its original speaker. Then assess how accurately it is used in the article. For example, the statement "separation of Church and State" was written by Thomas Jefferson. Where did that quotation come from? What was the context for that quotation? Whom did he say it to? Why did he say it? What did he mean by it?

Topic 3: What is Our Responsibility to the Environment?

When we think of religious or values issues, we often think of abortion, euthanasia, gay rights, and similar topics of personal or sexual behavior. New issues are emerging or receiving renewed

attention, such as war, global poverty, and care for the
ment. Religious groups are recognizing that proper care a...
ardship of the environment is a moral necessity; they believe that
the natural world is the creation of God, and they realize that its
condition affects the health and economic opportunities of all
human beings. Following are two statements from religious organizations that take different religious approaches toward the environment. Let's consider these readings together.

Climate Change: An Evangelical Call to Action

EVANGELICAL CLIMATE INITIATIVE

*The Evangelical Climate Initiative (ECI) is a group of evangelical
Christians who are concerned about global warming and consider it to be a moral problem, particularly for wealthy nations,
as they fear that poor nations will be most negatively affected by
climate change. They support government action such as federal
regulation of carbon emissions as well as government encouragement for businesses to find market-based solutions. The organization has received support from nearly one hundred evangelical
ministers as well as foundations such as the Pew Charitable
Trusts, the Hewlett Foundation, and the Rockefeller Brothers
Foundation. To learn more, you can find resources, press
releases, and answers to frequently asked questions on their web
site,* www.christiansandclimate.org.

*The Cornwall Alliance for the Stewardship of Creation is,
according to its web site, "a coalition of clergy, theologians, religious
leaders, scientists, academics, and policy experts committed to
bringing a balanced biblical view of stewardship to the critical
issues of environment and development." The alliance questions evidence of global warming, and as a result, they question proposed
policies. They are concerned that environmental activism by organizations such as the ECI is based on claims that remain to be proven,
and they also disagree with those organizations' interpretation of the
Bible and economic theory. To learn more, you will find resources,
press releases, their newsletter, and a blog on their web site,* www.
cornwallalliance.org.

◆

PREAMBLE

As American evangelical Christian leaders, we recognize both our opportunity and our responsibility to offer a biblically based moral witness that can help shape public policy in the most powerful nation on earth, and therefore contribute to the well-being of the entire world. *Whether* we will enter the public square and offer our witness there is no longer an open question. We are in that square, and we will not withdraw.

We are proud of the evangelical community's long-standing commitment to the sanctity of human life. But we also offer moral witness in many venues and on many issues. Sometimes the issues that we have taken on, such as sex trafficking, genocide in the Sudan, and the AIDS epidemic in Africa, have surprised outside observers. While individuals and organizations can be called to concentrate on certain issues, we are not a single-issue movement. We seek to be true to our calling as Christian leaders, and above all faithful to Jesus Christ our Lord. Our attention, therefore, goes to whatever issues our faith requires us to address.

Over the last several years many of us have engaged in study, reflection, and prayer related to the issue of climate change (often called "global warming"). For most of us, until recently this has not been treated as a pressing issue or major priority. Indeed, many of us have required considerable convincing before becoming persuaded that climate change is a real problem and that it ought to matter to us as Christians. But now we have seen and heard enough to offer the following moral argument related to the matter of human-induced climate change. We commend the four simple but urgent claims offered in this document to all who will listen, beginning with our brothers and sisters in the Christian community, and urge all to take the appropriate actions that follow from them.

CLAIM 1: HUMAN-INDUCED CLIMATE CHANGE IS REAL

Since 1995 there has been general agreement among those in the scientific community most seriously engaged with this issue that climate change is happening and is being caused mainly by human activities, especially the burning of fossil fuels. Evidence gathered since 1995 has only strengthened this conclusion.

Because all religious/moral claims about climate change are relevant only if climate change is real and is mainly human-induced, everything hinges on the scientific data. As evangelicals we have hesitated to speak on this issue until we could be more certain of the science of climate change, but the signatories now believe that the evidence demands action:

- The Intergovernmental Panel on Climate Change (IPCC), the world's most authoritative body of scientists and policy experts on the issue of global warming, has been studying this issue since the late 1980s. (From 1988–2002 the IPCC's assessment of the climate science was Chaired by Sir John Houghton, a devout evangelical Christian.) It has documented the steady rise in global temperatures over the last fifty years, projects that the average global temperature will continue to rise in the coming decades, and attributes "most of the warming" to human activities.
- The U.S. National Academy of Sciences, as well as all other G8 country scientific Academies (Great Britain, France, Germany, Japan, Canada, Italy, and Russia), has concurred with these judgments.
- In a 2004 report, and at the 2005 G8 summit, the Bush Administration has also acknowledged the reality of climate change and the likelihood that human activity is the cause of at least some of it.

In the face of the breadth and depth of this scientific and governmental concern, only a small percentage of which is noted here, we are convinced that evangelicals must engage this issue without any further lingering over the basic reality of the problem or humanity's responsibility to address it.

CLAIM 2: THE CONSEQUENCES OF CLIMATE CHANGE WILL BE SIGNIFICANT, AND WILL HIT THE POOR THE HARDEST

The earth's natural systems are resilient but not infinitely so, and human civilizations are remarkably dependent on ecological stability and well-being. It is easy to forget this until that stability and well-being are threatened.

Even small rises in global temperatures will have such likely impacts as: sea level rise; more frequent heat waves, droughts, and extreme weather events such as torrential rains and floods; increased tropical diseases in now-temperate regions; and hurricanes that are more intense. It could lead to significant reduction in agricultural output, especially in poor countries. Low-lying regions, indeed entire islands, could find themselves under water. (This is not to mention the various negative impacts climate change could have on God's other creatures.)

Each of these impacts increases the likelihood of refugees from flooding or famine, violent conflicts, and international instability, which could lead to more security threats to our nation.

Poor nations and poor individuals have fewer resources available to cope with major challenges and threats. The consequences of global warming will therefore hit the poor the hardest, in part because those areas likely to be significantly affected first are in the poorest regions of the world. *Millions of people could die in this century because of climate change, most of them our poorest global neighbors.*

CLAIM 3: CHRISTIAN MORAL CONVICTIONS DEMAND OUR RESPONSE TO THE CLIMATE CHANGE PROBLEM

While we cannot here review the full range of relevant biblical convictions related to care of the creation, we emphasize the following points:

- Christians must care about climate change because we love God the Creator and Jesus our Lord, through whom and for whom the creation was made. This is God's world, and any damage that we do to God's world is an offense against God Himself (Gen.1; Ps. 24; Col.1:16).
- Christians must care about climate change because we are called to love our neighbors, to do unto others as we would have them do unto us, and to protect, and care for the least of these as though each was Jesus Christ himself (Mt. 22:34–40; Mt. 7:12; Mt. 25:31–46).
- Christians, noting the fact that most of the climate change problem is human induced, are reminded that when God made humanity he commissioned us to exercise stewardship over the earth and its creatures. Climate change is the latest evidence of our failure to exercise proper stewardship, and constitutes a critical opportunity for us to do better (Gen. 1:26–28).

Love of God, love of neighbor, and the demands of stewardship are more than enough reason for evangelical Christians to respond to the climate change problem with moral passion and concrete action.

CLAIM 4: THE NEED TO ACT NOW IS URGENT. GOVERNMENTS, BUSINESSES, CHURCHES, AND INDIVIDUALS ALL HAVE A ROLE TO PLAY IN ADDRESSING CLIMATE CHANGE—STARTING NOW

The basic task for all of the world's inhabitants is to find ways now to begin to reduce the carbon dioxide emissions from the burning of fossil fuels that are the primary cause of human-induced climate change.

There are several reasons for urgency. First, deadly impacts are being experienced now. Second, the oceans only warm slowly, creating a lag in experiencing the consequences. Much of the climate change to which we are already committed will not be realized for several decades. The consequences of the pollution we create now will be visited upon our children and grandchildren. Third, as individuals and as a society we are making long-term decisions today that will determine how much carbon dioxide we will emit in the future, such as whether to purchase energy efficient vehicles and appliances that will last for 10–20 years, or whether to build more coal-burning power plants that last for 50 years rather than investing more in energy efficiency and renewable energy.

In the United States, the most important immediate step that can be taken at the federal level is to pass and implement national legislation requiring sufficient economy-wide reductions in carbon dioxide emissions through cost-effective, market-based mechanisms such as a cap-and-trade program. On June 22, 2005 the Senate passed the Domenici-Bingaman resolution affirming this approach, and a number of major energy companies now acknowledge that this method is best both for the environment and for business.

We commend the Senators who have taken this stand and encourage them to fulfill their pledge. We also applaud the steps taken by such companies as BP, Shell, General Electric, Cinergy, Duke Energy, and DuPont, all of which have moved ahead of the pace of government action through innovative measures implemented within their companies in the U.S. and around the world. In so doing they have offered timely leadership.

Numerous positive actions to prevent and mitigate climate change are being implemented across our society by state and local governments, churches, smaller businesses, and individuals. These commendable efforts focus on such matters as energy efficiency, the use of renewable energy, low CO_2 emitting technologies, and the purchase of hybrid vehicles. These efforts can easily be shown to save money, save energy, reduce global warming pollution as well as air pollution that harm human health, and eventually pay for themselves. There is much more to be done, but these pioneers are already helping to show the way forward.

Finally, while we must reduce our global warming pollution to help mitigate the impacts of climate change, as a society and as individuals we must also help the poor adapt to the significant harm that global warming will cause.

CONCLUSION

We the undersigned pledge to act on the basis of the claims made in this document. We will not only teach the truths communicated here but also seek ways to implement the actions that follow from them. In the name of Jesus Christ our Lord, we urge all who read this declaration to join us in this effort.

The Cornwall Declaration on Environmental Stewardship
CORNWALL ALLIANCE FOR THE STEWARDSHIP OF CREATION

The past millennium brought unprecedented improvements in human health, nutrition, and life expectancy, especially among those most blessed by political and economic liberty and advances in science and technology. At the dawn of a new millennium, the opportunity exists to build on these advances and to extend them to more of the earth's people.

At the same time, many are concerned that liberty, science, and technology are more a threat to the environment than a blessing to humanity and nature. Out of shared reverence for God and His creation and love for our neighbors, we Jews, Catholics, and Protestants, speaking for ourselves and not officially on behalf of our respective communities, joined by others of good will, and committed to justice and compassion, unite in this declaration of our common concerns, beliefs, and aspirations.

OUR CONCERNS

Human understanding and control of natural processes empower people not only to improve the human condition but also to do great harm to each other, to the earth, and to other creatures. As concerns about the environment have grown in recent decades, the moral necessity of ecological stewardship has become increasingly clear.

At the same time, however, certain misconceptions about nature and science, coupled with erroneous theological and anthropological positions, impede the advancement of a sound environmental ethic. In the midst of controversy over such matters, it is critically important to remember that while passion may energize environmental activism, it is reason—including sound theology and sound science—that must guide the decision-making process. We identify three areas of common misunderstanding:

1. Many people mistakenly view humans as principally consumers and polluters rather than producers and stewards. Consequently, they ignore our potential, as bearers of God's image, to add to the earth's abundance. The increasing realization of this potential has enabled people in societies blessed with an advanced economy not only to reduce pollution, while producing more of the goods and pollution. A clean environment is a costly good; consequently, growing affluence, techonological innovation, and the application of human and material captial are integral to environmental improvement. The tendency among some to oppose economic progress in the name of environmental stewardship is often sadly self-defeating.

2. Many people believe that "nature knows best," or that the earth—untouched by human hands—is the ideal. Such romanticism leads some to deify nature or oppose human dominion over creation. Our position, informed by revelation and confirmed by reason and experience, views human stewardship that unlocks the potential in creation for all the earths' inhabitants as good. Humanity alone of all the created order is capable of developing other resources and can thus enrich creation, so it can properly be said that the human person is the most valuable resource on earth. Human life, therefore, must be cherished and allowed to flourish. The alternative—denying the possibility of beneficial human management of the earth—removes all ratinale for environmental stewardship.

3. While some environmental concerns are well founded and serious, others are without foundation or greatly exaggerated. Some well-founded concerns focus on human health problems in the developing world arising from inadequate sanitation, widespread use of primitive biomass fuels like wood and dung, and primitive agricultural, industrial, and commercial practices; distorted resource consumption patterns driven by perverse economic incentives; and improper disposal of nuclear and other hazardous wastes in nations lacking adequate regulatory and legal safeguards. Some unfounded or

undue concerns include fears of destructive man-made global warming, overpopulation, and rampant species loss.

The real and merely alleged problems differ in the following ways:

1. The former are proven and well understood, while the latter tend to be speculative.
2. The former are often localized, while the latter are said to be global and cataclysmic in scope.
3. The former are of concern to people in developing nations especially, while the latter are of concern mainly to environmentalists in wealthy nations.
4. The former are of high and firmly established risk to human life and health, while the latter are of very low and largely hypothetical risk.
5. Solutions proposed to the former are cost effective and maintain proven benefit, while solutions to the latter are unjustifiably costly and of dubious benefit.

Public policies to combat exaggerated risks can dangerously delay or reverse the economic development necessary to improve not only human life but also human stewardship of the environment. The poor, who are most often citizens of developing nations, are often forced to suffer longer in poverty with its attendant high rates of malnutrition, disease, and mortality; as a consequence, they are often the most injured by such misguided, though well-intended, policies.

OUR BELIEFS

Our common Judeo-Christian heritage teaches that the following theological and anthropological principles are the foundation of environmental stewardship:

1. God, the Creator of all things, rules over all and deserves our worship and adoration.
2. The earth, and with it all the cosmos, reveals its Creator's wisdom and is sustained and governed by His power and loving kindness.
3. Men and women were created in the image of God, given a privileged place among creatures, and commanded to exercise stewardship over the earth. Human persons are moral agents for whom freedom is an essential condition of responsible action. Sound environmental stewardship must attend both to the demands of human well being and to a divine call for human beings to exercise caring dominion over the

earth. It affirms that human well being and the integrity of creation are not only compatible but also dynamically interdependent realities.

4. God's Law—summarized in the Decalogue and the two Great Commandments (to love God and neighbor), which are written on the human heart, thus revealing His own righteous character to the human person—represents God's design for shalom, or peace, and is the supreme rule of all conduct, for which personal or social prejudices must not be substituted.

5. By disobeying God's Law, humankind brought on itself moral and physical corruption as well as divine condemnation in the form of a curse on the earth. Since the fall into sin people have often ignored their Creator, harmed their neighbors, and defiled the good creation.

6. God in His mercy has not abandoned sinful people or the created order but has acted throughout history to restore men and women to fellowship with Him and through their stewardship to enhance the beauty and fertility of the earth.

7. Human beings are called to be fruitful, to bring forth good things from the earth, to join with God in making provision for our temporal well being, and to enhance the beauty and fruitfulness of the rest of the earth. Our call to fruitfulness, therefore, is not contrary to but mutually complementary with our call to steward God's gifts. This call implies a serious commitment to fostering the intellectual, moral, and religious habits and pracitces needed for free economies and genuine care for the environment.

OUR ASPIRATIONS

In light of these beliefs and concerns, we declare the following principled aspirations:

1. We aspire to a world in which human beings care wisely and humbly for all creatures, first and foremost for their fellow human beings, recognizing their proper place in the created order.

2. We aspire to a world in which objective moral principles—not personal prejudices—guide moral action.

3. We aspire to a world in which right reason (including sound theology and the careful use of scientific methods) guides the stewardship of human and ecological relationships.

4. We aspire to a world in which liberty as a condition of moral action is preferred over government-initiated management of the environment as a means to common goals.

5. We aspire to a world in which the relationships between stewardship and private property are fully appreciated, allowing people's natural incentive to care for their own property to reduce the need for collective ownership and control of resources and enterprises, and in which collective action, when deemed necessary, takes place at the most local level possible.

6. We aspire to a world in which widespread economic freedom—which is integral to private, market economies—makes sound ecological stewardship available to ever greater numbers.

7. We aspire to a world in which advancements in agriculture, industry, and commerce not only minimize pollution and transform most waste products into efficiently used resources but also improve the material conditions of life for people everywhere.

Connecting the Readings

Questions about Content

1. The position statements reflect contrasting approaches from two religious groups. Describe how their approaches toward the environment along with their interpretations of their religions differ.

2. Can you think of any points where they might be able to find common ground or agreement? What new information or arguments might eventually get them to agree?

Questions about Rhetorical Analysis

1. Compare and contrast how each organization addresses its readers. In what ways do they both strive to show respect for their audience? What strategy does the Evangelical Climate Initiative use in its introductory "preamble"? What strategy does the Cornwall Alliance use in its introductory paragraphs?

2. Both statements list various points using bullets or numbers or both. What is the purpose of providing information in the form of a list?

Topic 4: Is There a "Culture War" over Christmas?

Recently, some figures in the online, radio, and television talk show media have been arguing against what they perceive to be insults to those who celebrate the Christmas holiday. This debate features a different kind of disagreement, as the two sides not only disagree about the role of religious symbols in public life, they disagree over whether there is an actual problem to disagree about. One side perceives a real issue (their belief that Christmas is under attack), while the other side thinks the issue has been manufactured (their belief that no such attack exists). As a result, the following readings are really a debate about a debate. The writers, one liberal and one conservative, are exploring whether a problem exists.

This Season's War Cry: Commercialize Christmas, or Else

Adam Cohen

Adam Cohen is an assistant editor and frequent writer for the New York Times. *A graduate of Harvard Law School, he began his career as a lawyer specializing in education reform, and he later became a senior writer for* Time *magazine. He has become well known for writing articles about the law, the Constitution and Supreme Court, and legal issues regarding technology and the Internet, including a book titled* The Perfect Store: Inside eBay. *His articles for the* New York Times *are available online at* www.nytimes.com. *As you read, notice how Cohen uses history to advance his argument.*

◆

RELIGIOUS CONSERVATIVES HAVE A CAUSE THIS HOLIDAY SEASON: THE COMMERCIALIZATION OF CHRISTMAS. THEY'RE FOR IT.

The American Family Association is leading a boycott of Target for not using the words "Merry Christmas " in its advertising. (Target denies it has an anti-Merry-Christmas policy.) The Catholic League boycotted Wal-Mart in part over the way its web site treated searches for "Christmas." Bill O'Reilly, the Fox anchor who last year started a "Christmas Under Siege" campaign, has a chart on his web site of stores that use the phrase "Happy Holidays," along with a poll that asks, "Will you shop at stores that do not say 'Merry Christmas'?"

This campaign—which is being hyped on Fox and conservative talk radio—is an odd one. Christmas remains ubiquitous, and with its celebrators in control of the White House, Congress, the Supreme Court and every state supreme court and legislature, it hardly lacks for powerful supporters. There is also something perverse, when

Christians are being jailed for discussing the Bible in Saudi Arabia and slaughtered in Sudan, about spending so much energy on stores that sell "holiday trees."

What is less obvious, though, is that Christmas's self-proclaimed defenders are rewriting the holiday's history. They claim that the "traditional" American Christmas is under attack by what John Gibson, another Fox anchor, calls "professional atheists" and "Christian haters." But America has a complicated history with Christmas, going back to the Puritans, who despised it. What the boycotters are doing is not defending America's Christmas traditions, but creating a new version of the holiday that fits a political agenda.

The Puritans considered Christmas un-Christian, and hoped to keep it out of America. They could not find Dec. 25 in the Bible, their sole source of religious guidance, and insisted that the date derived from Saturnalia, the Roman heathens' wintertime celebration. On their first Dec. 25 in the New World, in 1620, the Puritans worked on building projects and ostentatiously ignored the holiday. From 1659 to 1681 Massachusetts went further, making celebrating Christmas "by forbearing of labor, feasting or in any other way" a crime.

The concern that Christmas distracted from religious piety continued even after Puritanism waned. In 1827, an Episcopal bishop lamented that the Devil had stolen Christmas "and converted it into a day of worldly festivity, shooting and swearing." Throughout the 1800's, many religious leaders were still trying to hold the line. As late as 1855, New York newspapers reported that Presbyterian, Baptist and Methodist churches were closed on Dec. 25 because "they do not accept the day as a Holy One." On the eve of the Civil War, Christmas was recognized in just 18 states.

Christmas gained popularity when it was transformed into a domestic celebration, after the publication of Clement Clarke Moore's "Visit from St. Nicholas" and Thomas Nast's Harper's Weekly drawings, which created the image of a white-bearded Santa who gave gifts to children. The new emphasis lessened religious leaders' worries that the holiday would be given over to drinking and swearing, but it introduced another concern: commercialism. By the 1920's, the retail industry had adopted Christmas as its own, sponsoring annual ceremonies to kick off the "Christmas shopping season."

Religious leaders objected strongly. The Christmas that emerged had an inherent tension: merchants tried to make it about buying, while clergymen tried to keep commerce out. A 1931 Times roundup of Christmas sermons reported a common theme: "the suggestion that Christmas could not survive if Christ were thrust into the background by materialism." A 1953 Methodist sermon broadcast on NBC—typical of countless such sermons—lamented that Christmas had become a "profit-seeking period." This ethic found popular expression in "A Charlie Brown Christmas." In the 1965 TV special, Charlie Brown ignores Lucy's advice to "get the biggest aluminum tree you can find" and her assertion that Christmas is "a big commercial racket," and finds a more spiritual way to observe the day.

This year's Christmas "defenders" are not just tolerating commercialization—they're insisting on it. They are also rewriting Christmas history on another key point: non-Christians' objection to having the holiday forced on them.

The campaign's leaders insist this is a new phenomenon—a "liberal plot," in Mr. Gibson's words. But as early as 1906, the Committee on Elementary Schools In New York City urged that Christmas hymns be banned from the classroom, after a boycott by more than 20,000 Jewish students. In 1945, the Rabbinical Assembly of America declared that calling on Jewish children to sing Christmas carols was "an infringement on their rights as Americans."

Other non-Christians have long expressed similar concerns. For decades, companies have replaced "Christmas parties" with "holiday parties," schools have adopted "winter breaks" instead of "Christmas breaks," and TV stations and stores have used phrases like "Happy Holidays" and "Season's Greetings" out of respect for the nation's religious diversity.

The Christmas that Mr. O'Reilly and his allies are promoting—one closely aligned with retailers, with a smack-down attitude toward nonobservers—fits with their campaign to make America more like a theocracy, with Christian displays on public property and Christian prayer in public schools.

It does not, however, appear to be catching on with the public. That may be because most Americans do not recognize this commercialized, mean-spirited Christmas as their own. Of course, it's not even clear the campaign's leaders really believe in it. Just a few days ago, Fox News's online store was promoting its "Holiday Collection" for shoppers. Among the items offered to put under a "holiday tree" was "The O'Reilly Factor Holiday Ornament." After bloggers pointed this out, Fox changed the "holidays" to "Christmases."

Questions about Content

1. Cohen says that "Christmas's self-proclaimed defenders are rewriting the holiday's history" and "America has a complicated history with Christmas." In what way, according to Cohen, are they rewriting the history of the holiday and what makes that history complicated?
2. In what ways is Christmas still a religious holiday? In what ways has it become secular or commercial? Could this change be for the better or for the worse?

Questions about Rhetorical Analysis

1. Cohen begins his article by saying that religious conservatives support the commercialization of Christmas, and later in the article he says they are "not just tolerating commercialization—they're insisting on it." With these statements, Cohen is using a strategy to reach his readers. Describe this strategy and assess its effectiveness.
2. What do you think Cohen's purpose is when he uses the Puritans and other evidence from history to support his claims?

"The Lord of Misrule" is Coming to Town
DAVID FRUM

David Frum, a graduate of Yale University and Harvard Law School, was a speechwriter and assistant to President George W. Bush and is currently a fellow at the American Enterprise Institute (AEI) and a columnist for the National Review. *He is the author of several books about politics, including* Dead Right, *which earned him much acclaim as a voice of the conservative movement. Frum writes opinion pieces for the* New York Times, *the* Wall Street Journal, *Great Britain's* Daily Telegraph, *and Canada's* National Post, *and he appears regularly on Fox News, CNN, and the BBC. More of his articles, as well as information about his books and the AEI, are available on his web site,* www.davidfrum.com. *As you read his article, notice how he uses history similarly, yet quite differently from Adam Cohen.*

◆

THE ONGOING "WAR AGAINST CHRISTMAS" WAS
LAUNCHED CENTURIES AGO—BY CHRISTIANS WHO
DESPISED ITS PAGAN ROOTS

Talk about your "war against Christmas": Until 1869, Boston schoolchildren could be expelled for the offence of skipping school on Christmas Day.

Premature political correctness? Not exactly. The Puritan founders of the Commonwealth of Massachusetts had long disliked and distrusted the Dec. 25 holiday—not because it was too Christian, but because they regarded it as not nearly Christian enough.

The carol, *The 12 Days of Christmas*, reminds us that in medieval times, Christmas in northern Europe extended for almost two weeks of drunken revelry: eating, boozing, gift-giving all presided over by a "Father Christmas"—usually one of the poorest villagers elevated suddenly to a kind of master of ceremonies. Yule logs were burnt, holly and mistletoe hung, evergreen trees decorated.

The founders of Massachusetts recognized all these customs for what they were: survivals of the pagan religions of pre-Christian Europe. "Yule" was the name of the winter solstice holiday of the ancient Germans. Mistletoe and holly were symbols of the immortality of the Norse gods. And "Father Christmas" was the "lord of misrule" who presided over the Roman midwinter holiday, Saturnalia.

Back in Europe, the godly Protestants who won the English Civil War had attempted to suppress these disorderly heathen festivities. In 1647, Parliament forbade Christmas feasts outright and ordered the Lord Mayor of London to compel shops and markets to open on Dec. 25.

The parliamentary ban on Christmas did not succeed, obviously. And yet it left behind an impact: Over the next two centuries, the more devout British Protestants downplayed the Christmas holiday. (Or Christ-tide, as they often named it, to eschew the Catholic word, "mass.")

In New England, however, the Puritan disapproval of Christmas exerted much more lingering influence. Well into the 19th century, Dec. 25 remained just another day on the calendar of the Congregationalist churches of Massachusetts and Connecticut.

In the 1840s and 1850s, the British revived some of their quaint medieval customs in sanitized forms. You can see the revival underway in Charles Dickens' famous story, *A Christmas Carol*, first published in 1843. Notice that when Ebenezer Scrooge wakes up reformed on Christmas morning, it is possible for him to buy a fat goose to give to the Cratchit family: The poultry shops are open. Apparently, the Lord Mayor's ordinances of the 1640s were still having their effect.

Americans took longer to change their minds about Christmas. In the 1840s and 1850s, the United States received a surge of Irish and German immigration. These newcomers, many of them Catholic, often behaved in ways that shocked and threatened their older-stock neighbors—and in reaction, those neighbors clung more firmly than ever to their Puritan beliefs and customs.

But Americans read their Dickens too, and the new Christmas customs were soon being adopted on this side of the Atlantic. The German-American (but staunchly Protestant!) cartoonist Thomas Nast drew his first Santa Claus for *Harper's Weekly* in 1863.

By the 1860s, New York was overtaking Boston as the cultural centre of America. New York had never had much use for Puritanism. Its Dutch founders had brought with them their own version of "Father Christmas." He was no more Christian than his English counterpart, but he had been retrofitted with the name of a fourth-century saint: Nicholas. An Episcopal clergyman in New York, Clement Moore, had invented the apparatus of sleigh, reindeer, red suit, pipe and fat, stomach in his poem, *The Night Before Christmas*.

Combined with another post-Civil War development—the department store—the modern American Christmas was launched.

Along the way, though, history took an ironic bounce. Christmas, once targeted by the most devout Christians, has instead become the special hate object of militant secularists. In reaction, the spiritual descendents of the devout Protestants who once tried to ban Christmas are now rallying to its defence.

And most ironically of all, the most fiercely contested of all Christmas symbols are precisely those about which Christians have historically been most dubious: the trees, boughs and Father Christmas.

These ironic facts point the way to a historic compromise.

We should recognize: There is nothing inherently Christian about the visual ornaments of the Christmas season. Quite the contrary: They are explicitly non-Christian objects that have been imbued with Christian symbolism hundreds and thousands of years afterward. A Christian can look at the Christmas evergreen and see a symbol of the eternal life promised by Jesus to his followers. But a non-Christian remains free to look at that same tree and see . . . just a tree.

Well, maybe not "just" a tree. These are trees that emerge from the ancient culture of northern Europe and the British Isles—a culture inherited by every English-speaking person, regardless of his or her particular creed of ethnicity. It is from that culture that we have derived our free society, our separation of church and state, and our rights to protest and complain.

So maybe those trees deserve a little veneration from everyone, Christian or not. And maybe, for just a few weeks of the year, those rights to protest and complain should go unexercised.

Questions about Content

1. In what ways, according to Frum, was a "war against Christmas" launched centuries ago? Frum says later that the history of this centuries-old war "took an ironic bounce." What does that "ironic bounce" refer to?

2. Describe the compromise Frum suggests at the end of the article. Is that compromise reasonable and fair to both sides of the debate?

Questions about Rhetorical Analysis

1. David Frum, like Adam Cohen, is using history for evidence. What is his purpose? How does it differ from Cohen's purpose?
2. Analyze Frum's approach to his audience. Who does he assume his readers are? What strategies does he employ to reach them?

Connecting the Readings

1. Consider the use of the term "war," which both articles use. Ultimately, how helpful is that word, "war," as a metaphor?
2. Because there is such a long history of disagreement over the meaning of Christmas, could we conclude that there has always been a "war" over Christmas and the current debate is just another part of this holiday's history? Or is the current disagreement different from past disagreements?
3. An *Atlantic Monthly* article by E. J. Dionne, "Why the Culture War Is the Wrong War" (January/February 2006, pages 130–135), suggests that we should rethink the whole idea that there is a culture war. Dionne observes that what we call the "culture war" really takes place in the media among those who earn a living arguing rather than among average Americans, who mostly live together in agreement or peaceful disagreement. If Dionne is correct, then the people who argue about Christmas are mostly bloggers and talk show hosts on radio and television, whereas the average person who gets a "Season's Greetings" card is not offended or did not consider being offended until someone in the media told them they should be. Is this view valid?

Writing Projects

1. Do a research project exploring one of the issues covered in this section or a different issue. Locate, evaluate, and use recent books, web pages, and articles from newspapers, magazines, and journals. Examples of issues might include these:
   - Allowing research using stem cells
   - Extending marriage to gay couples
   - Permitting displays of Christmas trees, crosses, menorahs, or other holiday symbols on public property
   - Recognizing a right to die or a right to physician-assisted suicide for terminally ill patients
   - Finding new solutions to global and national poverty
   - Responding to global threats with preemptive war

   As you research your topic, take an approach other than just deciding on one side or the other. Instead, take one of these approaches:
   - Analyze the rhetoric of the debate. What is the state of the discussion? Is it productive, or are people arguing past each other in ways that will probably

not yield solutions? What assumptions is each side of the debate making about the other? What terminology do writers use that carry loaded meanings? What is the tone of the debate?

- Search for a compromise solution, a "third way" to resolve the debate. Consider whether there might be a new way to conceive the issue that people on all sides of the debate might adopt.

2. David Kirkpatrick has said, "Each side can find ammunition for its perspective in almost any great historical figure or moment." How true is that? Choose one of the founders of the United States, such as Benjamin Franklin or Thomas Jefferson. Do research and find as many of that founder's statements about religion as you can. Then do some analysis. How religious or nonreligious was that founder? How big or how small a role for religion did this founder envision in the government? Does this founder's personal views about religion align with his views about government, or are they connected and complementary? Did this founder make statements that both sides of today's debates could use to advance their theses? The presentation of quotations and analysis could be done as an essay, or it could be a perfect project for a web page or blog.

Religion in Expository Writing

How are new cultural trends changing what we write about religion?

BACKGROUND

Some of the selections in this book tell stories about the past: personal narrative writing and narratives from sacred scriptures. Some are about the present: persuasive writing in the academic disciplines and in the public square. Now we come to expository writing that deals with current trends, situations that will impact the future of religion in our world. Expository writing explores a topic for readers. From the Latin *exponere*, meaning "to set forth," exposition may define and explain a concept, evaluate the validity or usefulness of something, identify causes or effects of a situation, or make predictions. A writer exploring trends in religion may use one, two, three, or all of these modes, including persuasion.

Trends that may affect the future of religion include the increasingly global economy, the rise of new international superpowers, changing immigration patterns, and the increasingly rapid development of new religions. In this chapter, we will focus our attention on three trends:

- The use of popular culture in religion,
- The growth of Islam in the United States, and
- The potential impact of new scientific discoveries on faith.

Popular Culture's Effect on Religion

Popular culture is the world of information and entertainment commercially produced for mass audiences of the general public. Often it incorporates religious themes. The plots of animated television cartoons such as *The Simpsons* and *South Park* include religious allusions or themes as part of their larger social satire. The Internet has numerous informational web sites about world faiths and organizational sites posted by particular religious groups. Devotional sites posted by individuals offer inspirational messages. Other sites posted by individuals or organizations offer arguments against belief.

More relevant to our purpose here, religion and popular culture meet when religious institutions adopt the methods of popular culture. Publishing companies have created new versions of the Bible to appeal to children, teenagers, and college students. One company, for example, has created a text messaging Bible. Another company is now publishing Bibles in the form of magazines for girls and boys. Many churches and religious organizations post pages on the Internet to announce their services, seek new members, request donations, and keep members of their congregation informed. Some churches, known as "mega-churches," offer entertainment, such as movies, live bands, and coffee shops.

These uses of popular culture for religious purposes raise concerns that faith is being trivialized in some way. Some might argue, for example, that a sacred book speaks words of divine mystery and eternal truth, and its messages should be read and studied with dedication and hard work. These messages, they might argue, are cheapened when they are changed for the convenience of readers. But others would argue that religion always changes with the times. New versions and translations of sacred texts have always been necessary to bring their messages to new populations. This is not a cheapening of faith, the argument goes; it is the strengthening of faith, a strength that comes from flexibility in new times and places. The question is where to draw the line. Is there a point of compromise? Is there a point where a religion must change so its core values can endure? Is there a point where a religion could change so much that it would risk losing its essential core values? As you read the following selection, consider: Is popular culture necessary to the survival of religion? If so, is there also a point at which popular culture could dilute the power of faith?

The Multimedia Spiritual Experience
Popular Culture and Faith
JONATHAN S. CULLICK

Jonathan S. Cullick is associate professor of English and director of the Writing Instruction Program at Northern Kentucky University. He teaches writing courses with service learning, philanthropy, and the topics of faith and religion. His literature courses include the Bible as literature and American literature focusing on the influence of religious belief on writers. As you read the following essay, notice how the writer is attempting to explore the issue broadly to understand and represent the concerns of all sides in the debate.

◆

Driving along a nearby interstate highway lined with industrial parks, I passed by a complex with a contemporary business-like building, copious parking space, and an exterior landscaped with fountains. A large marquee sign near the road announced that this building was a church. With bright multi-colored lights fit for competing against nearby billboards, the sign advertised its Sunday service, promising the faithful consumer "a multimedia worship experience." I began to wonder: Is the purpose of worship to have an "experience"? Do live bands with flashing lights, pyrotechnics, a cheering crowd, and wide plasma screens above the stage enhance the experience? Describing her own faith journey, Karen Armstrong concludes that the authentic spiritual experience, the "real test" of faith, is to see if you can find God "when there is just you on your knees" with no "aesthetic response" (130, 42). If her point is valid, then the implications for American religion would be enormous because the ways in which we develop and maintain religious faith are changing as quickly as popular culture itself changes.

Examples of these changes in American Christianity are ubiquitous and visible all around us. *USA Today* recently reported on the growing presence of religion on the Internet. "A survey last year by the Pew Internet and American Life Project found that more people used the Internet to look for religious and spiritual information than to download music, participate in online auctions or visit adult websites" (Barnett). The article further reports that more than one million sermons per month are now accessed on one web site alone, SermonAudio.com. Religious institutions, especially small ones, are using pod casting as a way for them to provide sermons at an inexpensive cost reaching an audience much larger than their church buildings can accommodate. GodTube has become "a Christian alternative to YouTube" reaching two million users per month (Barnett).[1]

Such technology is moving into the church buildings themselves. Some churches have created "high-tech collection plates" or "automatic tithe machines," ATM-type kiosks in which church members can make donations. Marty Baker, the pastor of a church using these machines, says that by doing business the way business is done in the culture at large, "We're just trying to connect with the culture." As one church volunteer, Dorna Adams, says, "We're here where society is at" ("The Lord Giveth, and Now He Takes Visa"). In a more controversial move, "across the country, hundreds of ministers and pastors desperate to reach young congregants have drawn concern and criticism through their use of an unusual recruiting tool: the immersive and violent video game Halo" (Richtel). Some churches are holding Halo nights, and "the question fits into a rich debate about how far churches should go to reach young people" (Richtel).

Not only is technology moving into the church; the church building itself is changing. Enormous churches with thousands of members are opening across the American landscape, developed on a business model. In fact, the work of advising religious entrepreneurs in opening their own churches has itself become a business. Lee McFarland is a minister and businessman who created a megachurch in Arizona by first moving to the area and doing market research to find out what kind of church experience would sell to local residents. As described by Jonathan Mahler in "The Soul of the New Exurb," McFarland created a church that would offer a weekend destination "to lure people away from other potential weekend destinations," a church with coffee shops and live bands and 50-inch plasma televisions and video games in the foyers. McFarland proudly says, "We want the church to look like a mall. We want you to come in here and say, 'Dude, where's the cinema?'" (Mahler).

The changes go even further than the church buildings: scripture itself is changing. New web sites offer the Bible in searchable databases on line. The SMS Bible will send daily Bible verses to the subscriber's cell phone. "In the beginning, God created the heavens and the earth." from Genesis 1:1 is translated "In da Bginnin God cre8d da heavens & da earth." "The Lord is my shepherd" from Psalm 23 is rendered, "U, Lord, r my shepherd." "For

God so loved the world" from John 3:16 is now "4 God so luvd da world" (www.biblesociety.com)[2]

The Thomas Nelson company, a well-established publisher that produces Bibles, is now publishing what we might call "Bible-zines," Bibles in the form of popular magazines for teenagers. The cover of *Refuel* for boys features the picture of a skateboarder, creating the look of a sports magazine, offering features such as "Men of the Sword: Dynamic Stories of Daring Men" and "Class Act: How to Attract Godly Girls" along with "lots of cool extras" and "hot movies, music & reads." Regular sections, such as one titled "Ways to Walk the Walk," give advice about values and advocate respecting girls and settling arguments peacefully rather than through violence. The cover of *Revolve* for girls looks like a teen beauty magazine. It promises "25 tips to make the most of your relationships," "Guys speak their minds," and "35 secrets on developing true beauty." The introduction tells the young reader that the Bible is "full of stories about girls and guys who made it their biggest priority to know God." It includes columns with advice such as "ask God to . . . help you see yourself the way he does. You're a knockout to him" and "a girl who shows the strength of genuine femininity is gorgeous to God, and she's a powerhouse for spreading his love."

Criticisms of the developments outlined above come from inside religion itself. Responding to the use of video games to draw teenagers to church, James Tonkowich, president of the Institute on Religion and Democracy, observes, "If you want to connect with young teenage boys and drag them into church, free alcohol and pornographic movies would do it . . . My own take is you can do better than that" (Richtel). Commenting on new Bibles, Martin Marty, professor emeritus of the University of Chicago Divinity School, says, "Marketing the Bible to youth culture isn't new" but it does present the danger of not approaching the Bible seriously (Haskell). Jeff Johnson, a director of children's ministeries, is more directly critical: "The Bible is a theological tool, not a barometer for our social needs" (Haskell). One reader of Mahler's article about megachurches was drawn to the idea of the church becoming like a shopping mall. "But why are we drawn to malls?" she asks in a letter she wrote to the editor, "I suspect it's because malls allow adults to act like children. We have all our needs and desires met in one convenient and entertaining place. Our only commitment is to show up and happily consume what is provided for us. For me, being a Christian is based on a mature commitment to God."[3]

That "mature commitment to God" is at the heart of assessing the influence of popular culture on religious faith. Does an iPod or a megachurch or a tithing kiosk foster faith or distract from it? Plenty of precedents exist to suggest that technology might be conducive to religion because changes in society and technology have always brought about changes in religious delivery systems. The switch to ATM kiosks is similar to the switch from cash to checks, which many congregation members use to give money. The move toward podcasts has its precedent in the move toward radio and television, which have made religious services more accessible, especially to those who are physically unable to attend a neighborhood church. As David Roozen, director of the Hartford Institute for Religion Research, notes, those technologies did not keep people away from church services, so most likely neither will the technology of pod casting (Barnett).

Some fear that Internet-based technologies might cause a sense of passivity and loss of community as religion, like entertainment in general, becomes self-directed and self-centered with individual users accessing the content they want from the comfort of their home computers. But this is no different from traditional churches, which have many members who stay at home on Sundays and many others who sit passively in the pews week after week. The argument could also be made that online users are showing active engagement in their faith by spending time and effort to locate material; they are also forming communities online in faith-based discussion boards, blogs, and chat rooms.

Even megachurches have precedent in an earlier kind of church that went out west and set up large tents for carnival-like revivals in rural areas. "The new breed of megachurches," Mahler points out, "has more in common with the frontier churches of the late 19th and early 20th centuries." And even the use of video games and the criticism it evokes have their precedents in the use of Bingo or casino nights, both of which employ gambling to raise money for churches.

John Leland, who has investigated "alt-evangelicalism," the use of alternative music and styles to attract younger converts, suggests that the use of alternative music is actually a move toward the traditional because it presents the traditional image of "the Christian as rebel or outsider, misunderstood, struggling against a world of conformity, commercialism, and manufactured pleasures." Tim Lucas, pastor of a new ministry called Liquid says, "[Young people] identify with being an underground movement, which is what Christianity was in the beginning." As a result, Leland says, "the changes are often more stylistic than doctrinal." Perhaps what we are seeing is that everything new is old again.

Past development of religion shows that change in the formation and delivery of faith is part of the evolution of religion. In his history of the image of Jesus, Stephen Prothero writes that the First Amendment, ratified in 1791, essentially created a marketplace of religion, a "market model that continues to characterize American religion. This new spiritual marketplace produced unprecedented religious creativity and intense religious competition" (45–46). According to Prothero, our thriving "spiritual marketplace" of today derives from the values upon which we were founded: "Inspired by republican rhetoric of liberty and equality, and by a popular revolt against deference and hierarchy, they [early Americans] rejected as well the authority of ministers, the veracity of creeds, and the importance of theology. The Bible remained authoritative, of course, but now Americans insisted on interpreting it for themselves" (47). Religion in America exists in a market-driven society in which preachers must "compete for souls not only with other preachers but also with the secular pleasures" and it is for this reason that preaching itself "entered the world of entertainment" (51).

We could extend Prothero's argument to say that the current technological and commercial revision of religion is our primary means of reinterpretation and reinvigoration of faith. This is no different from the use of television, radio, popular music or advertising going back to the 19th century. Early in America's history, the faith of the Puritans in the 17th century was Calvinist, based upon the doctrine that all human souls were predestined either to be saved or not, and the doctrine that God participated directly in human history, rewarding the faithful and punishing the wicked. Every natural disaster—earthquakes, fires—was interpreted as a sign from God telling the community that some of their members were weak in their faith and lax in their duties. That image of God in America has evolved through the 19th and 20th centuries into an image of Jesus as personal savior and comforter. The hymn, "What a Friend We Have in Jesus," came from the 19th century; it could not have been written in the 17th. With the evolution of faith, the modern commercialization of faith that we encounter today is nothing new.

Religious institutions have always used popular culture to reach their target populations. Ever since the Bible came into existence, it has been translated into new editions to make it more accessible to a wider demographic, and those new editions have often been met with criticism. When the Bible was translated into English from Greek and Latin, traditionalists saw this as an affront to God's word, yet those early translations, such as the King James Version, are revered by hundreds of millions of believers. Similarly, new versions of religious scriptures could be seen as opportunities to reach young people in ways they can identify with. Houses of worship, the counter-argument continues, have always been built to serve the needs of people by offering the stability and comfort of a community in times of celebration as well as times of need.

Religious institutions have always used the available technologies of their day. Preachers in the twentieth century began offering services by television and radio. Before those forms of communication were invented, itinerant preachers of the 18th and 19th centuries would travel the American frontier to bring tent revivals to populations in outlying, rural regions. One might even speculate that prophets from Moses to Muhammad would have used the Internet to get their messages out if it had existed in their day.

The only constant of faith is that faith is going to continue to change. Toby Lester has surveyed the religious landscape and found many new religions developing, too many to count. He predicts that "the new century will probably see religion explode in both intensity and variety. New religions are springing up everywhere. Old ones are mutating with Darwinian restlessness" (Lester 37). Precedent supports his thesis: "There's no reason to think that the religious movements of today are any less subject to change than were the religious movements of hundreds or even thousands of years ago" (37). Granted, the modern world has witnessed a trend toward secularization, "but religion seems to keep adapting to new social ecosystems in a process one might refer to as 'supernatural selection.' It shows no sign of extinction" (39).

Still, any kind of change, even change that we know has plenty of precedents in earlier changes, can be challenging on a visceral, emotional level. Alan Wolfe, professor of political science at Boston College, in his book, *The Transformation of American Religion: How We Actually Live Our Faith*, states, "American faith has met American culture—and American culture has triumphed" (Mahler). That is frightening for many believers who find in their faith a resource of support for confronting the challenges of a materialistic world that sometimes causes suffering, dismisses the suffering of others, demeans the search for purpose and meaning, and disrespects sexuality. The place of worship offers a refuge of reflection away from television and iPods and the shopping mall and the Internet. Putting worship into those elements of popular culture seems to plunge the believer right back into the very thing he or she needs to take a sabbatical from. When a place of worship shapes itself to compete against other cultural attractions, it runs the risk of losing the uniqueness of its message and becoming part of the noise of popular culture. The church or synagogue or temple on mosque can choose to do business the way the culture does, but can't people of faith at some point ask the culture to change and conduct its business in ways more reflective of faith and values? Must people of faith always change to conform to society? What about demanding that society change?

The problem is that change does not result from those kinds of simple demands; it results from the daily demands of millions of "consumers" and the corresponding independent decisions of millions of "producers." The supply and demand trend is toward more technology, more popular culture. Change is inevitable. This means that the greater concern is not how good or bad change is, but how we are going to react to it and what we are going to do with it.

So how should we react and what should we do? The answer may lie not in embracing popular culture or in rejecting it, but in using it in an intentional manner. The culture that we live in is like the air we breathe, so resisting it would result in a life of conflict. Besides, why resist it? If a podcast can give us access to an informative or inspiring message, why deny ourselves? We can use it, and as we do, we can be aware of how we are using it and what effect it is having upon us. Popular culture is a tool; it can foster faith or it can detract from it. The power lies with the user.

Faith always exists within culture, but it must also offer some quiet time and space apart from the world as well as in the world. It must provide room to reflect and explore, to search for purpose and meaning, to ask the most enduring questions and debate the most pressing questions of life. The Buddha left his home and went to the Bodhi tree to seek enlightenment. Moses went to the top of the mountain to encounter God and receive the law. Jesus went to the wilderness to pray and realize his mission. Mohammad journeyed out to the desert to hear the angel's call for him to recite. Moments of removal from the world are crucial to one's ability to rejoin the world with the will to persevere.

I know many people of faith who do not spend much time listening to podcast sermons or reading Bible-zines or attending shopping mall churches. These are people who use and enjoy popular culture as much as anyone else, but their faith takes them somewhere else. I know Buddhists who do the hard work of meditation and the quiet work of daily mindfulness and compassion. I know Jews who are committed to lives of study, self-examination, ethical action, and service. I know Christians who devote themselves daily to acts of charity, even using their annual vacation days to contribute their carpentry or nursing skills to individuals and communities in need. And yes, I know agnostics and atheists and humanists who marvel at the awesomeness of nature and engage in continual self-awareness and self-correction.

These are all individuals choosing to be thoughtful, serious, and wakeful, opening themselves like poet Walt Whitman to the discovery that the whole universe resides within one blade of grass and every single human being. They take time to look for that universe. They choose enduring periods of inspiration over ephemeral moments of stimulation. Somehow it seems to me that those people are finding the authentic spiritual experience.

Endnotes

1. My focus is on Christianity in America because it presents us with the most visible examples in daily life. However, it would certainly be worthwhile to study the effects of popular culture on other religions, especially in other countries. New kinds of scriptures and places of worship are appearing in other religions and countries. To mention just one example, a new generation of Muslims in America and around the world is making changes to Islam. New hotels and shopping centers are being constructed well in view of the Grand Mosque in the city of Mecca in Saudi Arabia, Islam's holiest site. An amusement park, fast food shops, and even a lingerie shop are now in the neighborhood (Fattah). Muslim scholar Reza Aslan suggests that what is really happening in Islam right now is a kind of reformation with revolutionary effects similar to the invention of the printing press. Islam is becoming decentralized with new translations of the Qur'an and Muslim televangelists and web sites. "Fifty years ago, if a Muslim in say, Malaysia, wanted a legal ruling on a disputed topic, he had access only to the religious opinion of his neighborhood cleric" Aslan reports. "Now, that Muslim can troll the vast databases of fatwa-online.com or Islamonline.net, both of which provide ready-made fatwas on every question imaginable. . . . And because no centralized religious authority exists in Islam to determine whose opinion is sound and whose is not, Muslims can simply follow whichever fatwa they like best. Welcome to the Islamic Reformation" (Aslan).
2. The sacred texts of other religions, such as the Qur'an of Islam and Bhagavad Gita of Hinduism, are also becoming available on line in searchable databases. Reza Aslan points out that the Qur'an has been translated into more languages in the past century alone than in all other centuries in the entire history of Islam combined.
3. Similarly, criticisms of popular culture in Islam are coming from Muslims. Reza Aslan points out that much of the violence by Muslim extremists today is being conducted by a very small minority of fundamentalists who are directing their anger toward those Muslims who are becoming moderate or progressive. It is the most fundamentalist of the fundamentalists reacting against the modernization of Islam.

Works Cited

Armstrong, Karen. *The Spiral Staircase*. New York: Knopf, 2005.

Aslan, Reza. "The War for Islam." *Boston Globe* 10 September 2006. 2 December 2007. http://www.rezaaslan.com.

Barnett, Ron. "Religious Teaching Straight to Your iPod: Downloadable Sermons Spread the Spiritual Word." *USA Today* 9 April 2008: 7D.

"Bible cre8td for a nu wrl: testaments by SMS." *Sydney Morning Herald* 6 October 2005: 30 November 2006. http://www.smh.com.au.

Fattah, Hassan M. "The Price of Progress: Transforming Islam's Holiest Site." *New York Times* 8 March 2007: A4.

Haskell, Kari. "Revelation Plus Makeup Advice." *New York Times* 16 May 2004: Section 4, p. 14.

Leland, John. "Christian Cool and the New Generation Gap." *New York Times* 16 May 2004: Section 4, pages 1, 14.

Lester, Toby. "Oh, Gods!" *The Atlantic Monthly* February 2002: 37–45.

"Lord Giveth, and Now He Takes Visa." *New York Times* 10 December 2006: 31.

Mahler, Jonathan. "The Soul of the New Exurb." *New York Times* 27 March 2005. 4 June 2007. http://www.nytimes.com.

Prothero, Stephen. *American Jesus: How the Son of God Became a National Icon*. New York: Farrar, Straus, and Giroux: 2004.

Refuel 2: The Complete New Testament. Nashville, Tennessee: Thomas Nelson, Inc., 2006.

Revolve 2007: The Complete New Testament. Nashville, Tennessee: Thomas Nelson, Inc., 2006.

Richtel, Matt. "Thou Shalt Not Kill, Except in a Popular Video Game at Church." *New York Times* 7 October 2007. 8 October 2007. http://www.nytimes.com.

Questions about Content

1. In the first paragraph, the writer uses the terms "faithful consumer" and "aesthetic response." How are the definitions of these terms related?
2. The essay weighs the pros and cons of popular culture in religion. What is the core argument against it? What is the central argument for it? What resolution does the essay finally endorse?

Questions about Rhetorical Analysis

1. Notice that the essay begins and concludes with personal reflections. Is this strategy effective or does it distract from the argument?
2. This essay is organized by moving from one type of example to another and then evaluating the impact of those examples. Create a paragraph-by-paragraph outline of this essay. Indicate not only what each paragraph is about but also, and more important, indicate what each paragraph is *doing*, what purpose it serves for the argument.

The Growth of Islam in the United States

Islam is one of the largest and fastest growing religions in the world today, but unfortunately, Americans have become more aware of it only through their recent encounters with its most extreme forms. Consequently, Islam is one of the least understood religions. This has led to some conflicts, for instance:

- The University of Michigan at Dearborn in 2007 installed footbaths in campus restrooms because Muslim students were washing their feet in the sinks. Because this kind of washing is a religious ritual for Muslims, some organizations on and off campus protested that the school was providing a special, unfair, and unconstitutional accommodation for religious purposes. The university countered that the footbaths were built primarily for safety after one person was injured in a fall and the janitorial staff alerted the administration that pools of water were dangerously collecting on the floors.

- In 2006, when a district in Minnesota elected Keith Ellison to the U.S. House of Representatives, he became the first Muslim ever elected to Congress. As Ellison planned to take his oath of office on the Qur'an rather than the Bible, outrage among a handful of political pundits and talk show hosts ensued. In a symbolic move intended to make a point about open-mindedness, Ellison took his oath upon a copy of the Qur'an he borrowed from the Library of Congress—the same copy that had been owned and read by Thomas Jefferson.

- Many residents of the city of Hamtramck, Michigan in 2004 protested when a local mosque applied for a permit to use amplifiers to make their call to prayer louder. City council members pointed out that this would be no different from churches ringing bells before their services to call their members to prayer, but as one resident complained, "It's against my constitutional rights to have to listen to another religion evangelize in my ear."

- Similar debates about mosques have played out in other towns and cities, sometimes in acrimonious ways. In the Texas town of Katy in 2006, a local landowner who lived next to a growing mosque built pig pens and a track for pig racing on his side of the fence separating his property from the mosque's property. Muslims consider pigs to be impure or "unclean," and though this move was offensive to the mosque, the landowner claimed that he had no malicious intent.

- In Minneapolis, some Muslim taxi drivers, citing their religious practices, complained about having to pick up airport passengers who were carrying alcohol. Because the drivers operate with publicly issued licenses giving them access to the airport's business, some argued that they must be required to serve all customers.

Why are these kinds of conflicts occurring? Most Americans did not think much about Islam until the terrorist attacks on September 11, 2001. Fear of another attack combined with a lack of knowledge and inflammatory rhetoric from the Internet and the radio-television talk show media has resulted in much Western misunderstanding. Radical terrorist organizations such as Al Qaeda are transnational and well known, but in actuality, they account for an extremely small number of Muslims. The vast majority of Muslims do not support terrorism. As scholar and writer Reza Aslan has pointed out, moderate and progressive Muslims in Middle Eastern countries have been the targeted victims of terrorist attacks much more than Westerners. In fact, after 9/11, many Muslim leaders and organizations around the world sharply criticized the actions of Al Qaeda and other terrorist groups, saying that such violence is anathema to Islam.

The following selections are examples of Muslim writers attempting to educate and put the fears of American readers to rest. As you read the following selections, consider: What is the future of the relationships between Islam and both Judaism and Christianity?

How Does It Feel?

MICHAEL WOLFE

Michael Wolfe has written The Hadj, *a book about his pilgrimage to Mecca, and* One Thousand Roads to Mecca, *an anthology of writings by other travelers who have made the pilgrimage over several centuries. Wolfe is also a filmmaker who hosted a documentary about the pilgrimage to Mecca on the ABC television show,* Nightline, *and has produced a PBS documentary film titled* Muhammad: Legacy of a Prophet *with Unity Productions Foundation. Wolfe is the editor of* Taking Back Islam: American Muslims Reclaim Their Faith, *a collection of writings about Islam in post-9/11 America as well as personal writings by Muslims. You can read more about his films at the Unity Productions Foundation site at www.upf.tv and more of his*

*articles on Beliefnet at www.beliefnet.com. As you read his article,
notice how he tries to establish common ground with a non-Muslim
audience of readers.*

———————————— ◆ ————————————

WHEN YOU BECOME A MUSLIM HERE, UNLESS YOU KEEP IT SECRET, THE PERKS HAVE A WAY OF DISAPPEARING RIGHT BEFORE YOUR EYES.

With Bob Dylan's 60th birthday in the news lately, I've found myself humming one of his Golden Oldies: "How does it feel/To be on your own/With no direction home/Like a Rolling Stone." These days, in addition to all its other applications, this song speaks personally to me about being a Muslim in America. How *does* it feel?

Dylan's question is rhetorical. You have to hear his freight-train nasal whine to get the meaning: He's not asking how you feel, as if he were curious. He's telling you that as a social creature, you might not always fit in as you'd hoped to, that it could just be, despite the TV jingles, that you don't "feel so fine" all of the time, that being "alone and on your own" without your usual comforts, your social expectations and constitutionally conferred rights, you may not feel as good as you'd hoped or wanted.

In the matter of constitutional rights, many Muslims these days have a split view of this country. On the one hand, most American Muslims know that simply by living here they have more freedoms guaranteed on paper than if they resided almost anywhere else on earth. On the other hand, they often feel they are strangers. And they are, all too often, treated as outright alliens at the most unexpected moments.

This sense of alienation has mixed causes in the United States, where race more often than faith triggers most mainstream discomfort. Half of America's Muslims were born here, but their race and ethnicity is rarely "European." The other half hail from dozens of nations around the globe. Muslims may think they are being criticized or rejected because of their faith, when the issue is often more plainly racial. Nonwhite Muslims, and Muslims of varying language or dress who don't immediately blend in, may THINK they are being singled out for their beliefs, when it is actually their appearance that is the sticking point.

America is the biggest island in the world, and its incessant and innumerable television cameras are almost entirely turned inward. Ours may be a "global" economy, but as a geographical entity, the United States still has a single dominant language, and despite great changes lately in the demographics of its urban population, a majority of Americans are white and of Christian background.

Perhaps Muslims in America tend to hang together because the surface pleasures of mainstream U.S. democracy have an unpleasant way of becoming a very icy bath at moments when you'd least expect it. This can cut across all race and gender lines. I, for example, am a white, college-educated fifty-something male. Now, in America a lot of perks and benefits go with that description. Yet when you become a Muslim here, unless you keep it secret, the perks and benefits have a way of disappearing right before your eyes.

Eyes were, in fact, the first testing ground of my new experience as a Muslim in the States. It was in the weeks when I was first preparing to go on the pilgrimage to Mecca, in 1990. A friend, hearing of my travel plans, suggested I should wear brown contact lenses to keep out of trouble with the Arabs. When I mentioned feeling safer in Morocco than Manhattan, my friend replied that perhaps I should move to Morocco. A week before I left for Mecca, I bought the brightest blue lenses I could find and wore them to his house to say good-bye. Later on in Mecca, I wore the lenses often, without comment.

Most Americans are wrong about the Arabs, just as they are wrong about Islam. The only Arabs they seem to know are the mug shots of brainwashed hit men employed by shabby tyrants. As for Islam, Americans still don't seem to know much about it. It rarely dawns on them that Islam is a religion, for example, rather than a set of political responses. They believe what they see on TV, and go from there—a very dangerous practice if you care about your mind. Despite the fact that the "news" specializes in tragedy and discord, most American viewers extrapolate from what they see, building on a sublimated base of fear whenever they're faced with racial or religious difference.

As every American worker knows, not a day goes by in the U.S. marketplace without employers' decisions and workplace attitudes being unpleasantly affected by issues of gender, race, and faith. Muslims, the new kids on the block here and probably the most sorely misunderstood, come in for more than a fair share of hard knocks in this regard. Every month like clockwork, a host of Muslim workers file complaints and often go to court to protect their rights to work and practice their religion.

Islam asks Muslims to pray five times a day; employers often try to oppose this stricture and frequently wind up in arbitration or in court. Last month, for example, Value City Department stores, in Columbus, Ohio, finally agreed to offer breaks and set aside a quiet room for Muslim employees to pray in. At about the same time, United Airlines announced changes in its uniform guidelines to permit Muslim women employees to cover their hair when they choose to. Meanwhile, in Washington, D.C., six Muslim firefighters filed a federal suit alleging that fire chief Ronnie Few interfered with their rights to wear beards, a practice many Muslims adopt in their effort to emulate the Prophet Muhammad. The lawsuit is being brought with help from the American Civil Liberties Union.

Disagreements like these reflect the usual, embattled give-and-take between established mainstream American social practices and fresh requirements introduced by newly emerging ethnic and religious populations that seek fair representation in exchange for the sweat of their brow. This process is business as usual in a democratic, multicultural society. One can only hope, in the case of Muslims, that the courts will continue to interpret the laws in their favor, maintaining the integrity of the U.S. Constitution, from which the laws spring.

Muslims are now experiencing what the Italian community, for instance, knows all too well: that stereotyping is a part of the American experience; that the violent acts of .1% of a group can and will be used against the other 99.9% of the community. One hopes that, in time, we will see Muslims emerge from the shadow of their own worst examples, as the Italian American community emerged from the shadow of, say, the Cosa Nostra to give us mayors and governors and senators and judges and, more important, a free run at the social and economic opportunities supposedly enjoyed here by us all.

Meanwhile, if you're a non-Muslim, take my advice: Get to know some Muslims. They're your neighbors, fellow workers, and fellow students. By and large, they're a worthwhile lot. You may well enjoy the experience. You might even learn something.

Questions about Content

1. Wolfe says, "In the matter of constitutional rights, many Muslims these days have a split view of this country." Describe the "split view" that he refers to.
2. "America is the biggest island in the world." How is the writer using the word "island" here?
3. According to Wolfe, is the challenge of being Muslim in America today more a matter of race or religion? Explain.

Questions about Rhetorical Analysis

1. Is the main audience for this article Muslims, non-Muslims, or both, and how do you know?
2. Describe Wolfe's tone throughout the article; how does he appeal to his non-Muslim readers in the introductory paragraph and in the concluding two paragraphs?

Discovering (not Uncovering) the Spirituality of Muslim Women

INGRID MATTSON

Ingrid Mattson is the president of the Islamic Society of North America, professor of Islamic Studies, the director of Islamic Chaplaincy, and the associate editor of The Muslim World *at the Macdonald Center for Islamic Studies and Christian-Muslim Relations at Hartford Seminary. With a Ph.D. in Islamic Studies from the University of Chicago, she teaches courses such as Introduction to Islamic Law, Contemporary Islamic Ethics, Islamic Ritual and Family Law, The Life of the Prophet Muhammad, Early Islamic History, Readings in Arabic Texts, Readings in Islamic Theology, and The Spirituality of Muslim Women. She is the author of* The Story of the Qur'an: Its History and Place in Muslim Life. *Many of her writings are posted at* http://macdonald.hartsem.edu/ mattson.htm. *As you read her essay, notice how she blends personal observations with more objective historical and cultural information to teach her non-Muslim readers about the clothes that many Muslim women wear.*

◆

It was almost midnight when I parked my car in front of the low plain building. Clearly there were no meaningful zoning regulations in this neighborhood where an Islamic elementary school backed onto the yard of an auto body shop. The Muslims were not complaining—after all, it was a regulatory vacuum in this unincorporated village just outside of Chicago that allowed them to build in the first place. Muslims in other, more organized suburbs had felt the power of zoning when their applications to build mosques and schools had been rejected. So I wasn't surprised to see a building like this—previously used as a warehouse or for small manufacturing—stretching out beside a residential home. I was a little surprised that this is where the women would be spending the night in prayer. I got out of the car, walked through the dreary foyer and into a large room where a dozen women stood praying on a sheet spread on the concrete floor.

The imam ("leader") had a lovely voice. She stood in the middle of the line of women and recited Qur'an from memory. They listened quietly, said "amen" when she finished a passage and followed as she led them in the bowing and prostrating of prayer. Perhas she was a *bafiz*—one who has memorized the complete scripture. In any case, it was evident that she had memorized at least a significant portion of the Qur'an, and was proficient in the art of recitation.

The women were friends from the neighborhood. All of them had been born in the Middle East or North Africa and had moved to the United States as young adults. Most of the women were in middle age; some taught at the religious school; most were home-makers. They were the kind of women who took pride in their cook-ing, in helping neighbors, and in maintaining a simple, but welcom-ing home. Whenever I visit my friend, who had invited me to the gathering when she heard I was in town, she always looks lovely and is ready to serve me homemade soup or bread fresh from the oven.

I joined their prayer that night, then sat with them for a while. They said they wanted to talk to me about being a Muslim in America. I thought this was a rather odd topic, given the length of time most of these women had been in the country. But they told me they had a hard time talking with people outside their community. They had realized, especially in the last few years, that so many Americans have a very negative image of Muslims. They wanted to make themselves better known. They were not interested in giving speeches or going to organized events—they just wanted to have friendlier encounters with the non-Muslim Americans they met in their daily lives. In their experience, this was difficult, and they were convinced that their dress was the main barrier.

When these Muslim women, who wear figure-flattering dresses at home leave the house, they wear a headscarf and a long, loose coat known in Arabic as *jilbab*. This practice of *hijab*—covering one's body in public—is practiced across the Muslim world. It's origin lies in the Qur'an and in the guidance given by the Prophet Muhammad to his community. Hijab is one aspect of a comprehensive system of behavior practiced by Muslim men and women to support chastity and propriety. Some people interpret the practice of hijab as a way to "control women's sexuality," but this is a misunderstanding—or perhaps, an incomplete understanding. Islam requires both men and women to control their sexuality so that intimate relations occur only within marriage. But Islam does not encourage prudity nor does it demean sexuality. Sex is a vital part of marriage—it is an end in itself, not just a means to reproduction. To encourage inti-macy in the home, these women change into comfortable but attrac-tive clothes as soon as they return home. To guard this special inti-mate relationship, *hijab* is worn upon leaving the house.

In America, we have been taught, "Don't judge a book by its cover," but as Derrida taught us, the book has no meaning except what we bring to it. So how do non-Muslim Americans "read" a

Muslim woman covered in hijab? What meaning do we impart to the "veiled woman"? I fear that it is difficult for many Americans to free themselves of the long sad history of orientalist voyeurism associated with hijab. How many books and articles about Islam use these metaphors: "unveiling Islam," "beyond the veil," "behind the veil"? In the veil we see deceit, secrets, double lives but also mystery and exoticism. This spring, *US News and World Report* played on this creepy fascination with a special issue on Islam. Entitled, "Secrets of Islam," the cover featured a close-up of a woman (or is it a man?) with her face and hair clothed in a black veil. The ambiguous gender of the model adds another level of discomfort. Perhaps this is a male terrorist dressing as a woman, or perhaps there is a more sinister aspect to the veiled Muslim woman than we realized.

Unfortunately, the politicization of dress in the modern Muslim world also affects our understanding of hijab. In Saudi Arabia, Iran and Afghanistan under the Taliban, women were forced to adopt a particular form of dress. Americans are given little context to understand these events. We may not be aware that these governments have also forced men to adopt certain forms of dress, nor are we aware that in most Muslim majority countries, men and women are free to dress as they like. Many women in these countries choose to observe some form of hijab because they believe it to be appropriate public dress. Most Americans are probably also not aware that in certain Muslim majority countries that espouse an extremist form of secularism, women are forbidden from wearing hijab in schools, colleges and government institutions. At Hartford Seminary, we have are a number of young Turkish women who left their country because they could not continue their studies while wearing a headscarf.

All these associations came to mind, as I sat with the women that night in the industrial park outside of Chicago. I acknowledged their observation that hijab did present an initial obstacle to connecting for many Americans. Perhaps the most compassionate advise would be to tell the women to change their dress. But why should they have to strip themselves of something so important to them? After all, these were not just pieces of cloth, but one aspect of a way of interacting in the world that was essential to their sense of self, family and community. So I counseled the woman about ways to engage in small talk and how to use body language to allow others to relax around them. Certainly there would always be some negative reactions, but with patience, confidence and kindness, they should be able to connect to others.

I left the building just past midnight. It was a cold April night and the women would continue their devotions for some time. They met every month, spending the day in fasting and the night in prayer.

I knew that their prayers were only for the sake of God. They did not care if anyone else knew about the rich spiritual lives they experienced behind the doors of this nondescript building. But I cared.

We hear so much about the oppression of Muslim women. Certainly Islam can be used as a source of repression. But this is true of any religion and any value system. The dominant normative discourse of any society will always be engaged to justify divergent actions and policies. In secular societies, nationalism and patriotism can as easily be used to justify oppression as Islam can be used for this purpose in Muslim societies. But this is not the essence of Islam, nor is oppression the normal experience of Muslim women. Islam is a deep source of spirituality and dignity for many Muslim women. Every place I have travelled in the Muslim world, I find women who have organized themselves to express their sisterhood and develop their own models of religious leadership. Through prayer, fasting, and other rituals of Islam, these women experience the deep joy of connecting with their merciful Creator. We do not need to rip the covers off books to understand what is inside. We can only hope to understand something about a book if we have the humility to realize that it can teach us something new—perhaps even about ourselves.

Questions about Content

1. What is hijab, and what, according to Mattson, is the misunderstanding about it?
2. Mattson refers to "orientalist voyeurism." What does that term mean? (If necessary, look up those words in a collegiate dictionary.) More specifically, how does that term apply to Americans looking at a Muslim woman wearing hijab?

Questions about Rhetorical Analysis

1. Who is Mattson's intended audience and what does she hope those readers will do or think differently after reading her essay?
2. Notice how much of the essay is a personal narrative, and consider how this serves the essay's purpose. Why does she tell her reader about her own experience that evening?

Connecting the Readings

1. These writers voice similar concerns, but in what ways do their perspectives differ? Do Wolfe's and Mattson's experiences differ because of their genders?
2. Each writer's concluding sentences ask or challenge readers to change their thinking, but those ending sentences are quite different in tone. Describe those differences in the conclusions.

New Discoveries in the Science of Faith

Does science challenge faith? Could science eventually make belief in God obsolete? New discoveries are making questions about faith more relevant and more provocative than ever. If neuroscientists and psychologists discover a mechanism in the human brain that makes faith possible, will that discovery affect faith? If geneticists eventually isolate a single gene that makes faith possible, will that discovery have any effect on faith? If physicists discover a unifying theory to describe and predict the behavior of all matter and energy in the universe, will the discovery have an effect on faith? If astronomers discover intelligent life on a distant planet, will the discovery affect belief?

Will any of these discoveries undermine human belief in God? Or will these discoveries enhance belief? Will scientific knowledge supplant faith in God? Or will it deepen appreciation for the world God created?

Tension exists between scientific knowledge and religious belief. Throughout history, religious people and institutions have feared that science usurps God's role by pushing God to the margins. This idea is referred to as the "god of the gaps" concept, a belief in God that develops in the gaps of human knowledge; when science cannot yet explain some phenomenon, humanity may attribute that phenomenon to God. The problem with holding this kind of belief is that as human knowledge expands, the room for faith in God will contract.

For example, Puritans believed that lightning and other natural phenomena were expressions of God's power and anger. William Bradford, a pilgrim who came to the "New World" on the Mayflower and became the governor of the Plymouth colony, interpreted an earthquake as God's displeasure with those Puritans who were not strong in their faith. Jonathan Edwards, a famous eighteenth century minister, was inspired to believe in God while experiencing the lightning and thunder of a storm. Benjamin Franklin investigated lightning and discovered that it was the same phenomenon as the electricity that he could produce in his laboratory. Realizing that the effects of lightning could be controlled, Franklin invented the lightning rod, earning him international praise, but some ministers criticized him for interfering with God's power. Franklin had explained a major element of nature that had not been understood previously. No longer cited as the reason for lightning, God would have to be used to explain other phenomena that were not yet understood. The problem with keeping science and faith in this kind of relationship is that the more science understands—and science will continue to explain more and more—the less space there will be for faith.

On the other hand, some people of faith argue that this notion of God incorrectly assumes that God can be limited only to areas where human knowledge is lacking; thus, it could be argued that scientific discovery does not actually have a negative effect on faith. In fact, one could say that science only enhances human appreciation for the world God created. In an *Atlantic Monthly* article titled "Oh, Gods!" (February, 2002), writer Toby Lester observes, "Religion didn't begin to wither away during the twentieth century, as some academic experts had prophesized," he notes. "And the new century," he predicts, "will probably see religion explode—in both intensity and variety."

Where do you stand on the religion vs. science conflict? Is there even a conflict? While reading the selections below, consider: As sciences such as genetics, neuroscience, and evolutionary biology and psychology discover more about how the human mind performs the act of believing, what will be the impact on religion? As astronomy and physics seek greater knowledge about the workings of the world and the presence of life in the universe, how will religion be challenged to change?

E.T. and God
PAUL DAVIES

Paul Davies is a professor of theoretical physics and the founder and director of the Beyond Center for Fundamental Concepts in Science at Arizona State University. Davies is the author of many articles in magazines, newspapers, and scientific journals and has participated in several radio and television documentaries about science. Among the numerous books he has written or edited, he is the author of The Goldilocks Enigma: Why Is the Universe Just Right for Life? *and* Are We Alone: The Philosophical Basis of the Search for Extraterrestrial Life. *In 1995 Davies received the prestigious Templeton Prize for Progress in Religion. His main research interest is astrobiology, the study of life in the universe. Read about Davies at* http://cosmos.asu.edu, *the Beyond Center at* http://beyond.asu.edu, *and the Templeton Prize at* www.templeton.org. *As you read the article, notice how the writer challenges himself to think creatively with a unique topic: what would happen to religion on earth if scientists discovered life elsewhere in the universe?*

◆

COULD EARTHLY RELIGIONS SURVIVE THE DISCOVERY OF LIFE ELSEWHERE IN THE UNIVERSE?

The recent discovery of abundant water on Mars, albeit in the form of permafrost, has raised hopes; for finding traces of life there. The Red Planet has long been a favorite location for those speculating about extraterrestrial life, especially since the 1890s, when H. G. Wells wrote The War of the Worlds and the American astronomer Percival Lowell claimed that he could see artificial canals etched into the planet's parched surface. Today, of course, scientists expect to find no more than simple bacteria dwelling deep underground, if even that. Still, the discovery of just a single bacterium somewhere beyond Earth would force us to revise our understanding of who we are and where we fit into the cosmic scheme of things, throwing us into a deep: spiritual identity crisis that would be every bit as dramatic as the one Copernicus brought about in the early 1500s, when he asserted that Earth was not at the center of the universe.

Whether or not we are alone is one of the great existential questions that confront us today. Probably because of the high emotional stakes, the search for life beyond Earth is deeply fascinating to the public. Opinion polls and Web-site hits indicate strong support for and interest in space missions that are linked even obliquely to this search. Perceiving the public's interest, NASA has reconfigured its research strategy and founded the NASA Astrobiology Institute, dedicated to the study of life in the cosmos. At the top of the agenda, naturally, is the race to find life elsewhere in the solar system.

Researchers have long focused on Mars in their search for extraterrestrial life because of its relative proximity. But twenty-five years ago, as a result of the 1976 Viking mission, many of them became discouraged. A pair of spacecraft had passed through the planet's extremely thin atmosphere, touched down on the surface, and found it to be a freeze dried desert drenched with deadly ultraviolet rays. The spacecraft, equipped with robotic arms, scooped up Martian dirt so that it could be examined for signs of biological activity. The results of the analysis were inconclusive but generally negative, and hopes faded for finding even simple microbes on the surface of Mars.

The outlook today is more optimistic. Several probes are scheduled to visit Mars in the coming months, and all will be searching for signs of life. This renewed interest is due in part to the discovery of organisms living in some remarkably hostile environments on Earth (which opens up the possibility of life on Mars in places the Viking probes didn't examine), and in part to better information about the planet's ancient history. Scientists now believe that Mars once had a much thicker atmosphere, higher temperatures, rivers, floods, and extensive volcanic activity—all conditions considered favorable to the emergence of life.

The prospects for finding living organisms on Mars remain slim, of course, but even traces of past life would represent a discovery of unprecedented scientific value. Before any sweeping philosophical or theological conclusions could be drawn, however, it would be necessary to determine whether this life was the product of a second genesis—that is, whether its origin was independent of life on Earth. Earth and Mars are known to trade material in the form of rocks blasted from the planets' surfaces by the violent impacts of asteroids and comets. Microbes could have hitched a ride on this detritus, raising the possibility that life started on Earth and was transferred to Mars, or vice versa. If traces of past life were discovered on Mars but found to be identical to some form of terrestrial life, transportation by ejected rocks would be the most plausible explanation, and we would still lack evidence that life had started from scratch in two separate locations.

The significance of this point is crucial. In his theory of evolution Charles Darwin provided a persuasive account of how life evolved over billions of years, but he pointedly omitted any explanation of how life got started in the first place. "One might as well think of origin of matter," he wrote in a letter to a friend. A century and a half later, scientists still have little understanding of how the first living filling came to be.

Some scientists believe that life on Earth is a freak accident of chemistry, and as such must be unique. Because even the simplest known microbe is breathtakingly complex, they argue, the chances that one formed by blind molecular shuffling are infinitesimal; the probability that the process would occur twice, in separate locations, is virtually negligible. The French biochemist and Nobel laureate Jacques Monod was a firm believer in this view. "Man at last knows he is alone in the unfeeling immensity of the universe, out of which he has emerged only by chance," he wrote in 1971. He used this bleak assessment as a springboard to argue for atheism and the absurdity and pointlessness of existence. As Monod saw it, we are merely chemical extras in a majestic but impersonal cosmic drama—an irrelevant, unintended sideshow.

But suppose that's not what happened. Many scientists believe that life is not a freakish phenomenon (the odds of life's starting by chance, the British cosmologist Fred Hoyle once suggested, are comparable to the odds of a whirlwind's blowing through a junkyard and assembling a functioning Boeing 747) but instead is written into the laws of nature. "The universe must in some sense have known we were coming," the physicist Freeman Dyson famously observed. No one can say precisely in what sense the universe might be pregnant with life, or how the general expectancy Dyson spoke of might translate into specific physical processes at the molecular level. Perhaps matter and energy always get fast-tracked along the road to life by what's often called "self-organization." Or perhaps the power of Darwinian evolution is somehow harnessed at a pre-biotic molecular stage. Or maybe some efficient and as yet unidentified physical process (quantum mechanics?) sets the gears in motion, with organic life as we know it taking over the essential machinery at a later stage. Under any of these scenarios life becomes a fundamental rather than an incidental product of nature. In 1994, reflecting on this same point, another Nobel laureate, the Belgian biochemist Christian de Duve, wrote, "I view this universe not as a 'cosmic joke,' but as a meaningful entity—made in such a way as to generate life and mind, bound to give birth to thinking beings able to discern truth, apprehend beauty, feel love, yearn after goodness, define evil, experience mystery."

Absent from these accounts is any mention of miracles. Ascribing the origin of life to a divine miracle not only is anathema to scientists but also is theologically suspect. The term "God of the gaps" was coined to deride the notion that God can be invoked as an explanation whenever scientists have gaps in their understanding. The trouble with invoking God in this way is that as science advances, the gaps close, and God gets progressively squeezed out of the story of nature. Theologians long ago accepted that they would forever be fighting a rearguard battle if they tried to challenge science on its own ground. Using the formation of life to prove the existence of God is a tactic that risks instant demolition should someone succeed in making life in a test tube. And the idea that God acts in fits and starts, moving atoms around on odd occasions in competition with natural forces, is a decidedly uninspiring image of the Grand Architect.

The theological battle line in relation to the formation of life is not, therefore, between the natural and the miraculous but between sheer chance and lawlike certitude. Atheists tend to take the first side, and theists line up behind the second; but these divisions are general and by no means absolute. It's perfectly possible to be an atheist and believe that life is built ingeniously into the nature of the universe. It's also possible to be a theist and suppose that God engineered just one planet with life, with or without the help of miracles.

Though the discovery of microbes on Mars or elsewhere would ignite a passionate theological debate, the truly difficult issues surround the prospect of advanced alien beings in possession of intelligence and technology. Most scientists don't think that such beings exist, but for forty years a dedicated band of astronomers has been sweeping the skies with radio telescopes in hopes of finding a message from a civilization elsewhere in the galaxy. Their project is known as SETI (Search for Extraterrestrial Intelligence).

Because our solar system is relatively young compared with the universe overall, any alien civilization the SETI researchers might discover is likely to be much older, and presumably wiser, than ours. Indeed, it might have achieved our level of science and technology millions or even billions of years ago. Just contemplating the possibility of such advanced extraterrestrials appears to raise additional uncomfortable questions for religion.

The world's main faiths were all founded in the prescientific era, when Earth was widely believed to be at the center of the universe and humankind at the pinnacle of creation. As scientific discoveries have piled up over the past 500 years, our status has been incrementally diminished. First Earth was shown to be just one planet of several orbiting the Sun. Then the solar system itself was relegated to the outer suburbs of the galaxy, and the Sun classified as an insignificant dwarf star among billions. The theory of evolution proposed that human beings occupied just a small branch on a complex evolutionary tree. This pattern continued into the twentieth century, when the supremacy of our much vaunted intelligence came under threat. Computers began to outsmart us. Now genetic engineering has raised the specter of designer babies with superintellects that leave ours far behind. And we must consider the uncomfortable possibility that in astrobiological terms, God's children may be galactic also-rans.

Theologians are used to putting a brave face on such developments. Over the centuries the Christian church, for example, has time and again been forced to accommodate new scientific facts that challenge existing doctrine. But these accommodations have usually been made reluctantly and very belatedly. Only recently, for example, did the Pope acknowledge that Darwinian evolution is more than just a theory. If SETI succeeds, theologians will not have the luxury of decades of careful deliberation to assess the significance of the discovery. The impact will be instant.

The discovery of alien superbeings might not be so corrosive to religion if human beings could still claim special spiritual status. After all, religion is concerned primarily with people's relationship to God, rather than with their biological or intellectual qualities. It is possible to imagine alien beings who are smarter and wiser than we are but who are spiritually inferior, or just plain evil. However, it is more likely that any civilization that had surpassed us scientifically would have improved on our level of moral development, too. One may even speculate that an advanced alien society would sooner or later find some way to genetically eliminate evil behavior, resulting in a race of saintly beings.

Suppose, then, that E.T. is far ahead of us not only scientifically and technologically but spiritually, too. Where does that leave mankind's presumed special relationship with God? This conundrum poses a particular difficulty for Christians, because of the unique nature of the Incarnation. Of all the world's major religions, Christianity is the most species-specific. Jesus Christ was humanity's savior and redeemer. He did not die for the dolphins or the gorillas, and certainly not for the proverbial little green men. But what of deeply spiritual aliens? Are they not to be saved? Can we contemplate a universe that contains perhaps a trillion worlds of saintly beings, but in which the only beings eligible for salvation inhabit a planet where murder, rape, and other evils remain rife?

Those few Christian theologians who have addressed this thorny issue divide into two camps. Some posit multiple incarnations and even multiple crucifixions—God taking on little green flesh to save little green men, as a prominent Anglican minister once told me. But most are appalled by this idea or find it ludicrous. After all, in the Christian view of the world, Jesus was God's only son. Would God have the same person born, killed, and resurrected in endless succession on planet after planet? This scenario was lampooned as long ago as 1794, by Thomas Paine. "The Son of God," he wrote in The Age of Reason, "and sometimes God himself, would have nothing else to do than to travel from world to world, in an endless succession of death, with scarcely a momentary interval of life." Paine went on to argue that Christianity was simply incompatible with the existence of extraterrestrial beings, writing, "He who thinks he believes in both has thought but little of either."

Catholics tend to regard the idea of multiple incarnations as verging on heresy, not because of its somewhat comic aspect but because it would seem to automate an act that is supposed to be God's singular gift, "God chose a very specific way to redeem human beings," writes George Coyne, a Jesuit priest and the director of the Vatican Observatory, whose own research includes astrobiology. "He sent his only son, Jesus, to them, and Jesus gave up his life so that human beings would be saved from their sin. Did God do this for extraterrestrials? . . . The theological implications about God are getting even more serious."

Paul Tillich, one of the few prominent Protestant theologians to give serious consideration to the issue of alien beings, took a more positive view. "Man cannot claim to occupy the only possible place for incarnation," he wrote. The Lutheran theologian Ted Peters, of the Center for Theology and the Natural Sciences, in Berkeley, California, has made a special study of the impact on religious faith of belief in extraterrestrials. In discussing the tradition of debate on this topic, he writes, "Christian theologians have routinely found ways to address the issue of Jesus Christ as God incarnate and to conceive of God's creative power and saving power exerted in other worlds." Peters believes that Christianity is robust enough and flexible enough to accommodate the discovery of extraterrestrial intelligence, or ETI. One theologian who is emphatically not afraid of that challenge is Robert Russell, also of the Center for Theology and the Natural Sciences. "As we await 'first contact,'" he has written, "pursuing these kinds of questions and reflections will be immensely valuable."

Clearly, there is considerable diversity—one might even say muddle—on this topic in theological circles. Eman McMullin, a professor emeritus of philosophy at Notre Dame University, affirms that the central difficulty stems from Christianity's roots in a pre-scientific cosmology. "It was easier to accept the idea of God's becoming man," he has written, "when humans and their abode both held a unique place in the universe." He acknowledges that Christians especially face a stark predicament in relation to ETI, but feels that Thomas Paine and his like-minded successors have presented the problem too simplistically. Pointing out that concepts such as original sin, incarnation, and salvation are open to a variety of interpretations, McMullin concludes that there is also widespread divergence among Christians on the correct response to the ETI challenge. On the matter of multiple incarnations he writes. "Their answers could range . . . from 'yes, certainly' to 'certainly not.' My own preference would be a cautious 'maybe.'"

Even for those Christians who dismiss the idea of multiple incarnations there is an interesting fallback position: perhaps the course of evolution has an element of directionality, with human-like beings the inevitable end product. Even if Homo sapiens as such may not be the unique focus of God's attention, the broader class of all humanlike beings in the universe might be. This is the basic idea espoused by the philosopher Michael Ruse, an ardent Darwinian and an agnostic sympathetic to Christianity. He sees the incremental progress of natural evolution as God's chosen mode of creation, and the history of life as a ladder that leads inexorably from microbes to man.

Most biologists regard a "progressive evolution," with human beings its implied preordained goal, as preposterous. Stephen Jay Gould once described the very notion as "noxious." After all, the essence of Darwinism is that nature is blind. It cannot look ahead. Random chance is the driving force of evolution, and randomness by definition has no directionality. Gould insisted that if the evolutionary tape were replayed, the result would be very different from what we now observe. Probably life would never get beyond microbes next time around.

But some respected biologists disagree sharply with Gould on this point. Christian de Duve does not deny that the fine details of evolutionary history depend on happenstance, but he believes that the broad thrust of evolutionary change is somehow innately predetermined—that plants and animals were almost destined to emerge amid a general advance in complexity. Another Darwinian biologist, Simon Conway Morris, of Cambridge University makes his own case for a "ladder of progress," invoking the phenomenon of convergent evolution—the tendency of similar-looking organisms to evolve independently in similar ecological riches. For example, the Tasmanian tiger (now extinct) played the role of the big cat in Australia even though, as a marsupial, it was genetically far removed from placental mammals. Like Ruse, Conway Morris maintains that the "humanlike niche" is likely to be filled on other planets that have advanced life. He even goes so far as to argue that extraterrestrials would have a humanoid form. It is not a great leap from this conclusion to the belief that extraterrestrials would sin, have consciences, struggle with ethical questions, and fear death.

The theological difficulties posed by the possibility of advanced alien beings are less acute for Judaism and Islam. Muslims, at least, are prepared for ETI: the Koran states explicitly, "And among His Signs is the creation of the heavens and the earth, and the living creatures that He has scattered through them."

Nevertheless, both religions stress the specialness of human beings—and, indeed, of specific, well-defined groups who have been received into the faith. Could an alien become a Jew or a Muslim? Does the concept even make sense? Among the major religious communities, Buddhists and Hindus would seem to be the least threatened by the prospect of advanced aliens, owing to their pluralistic concept of God and their traditionally much grander vision of the cosmos.

Among the world's minority religions, some would positively welcome the discovery of intelligent aliens. The Raëlians, a Canada-based cult recently propelled to fame by its claim to have cloned a human being, believe that the cult's leader, Raël, a

French former journalist originally named Claude Vorilhon, received revelations from aliens who briefly transported him inside a flying saucer in 1973. Other fringe religious organizations with an extraterrestrial message include the ill-fated Heaven's Gate cult and many UFO groups. Their adherents share a belief that aliens are located further up not only the evolutionary ladder but also the spiritual ladder, and can therefore help us draw closer to God and salvation. It is easy to dismiss such beliefs as insignificant to serious theological debate, but if evidence for alien beings were suddenly to appear, these cults might achieve overnight prominence while established religions floundered in doctrinal bewilderment.

Ironically, SETI is often accused of being a quasi-religious quest. But Jill Tarter, the director of the SETI Institute's Center for SETI Research, in Mountain View, California, has no truck with religion and is contemptuous of the theological gymnastics with which religious scholars accommodate the possibility of extraterrestrials. "God is our own invention," she has written. "If we're going to survive or turn into a long-lived technological civilization, organized religion needs to be outgrown. If we get a message [from an alien civilization] and it's secular in nature, I think that says that they have no organized religion—that they've outgrown it." Tartar's dismissal is rather naive, however. Though many religious movements have come and gone throughout history, some sort of spirituality seems to be part of human nature. Even atheistic scientists profess to experience what Albert Elnstein called a "cosmic religious feeling" when contemplating the awesome majesty of the universe.

Would advanced alien beings share this spiritual dimension, even though they might long ago have "outgrown" established religion? Steven Dick, a science historian at the U.S. Naval Observatory, believes they would. Dick is an expert on the history of speculation about extraterrestrial life, and he suggests that mankind's spirituality would be greatly expanded and enriched by contact with an alien civilization. However, he envisages that our present concept of God would probably require a wholesale transformation. Dick has outlined what he calls a new "cosmotheology," in which human spirituality is placed in a full cosmological and astrobiological context. "As we learn more about our place in the universe," he has written, "and as we physically move away from our home planet, our cosmic consciousness will only increase." Dick proposes abandoning the transcendent God of monotheistic religion in favor of what he calls a "natural God"—a superbeing located within the universe and within nature. "With due respect for present religious traditions whose history stretches back nearly four millennia," he suggests, "the natural God of cosmic evolution and the biological universe, not the supernatural God of the ancient Near East, may be the God of the next millennium."

Some form of natural God was also proposed by Fred Hoyle, in a provocative book titled *The Intelligent Universe*. Hoyle drew on his work in astronomy and quantum physics to sketch the notion of a "superintellect"—a being who had, as Hoyle liked to say, "monkeyed with physics," adjusting the properties of the various fundamental particles and forces of nature so that carbon-based organisms could thrive and spread across the galaxy. Hoyle even suggested that this cosmic engineer might communicate with us by manipulating quantum processes in the brain. Most scientists shrug off Hoyle's speculations, but his ideas do show how far beyond traditional religious doctrine some people feel they need to go when they contemplate the possibility of advanced life forms beyond Earth.

Though in some ways the prospect of discovering extraterrestrial life undermines established religions, it is not all bad news for them. Astrobiology has also led to a surprising resurgence of the so-called "design argument" for the existence of God. The original design argument, as articulated by William Paley in the eighteenth century, was that living organisms' intricate adaptation to their environments pointed to the providential hand of a benign Creator. Darwin demolished the argument by showing how evolution driven by random mutation and natural selection could mimic design. Now a revamped design argument has emerged that fully embraces the Darwinian account of evolution and focuses instead on the origin of life. (I must stress that I am not referring here to what has recently become known as the Intelligent Design movement, which relies on an element of the miraculous.) If life is found to be widespread in the universe, the new design argument goes, then it must emerge rather easily from nonliving chemical mixtures, and thus the laws of nature must be cunningly contrived to unleash this remarkable and very special state of matter, which itself is a conduit to an even more remarkable and special state: mind. This sort of exquisite bio-friendliness would represent an extraordinary and unexpected bonus among nature's inventory of principles—one that could be interpreted by those of a religious persuasion as evidence of God's ingenuity and foresight. In this version of cosmic design, God acts not by direct intervention but by creating appropriate natural laws that guarantee the emergence of life and mind in cosmic abundance. The universe, in other words, is one in which there are no miracles except the miracle of nature itself.

The E.T. debate has only just begun, but a useful starting point is simply to acknowledge that the discovery of extraterrestrial life would not have to be theologically devastating. The revamped design argument offers a vision of nature distinctly inspiring to the spiritually inclined—certainly more so than that of a cosmos sterile everywhere but on a single planet. History is instructive in this regard. Four hundred years ago Giordano Bruno was burned at the stake by the Church in Rome for, among other things, espousing the notion of a plurality of inhabited worlds. To those whose theological outlook depended on a conception of Earth and its life forms as a singular miracle, the very notion of extraterrestrial life proved deeply threatening. But today the possibility of extraterrestrial life is anything but spiritually threatening. The more one accepts the formation of life as a natural process (that is, the more deeply embedded one believes it is in the overall cosmic scheme), the more ingenious and contrived (dare one say "designed"?) the universe appears to be.

Questions about Content

1. Reread the final sentence of the first paragraph: "Still, the discovery of just a single bacterium somewhere beyond Earth would force us to revise our understanding of who we are and where we fit into the cosmic scheme of things, throwing us into a deep spiritual identity crisis." Do you agree with this statement, and why?
2. Davies talks about a "second genesis." What does this term mean and why could it be significant?
3. Davies redefines the "theological battle line," saying it is "not, therefore, between the natural and the miraculous but between sheer chance and law-like certitude." How could this redefinition change the debate?
4. According to this article, what has been the historical relationship between science and religion? In what ways has one accommodated the other?
5. Ultimately, how does Davies answer the question, "Could earthly religions survive the discovery of life elsewhere in the universe?"

Questions about Rhetorical Analysis

1. Davies states, "Just contemplating the possibility of such advanced extraterrestrials appears to raise additional uncomfortable questions for religion." Do the questions strike you as exciting? Do they seem to challenge faith?
2. Consider the writer's tone throughout the article. What seems to be his attitude toward his material? Is he concerned and worried, or is he fascinated and curious? Is he warning the reader or inviting the reader? Select a word or phrase and explain how it communicates his tone.

Is God an Accident?

PAUL BLOOM

Paul Bloom is a professor of psychology at Yale University, the past president of the Society for Philosophy and Psychology, and coeditor of a major journal in science, Behavioral and Brain Sciences. *Having received his Ph.D. from the Massachusetts Institute of Technology, he has received many awards for his research and teaching and has written numerous articles for scientific journals as well as major newspapers and magazines such as the* New York Times, *the* Guardian, *and* Atlantic Monthly. *His books include* Descartes' Baby: How the Science of Child Development Explains What Makes Us Human *and* How Children Learn the Meanings of Words. *You can learn more about his research and read some of his publications at* http://pantheon.yale.edu/~pb85. *As you read Bloom's article that follows, notice how he chooses a unique, creative topic to write about: As science discovers more about how the human mind adopts beliefs in supernatural phenomena, what is the future of faith?*

───────────── ✦ ─────────────

Despite the vast number of religions, nearly everyone in the world believes in the same things: the existence of a soul, an afterlife, miracles, and the divine creation of the immerse. Recently psychologists doing research on the minds of infants have discovered two related facts that may account for this phenomenon. One: human beings come into the world with a predisposition to believe in supernatural phenomena. And two: this predisposition is an incidental by-product of cognitive functioning gone awry. Which leads to the question . . .

I. GOD IS NOT DEAD

When I was a teenager my rabbi believed that the Lubavitcher Rebbe, who was living in Crown Heights, Brooklyn, was the Messiah, and that the world was soon to end. He believed that the earth was a few thousand years old, and that the fossil record was a consequence of the Great Flood. He could describe the afterlife, and was able to answer adolescent questions about the fate of Hitler's soul.

My rabbi was no crackpot; he was an intelligent and amiable man, a teacher and a scholar. But he held views that struck me as

He sounds contradictive.

strange, even disturbing. Like many secular people. I am comfortable with religion as a source of spirituality and transcendence, tolerance and love, charity and good works. Who can object to the faith of Martin Luther King Jr. or the Dalai Lama—at least as long as that faith grounds moral positions one already accepts? I am uncomfortable, however, with religion when it makes claims about the natural world, let alone a world beyond nature. It is easy for those of us who reject supernatural beliefs to agree with Stephen Jay Gould that the best way to accord dignity and respect to both science and religion is to recognize that they apply to "non-overlapping magisterial: science gets the realm of facts, religion the realm of values.

For better or worse, though, religion is much more than a set of ethical principles or a vague sense of transcendence. The anthropologist Edward Tylor got it right in 1871, when he noted that the "minimum definition of religion" is a belief in spiritual beings, in the supernatural. My rabbi's specific claims were a minority view in the culture in which I was raised, but those sorts of views—about the creation of the universe, the end of the world, the fates of souls—define religion as billions of people understand and practice it.

The United States is a poster child for supernatural belief. Just about everyone in this country—96 percent in one poll—believes in God. Well over half of Americans believe in miracles, the devil, and angels. Most believe in an afterlife—and not just in the mushy sense that we will live on in the memories of other people, or in our good deeds; when asked for details, most Americans say they believe that after death they will actually reunite with relatives and get to meet God. Woody Allen once said, "I don't want to achieve immortality through my work. I want to achieve it through not dying." Most Americans have precisely this expectation.

But America is an anomaly, isn't it? These statistics are sometimes taken as yet another indication of how much this country differs from, for instance, France and Germany, where secularism holds greater sway. Americans are fundamentalists, the claim goes, isolated from the intellectual progress made by the rest of the world.

There are two things wrong with this conclusion. First, even if a gap between America and Europe exists. It is not the United States that is idiosyncratic. After all, the rest of the world—Asia, Africa, the Middle East—is not exactly filled with hard-core atheists. If one is to talk about exceptionalism, it applies to Europe, not the United States.

Second, the religious divide between Americans and Europeans may be smaller than we think. The sociologists Rodney Stark, of Baylor University, and Roger Finke, of Pennsylvania State

He sounds objective about Religion in Europe & U.S.

University, write that the big difference has to do with church attendance, which really is much lower in Europe. (Building on the work of the Chicago-based sociologist and priest Andrew Greeley, they argue that this is because the United States has a rigorously free religious market, in which churches actively via for parishioners and constantly improve their product, whereas European churches are often under state control and, like many government monopolies, have become inefficient.) Most polls from European countries show that a majority of their people are believers. Consider Iceland, To judge by rates of churchgoing, Iceland is the most secular country on earth, with a pathetic two percent weekly attendance. But four out of five icelanders say that they pray, and the same proportion believe in life after death.

In the United States some liberal scholars posit a different sort of exceptionalism, arguing that belief in the supernatural is found mostly in Christian conservatives—those infamously described by the Washington Post reporter Michael Weisskopf in 1993 as "largely poor, uneducated, and easy to command." Many people saw the 2004 presidential election as pitting Americans who are religious against those who are not.

Finally, consider scientists. They are less likely than nonscientists to be religious—but not by a huge amount. A 1996 poll asked scientists whether they believed in God, and the polisters set the bar high—no mealy-mouthed evasions such as "I believe in the totality of all that exists" or "in what is beautiful and unknown"; rather, they insisted on a real biblical God, one believers could pray to and actually get an answer from. About 40 percent of scientists said yes to a belief in this kind of God—about the same percentage found in a similar poll in 1916. Only when we look at the most elite scientists—members of the National Academy of Sciences—do we find a strong majority of atheists and agnostics.

These facts are an embarrassment for those who see supernatural beliefs as a cultural anachronism, soon to be eroded by scientific discoveries and the spread of cosmopolitan values. They require a new theory of why we are religious—one that draws on research in evolutionary biology, cognitive neuroscience, and developmental psychology.

II. OPIATES AND FRATERNITIES

One traditional approach to the origin of religious belief begins with the observation that it is difficult to be a person. There is evil all around; everyone we love will die; and soon we ourselves will die—either slowly and probably unpleasantly or quickly and probably unpleasantly. For all but a pampered and lucky few life really is nasty, brutish, and short. And if our lives have some greater meaning, it is hardly obvious.

So perhaps, as Marx suggested, we have adopted religion as an opiate, to soothe the pain of existence. As the philosopher Susanne K. Langer has put it, man "cannot deal with Chaos"; supernatural beliefs solve the problem of this chaos by providing meaning. We are not mere things; we are lovingly crafted by God, and serve his purposes. Religion tells us that this is a just world, in which the good will be rewarded and the evil punished. Most of all, it addresses our fear of death. Freud summed it all up by describing a "three-fold task" for religious beliefs: "they must exercise the terrors of nature, they must reconcile men to the cruelty of Fate, particularly as it is shown in death, and they must compensate them for the sufferings and privations which a civilized life in common has imposed on them."

Religions can sometimes do all these things, and it would be unrealistic to deny that this partly explains their existence. Indeed, sometimes theologians use the foregoing arguments to make a case for why we should believe: if one wishes for purpose, meaning, and eternal life, there is nowhere to go but toward God.

One problem with this view is that, as the cognitive scientist Steven Pinker reminds us, we don't typically get solace from propositions that we don't already believe to be true. Hungry people don't cheer themselves up by believing that they just had a large meal. Heaven is a reassuring notion only insofar as people believe such a place exists; it is this belief that an adequate theory of religion has to explain in the first place.

Also, the religion-as-opiate theory fits best with the monotheistic religions most familiar to us. But what about those people (many of the religious people in the world) who do not believe in an all-wise and just God? Every society believes in spiritual beings, but they are often stupid or malevolent. Many religions simply don't deal with metaphysical or teleological questions; gods and ancestor spirits are called upon only to help cope with such mundane problems as how to prepare food and what to do with a corpse—not to elucidate the Meaning of it All. As for the reassurance of heaven, justice, or salvation, again, it exists in some religions but by no means all. (In fact, even those religions we are most familiar with are not always reassuring. I know some older Christians who were made miserable as children by worries about eternal damnation; the prospect of oblivion would have been far preferable.) So the opiate theory is ultimately an unsatisfying explanation for the existence of religion.

The major alternative theory is social: religion brings people together, giving them an edge over those who lack this social glue.

Sometimes this argument is presented in cultural terms, and sometimes it is seen from an evolutionary perspective: survival of the fittest working at the level not of the gene or the individual but of the social group. In either case the claim is that religion thrives because groups that have it outgrow and outlast those that do not.

In this conception religion is a fraternity, and the analogy runs deep. Just as fraternities used to paddle freshmen on the rear end to instlii loyalty and commitment, religions have painful initiation rites—for example, snipping off part of the penis. Also, certain puzzling features of many religions, such as dietary restrictions and distinctive dress, make perfect sense once they are viewed as tools to ensure group solidarity.

The fraternity theory also explains why religions are so harsh toward those who do not share the faith, reserving particular ire for apostates. This is clear in the Old Testament, in which "a jealous God" issues commands such as

> Should your brother, your mother's son, or your son or your daughter or the wife of your bosom or your companion who is like your own self incite you in secret, saying 'Let us go and worship other gods' - you shall surely kill him. Your hand shall be against him first to put him to death and the hand of all the people last. And you shall stone him and he shall die, for he sought to thrust you away from the LORD your God who brought you out of the land of Egypt, from the house of slaves.— Deuteronomy 13, 7–11

sarcasm

This theory explains almost everything about religion— except the religious part. It is clear that rituals and sacrifices can bring people together, and it may well be that a group that does such things has an advantage over one that does not. But it is not clear why a religion has to be involved. Why are gods, souls, an afterlife, miracles, divine creation of the universe, and so on brought in? The theory doesn't explain what we are most interested in, which is belief in the supernatural.

III. BODIES AND SOULS

Enthusiasm is building among scientists for a quite different view—that religion emerged not to serve a purpose but by accident.

This is not a value judgment. Many of the good things in life are, from an evolutionary perspective, accidents. People sometimes give money, time, and even blood to help unknown strangers in faraway countries whom they will never see. From the perspective of one's genes this is disastrous—the suicidal squandering of resources for no benefit. But its origin is not magical; long-distance altruism is most likely a by-product of other, more adaptive traits, such as empathy and abstract reasoning. Similarly, there is no reproductive advantage to the pleasure we get from paintings or movies. It just so happens that our eyes and brains, which evolved to react to three-dimensional objects in the real world, can respond to two-dimensional projections on a canvas or a screen.

Supernatural beliefs might be explained in a similar way. This is the religion-as-accident theory that emerges from my work and the work of cognitive scientists such as Scott Atran, Pascal Boyer, Justin Barrett, and Deborah Kelemen. One version of this theory begins with the notion that a distinction between the physical and the psychological is fundamental to human thought. Purely physical things, such as rocks and trees, are subject to the pitiless laws of Newton. Throw a rock, and it will fly through space on a certain path; if you put a branch on the ground, it will not disappear, scamper away, or fly into space. Psychological things, such as people, possess minds, intentions, beliefs, goals, and desires. They move unexpectedly, according to volition and whim; they can chase or run away. There is a moral difference as well: a rock cannot be evil or kind; a person can.

Where does the distinction between the physical and the psychological come from? Is it something we learn through experience, or is it somehow pre-wired into our brains? One way to find out is to study babies. It is notoriously difficult to know what babies are thinking, given that they can't speak and have little control over their bodies. (They are harder to test than rats or pigeons, because they cannot run mazes or peck levers.) But recently investigators have used the technique of showing them different events and recording how long they look at them, exploiting the fact that babies, like the rest of us, tend to look longer at something they find unusual or bizarre.

This has led to a series of striking discoveries. Six-month-olds understand that physical objects obey gravity. If you put an object on a table and then remove the table, and the object just stays there (held by a hidden wire), babies are surprised; they expect the object to fall. They expect objects to be solid, and contrary to what is still being taught in some psychology classes, they understand that objects persist over time even if hidden. (Show a baby an object and then put it behind a screen. Wait a little while and then remove the screen. If the object is gone, the baby is surprised.) Five-month-olds can even do simple math, appreciating that if first one object and then another is placed behind a screen, when the screen drops there should be two objects, not one or three. Other experiments find the same numerical understanding in nonhuman primates, including macaques and tamarins, and in dogs.

Similarly precocious capacities show up in infants' understanding of the social world. Newborns prefer to look at faces over anything else, and the sounds they most like to hear are human voices—preferably their mothers'. They quickly come to recognize different emotions, such as anger, fear, and happiness, and respond appropriately to them. Before they are a year old they can determine the target of an adult's gaze, and can learn by attending to the amotions of others; if a baby is crawling toward an area that might be dangerous and an adult makes a horrified or disgusted face, the baby usually knows enough to stay away.

A skeptic might argue that these social capacities can be explained as a set of primitive responses, but there is some evidence that they reflect a deeper understanding. For instance, when twelve-month-olds see one object chasing another, they seem to understand that it really is chasing, with the goal of catching; they expect the chaser to continue its pursuit along the most direct path, and are surprised when it does otherwise. In some work I've done with the psychologists Valerie Kuhlmeier, of Queen's University, and Karen Wynn, of Yale, we found that when babies see one character in a movie help an individual and a different character hurt that individual, they later expect the individual to approach the character that helped it and to avoid the one that hurt it.

Understanding of the physical world and understanding of the social world can be seen as akin to two distinct computers in a baby's brain, running separate programs and performing separate tasks. The understandings develop at different rates: the social one emerges somewhat later than the physical one. They evolved at different points in our prehistory: our physical understanding is shared by many species, whereas our social understanding is a relatively recent adaptation, and in some regards might be uniquely human.

That these two systems are distinct is especially apparent in autism, a developmental disorder whose dominant feature is a lack of social understanding. Children with autism typically show impairments in communication (about a third do not speak at all), in imagination (they tend not to engage in imaginative play), and most of all in socialization. They do not seem to enjoy the company of others; they don't hug; they are hard to reach out to. In the most extreme cases children with autism see people as nothing more than objects—objects that move in unpredictable ways and make unexpected noises and are therefore frightening. Their understanding of other minds is impaired, though their understanding of material objects is fully intact.

At this point the religion-as-accident theory says nothing about supernatural beliefs. Babies have two systems that work in a cold-bloodedly rational way to help them anticipate and understand—and, when they get older, to manipulate—physical and social entities. In other words, both these systems are biological adaptations that give human beings a badly needed head start in dealing with objects and people. But these systems go awry in two important ways that are the foundations of religion. First, we perceive the world of objects as essentially separate from the world of minds, making it possible for us to envision soulless bodies and bodiless souls. This helps explain why we believe in gods and an afterlife. Second, as we will see, our system of social understanding overshoots, inferring goals and desires where none exist. This makes us animists and creationists.

IV. NATURAL-BORN DUALISTS

For those of us who are not autistic, the separateness of these two mechanisms, one for understanding the physical world and one for understanding the social world, gives rise to a duality of experience. We experience the world of material things as separate from the world of goals and desires. The biggest consequence has to do with the way we think of ourselves and others. We are dualists; It seems intuitively obvious that a physical body and a conscious entity—a mind or soul—are genuinely distinct. We don't feel that we are our bodies. Rather, we feel that we occupy them, we possess them, we own them.

This duality is immediately apparent in our imaginative life. Because we see people as separate from their bodies, we easily understand situations in which people's bodies are radically changed while their personhood stays intact. Kafka envisioned a man transformed into a gigantic insect; Homer described the plight of men transformed into pigs; in Shrek 2 an ogre is transformed into a human being, and a donkey into a steed; in Star Trek a scheming villain forcibly occupies Captain Kirk's body so as to take command of the Enterprise; in The Tale of the Body Thief, Anne Rice tells of a vampire and a human being who agree to trade bodies for a day; and in 13 Going on 30 a teenager wakes up as thirty-year-old Jennifer Garner. We don't think of these events as real, of course, but they are fully understandable; it makes intuitive sense to us that people can be separated from their bodies, and similar transformations show up in religions around the world.

This notion of an immaterial soul potentially separable from the body clashes starkly with the scientific view. For psychologists and neuroscientists, the brain is the source of mental life; our consciousness, emotions, and will are the products of neural processes. As the claim is sometimes put, The mind is what the brain does. I

great examples

don't want to overstate the consensus here; there is no accepted theory as to precisely how this happens, and some scholars are skeptical that we will ever develop such a theory. But no scientist takes seriously Cartesian dualism, which posits that thinking need not involve the brain. There is just too much evidence against it.

Still, it feels right, even to those who have never had religious training, and even to young children. This became particularly clear to me one night when I was arguing with my six-year-old son, Max. I was telling him that he had to go to bed, and he said, "You can make me go to bed, but you can't make me go to sleep. It's my brain!" This piqued my interest, so I began to ask him questions about what the brain does and does not do. His answers showed an interesting split. He insisted that the brain was involved in perception—in seeing, hearing, tasting, and smelling—and he was adamant that it was responsible for thinking. But, he said, the brain was not essential for dreaming, for feeling sad, or for loving his brother. "That's what I do," Max said, "though my brain might help me out."

Max is not unusual. Children in our culture are taught that the brain is involved in thinking, but they interpret this in a narrow sense, as referring to conscious problem solving, academic rumination. They do not see the brain as the source of conscious experience; they do not identify it with their selves. They appear to think of it as a cognitive prosthesis—there is Max the person, and then there is his brain, which he uses to solve problems just as he might use a computer. In this commonsense conception the brain is, as Steven Pinker puts it, "a pocket PC for the soul."

If bodies and souls are thought of as separate, there can be bodies without souls. A corpse is seen as a body that used to have a soul. Most things—chairs, cups, trees—never had souls; they never had will or consciousness. At least some nonhuman animals are seen in the same way, as what Descartes described as "beast-machines," or complex automata. Some artificial creatures, such as industrial robots, Haitian zombies, and Jewish golems, are also seen as soulless beings, lacking free will or moral feeling.

Then there are souls without bodies. Most people I know believe in a God who created the universe, performs miracles, and listens to prayers. He is omnipotent and omniscient, possessing infinite kindness, justice, and mercy. But he does not in any literal sense have a body. Some people also believe in lesser noncorporeal beings that can temporarily take physical form or occupy human beings or animals: examples include angels, ghosts, poltergeists, succubi, dybbuks, and the demons that Jesus so frequently expelled from people's bodies.

This belief system opens the possibility that we ourselves can survive the death of our bodies. Most people believe that when the body is destroyed, the soul lives on. It might ascend to heaven, descend to hell, go off into some sort of parallel world, or occupy some other body, human or animal. Indeed, the belief that the world teems with ancestor spirits—the souls of people who have been liberated from their bodies through death—is common across cultures. We can imagine our bodies being destroyed, our brains ceasing to function, our bones turning to dust, but it is harder—some would say impossible—to imagine the end of our very existence. The notion of a soul without a body makes sense to us.

Others have argued that rather than believing in an afterlife because we are dualists, we are dualists because we want to believe in an afterlife. This was Freud's position. He speculated that the "doctrine of the soul" emerged as a solution to the problem of death: If souls exist, then conscious experience need not come to an end. Or perhaps the motivation for belief in an afterlife is cultural; we believe it because religious authorities tell us that it is so, possibly because it serves the interests of powerful leaders to control the masses through the carrot of heaven and the stick of hell. But there is reason to favor the religion-as-accident theory.

In a significant study the psychologists Jesse Bering, of the University of Arkansas, and David Bjorklund, of Florida Atlantic University: told young children a story about an alligator and a mouse, complete with a series of pictures, that ended in tragedy: "Uh oh! Mr. Alligator sees Brown Mouse and is coming to get him!" [The children were shown a picture of the alligator eating the mouse.] "Well, it looks like Brown Mouse got eaten by Mr. Alligator. Brown Mouse is not alive anymore."

The experimenters asked the children a set of questions about the mouse's biological functioning—such as "Now that the mouse is no longer alive, will he ever need to go to the bathroom? Do his ears still work? Does his brain still work?"—and about the mouse's mental functioning, such as "Now that the mouse is no longer alive, is he still hungry? Is he thinking about the alligator? Does he still want to go home?"

As predicted, when asked about biological properties, the children appreciated the effects of death: no need for bathroom breaks; the ears don't work, and neither does the brain. The mouse's body is gone. But when asked about the psychological properties, more than half the children said that these would continue: the dead mouse can feel hunger, think thoughts, and have desires. The soul survives. And children believe this more than adults do, suggesting that although we have to learn which specific afterlife people in our culture believe in (heaven, reincamation, a spirit world, and so on), the notion that life after death is possible is not learned at all. It is a by-product of how we naturally think about the world.

V. WE'VE EVOLVED TO BE CREATIONISTS

This is just half the story. Our dualism makes it possible for us to think of supernatural entities and events; it is why such things make sense. But there is another factor that makes the perception of them compelling, often irresistible. We have what the anthropologist Pascal Boyer has called a hypertrophy of social cognition. We see purpose, intention, design, even when it is not there.

In 1944 the social psychologists Fritz Heider and Mary-Ann Simmel made a simple movie in which geometric figures—circles, squares, triangles—moved in certain systematic ways, designed to tell a tale. When shown this movie, people instinctively describe the figures as if they were specific types of people (bullies, victims, heroes) with goals and desires, and repeat pretty much the same story that the psychologists intended to tell. Further research has found that bounded figures aren't even necessary—one can get much the same effect in movies where the "characters" are not single objects but moving groups, such as swarms of tiny squares.

Stewart Guthrie, an anthropologist at Fordham University, was the first modern scholar to notice the importance of this tendency as an explanation for religious thought. In his book *Faces in the Clouds*, Guthrie presents anecdotes and experiments showing that people attribute human characteristics to a striking range of real-world entities, including bicycles, bottles, clouds, fire, leaves, rain, volcanoes, and wind. We are hypersensitive to signs of agency—so much so that we see intention where only artifice or accident exists. As Guthrie puts it, the clothes have no emperor.

Our quickness to over-read purpose into things extends to the perception of intentional design. People have a terrible eye for randomness. If you show them a string of heads and tails that was produced by a random-number generator, they tend to think it is rigged—it looks orderly to them, too orderly. After 9/11 people claimed to see Satan in the billowing smoke from the World Trade Center. Before that some people were stirred by the Nun Bun, a baked good that bore an eerie resemblance to Mother Teresa. In November of 2004 someone posted on eBay a ten-year old grilled cheese sandwich that looked remarkably like the Virgin Mary; it sold for $28,000. (In response pranksters posted a grilled cheese sandwich bearing images of the Olsen twins, Mary-Kate and Ashley.) There are those who listen to the static from radios and other electronic devices and hear messages from dead people—a phenomenon presented with great seriousness in the Michael Keaton movie *White Noise*. Older readers who lived their formative years before CDs and MPEGs might remember listening intently for the significant and sometimes scatological messages that were said to come from records played backward.

Sometimes there really are signs of non random and functional design. We are not being unreasonable when we observe that the eye seems to be crafted for seeing, or that the leaf insect seems colored with the goal of looking very much like a leaf. The evolutionary biologist Richard Dawkins begins The Blind Watchmaker by conceding this point: "Biology is the study of complicated things that give the appearance of having been designed for a purpose." Dawkins goes on to suggest that anyone before Darwin who did not believe in God was simply not paying attention.

Darwin changed everything. His great insight was that one could explain complex and adaptive design without positing a divine designer. Natural selection can be simulated on a computer; in fact, genetic algorithms, which mimic natural selection, are used to solve otherwise intractable computational problems. And we can see natural selection at work in case studies across the world, from the evolution of beak size in Galapagos finches to the arms race we engage in with many viruses, which have an unfortunate capacity to respond adaptively to vaccines.

Richard Dawkins may well be right when he describes the theory of natural selection as one of our species' finest accomplishments; it is an intellectually satisfying and empirically supported account of our own existence. But almost nobody believes it. One poll found that more than a third of college undergraduates believe that the Garden of Eden was where the first human beings appeared. And even among those who claim to endorse Darwinian evolution, many distort it in one way or another, often seeing it as a mysterious internal force driving species toward perfection. (Dawkins writes that it appears almost as if "the human brain is specifically designed to misunderstand Darwinism.") And if you are tempted to see this as a red state-blue state issue, think again: although it's true that more Bush voters than Kerry voters are creationists, just about half of Kerry voters believe that God created human beings in their present form, and most of the rest believe that although we evolved from less-advanced life forms, God guided the process. Most Kerry voters want evolution to be taught either alongside creationism or not at all.

What's the problem with Darwin? His theory of evolution does clash with the religious beliefs that some people already hold. For Jews and Christians, God willed the world into being in six days, calling different things into existence. Other religions posit more physical processes on the part of the creator or creators, such as vomiting, procreation, masturbation, or the molding of clay. Not much room here for random variation and differential reproductive success.

But the real problem with natural selection is that it makes no intuitive sense. It is like quantum physics; we may intellectually grasp it, but it will never feel right to us. When we see a complex structure, we see it as the product of beliefs and goals and desires. Our social mode of understanding leaves it difficult for us to make sense of it any other way. Our gut feeling is that design requires a designer—a fact that is understandably exploited by those who argue against Darwin.

It's not surprising, then, that nascent creationist views are found in young children. Four-year-olds insist that everything has a purpose, including lions ("to go in the zoo") and clouds ("for raining"). When asked to explain why a bunch of rocks are pointy, adults prefer a physical explanation, while children choose a functional one, such as "so that animals could scratch on them when they get itchy." And when asked about the origin of animals and people, children tend to prefer explanations that involve an intentional creator, even if the adults raising them do not. Creationism—and belief in God—is bred in the bone.

VI. RELIGION AND SCIENCE WILL ALWAYS CLASH

Some might argue that the preceding analysis of religion, based as it is on supernatural beliefs, does not apply to certain non-Western faiths. In his recent book, The End of Faith, the neuroscientist Sam Harris mounts a fierce attack on religion, much of it directed at Christianity and Islam, which he criticizes for what he sees as ridiculous factual claims and grotesque moral views. But then he turns to Buddhism, and his tone shifts to admiration—it is "the most complete methodology we have for discovering the intrinsic freedom of consciousness, unencumbered by any dogma." Surely this religion, if one wants to call it a religion, is not rooted in the dualist and creationist views that emerge in our childhood.

Fair enough. But while it may be true that "theologically correct" Buddhism explicitly rejects the notions of body-soul duality and immaterial entities with special powers, actual Buddhists believe in such things. (Harris himself recognizes this; at one point he complains about the millions of Buddhists who treat the Buddha as a Christ figure.) For that matter, although many Christian theologians are willing to endorse evolutionary biology—and it was legitimately front-page news when Pope John *Paul II* conceded that Darwin's theory of evolution might be correct—this should not distract us from the fact that many Christians think evolution is nonsense.

Or consider the notion that the soul escapes the body at death. There is little hint of such an idea in the Old Testament, although it enters into Judaism later on. The New Testament is notoriously unclear about the afterlife, and some Christian theologians have argued, on the basis of sources such as *Paul's* letters to the Corinthians, that the idea of a soul's rising to heaven conflicts with biblical authority. In 1999 the pope himself cautioned people to think of heaven not as an actual place but, rather, as a form of existence—that of being in relation to God.

Despite all this, most Jews and Christians, as noted, believe in an afterlife—in fact, even people who claim to have no religion at all tend to believe in one. Our afterlife beliefs are clearly expressed in popular books such as The Five People You Meet in Heaven and A Travel Guide to Heaven. As the Guide puts it.

> Heaven is dynamic. It's bursting with excitement and action.
> It's the ultimate playground, created purely for our enjoyment, by someone who knows what enjoyment means, because He invented it. It's Disney World, Hawaii, Paris, Rome, and New York all rolled up into one. And it's forever! Heaven truly is the vacation that never ends.

(This sounds a bit like hell to me, but it is apparently to some people's taste.)

Religious authorities and scholars are often motivated to explore and reach out to science, as when the pope embraced evolution and the Dalai Lama became involved with neuroscience. They do this in part to make their world view more palatable to others, and in part because they are legitimately concerned about any clash with scientific findings. No honest person wants to be in the position of defending a view that makes manifestly false claims, so religious authorities and scholars often make serious efforts toward reconciliation—for instance, trying to interpret the Bible in a way that is consistent with what we know about the age of the earth.

If people got their religious ideas from ecclesiastical authorities, these efforts might lead religion away from the supernatural. Scientific views would spread through religious communities. Supernatural beliefs would gradually disappear as the theologically correct version of a religion gradually became consistent with the secular world view. As Stephen Jay Gould hoped, religion would stop stepping on science's toes.

But this scenario assumes the wrong account of where supernatural ideas come from. Religious teachings certainly shape many of the specific beliefs we hold; nobody is born with the idea that the birthplace of humanity was the Garden of Eden, or that the soul enters the body at the moment of conception, or that martyrs will be rewarded with sexual access to scores of virgins. These ideas are learned. But the universal themes of religion are not learned. They emerge as accidental by-products of our mental systems. They are part of human nature.

Enthusiasm is building among scientists for the view that religion emerged not to serve a purpose—not as an opiate or a social glue—but by accident. It is a by-product of biological adaptations gone awry.

We see the world of objects as separate from the world of minds, allowing us to envision souls and an afterlife; and our system of social understanding infers goals and desires where none exist, making us animiste and creationists.

Nobody is born with the idea that humanity started in the Garden of Eden, or that martyrs will be rewarded in heaven; these ideas are learned. But the universal themes of religion are not learned They are part of human nature.

The theory of natural selection is an empirically supported account of our existence. But almost nobody believes it. We may intellectually grasp it, but it will never feel right. Our gut feeling is that design requires a designer.

Questions about Content

1. Bloom surveys several theories that could account for the existence of faith. Which one of those theories seems most compelling or worth pursuing? Which one seems weakest? Explain your choices.
2. What does Bloom mean in saying that human beings are natural-born dualists? How useful, or how limiting, is this trait for human beings?
3. What does the writer mean in saying that "we have evolved to be creationists"? What are some examples of this? In what kinds of situations do you think this trait could be beneficial, and in what kinds of situations could it lead human beings into error?

Questions about Rhetorical Analysis

1. Bloom uses the word *accident*, a word that could be offensive, but that word is actually a "term of art," a term that has a special meaning in a particular field of study. What does the word *accident* mean as a term of art in the field of evolutionary theory?
2. The writer uses a variety of strategies, such as personal narrative, explanation and refutation of theoretical concepts, descriptions of experiments as examples, and references to authorities. Select one section of this article and describe how he uses these or other strategies to fulfill the purpose of his article.

Connecting the Readings

1. How would Davies and Bloom answer this question: Do advances in science undermine faith? Or will there be a need and role for religion regardless of scientific discovery?

2. Both writers are scientists writing for a general audience in a popular magazine, the *Atlantic Monthly*. Assess how these writers try to appeal to this audience of nonspecialists. What strategies do they employ to make their arguments accessible to people who are not familiar with the concepts and terminology of the sciences?

Writing Projects

1. **Popular Culture's Effect on Religion:**

   a. Do some research to discover ways in which religion appears in popular culture. You could explore a television show, such as *The Simpsons*. You could analyze a movie or a video game. What religious references do they make? What patterns of thought do you see in the way religion is represented? Are Eastern and Western religions treated differently? In what ways does the popular culture you are examining reinforce misunderstandings or prejudices of a particular religion?

   b. Create a catalog of religion in popular culture. You could create a web page or blog of links to advertisements, animated cartoons, games, films, videos, and audio files.

2. **The Growth of Islam in the United States:**

   a. Observe how Islam is presented in American media and write a summary of your observations with commentary. What messages are repeated in television and Internet news? Are claims made that could be explored in depth? What additional information about Islam would make a particular news story more informative?

   b. Create your own "religious literacy quiz" about Islam, give it to people you know, and write a report on the results. What do others understand about Islam? What do they misunderstand? What areas do they need more information about?

3. **New Discoveries in the Science of Faith:**

   a. Examine and explore in writing some of the questions basic to all belief: Is it possible to prove that a god or gods exist? Do research to discover the prevailing arguments that have been advanced on both sides of this debate. What are the strengths and weaknesses of the arguments?

   b. Examine and explore in writing the question: Are science and faith incompatible? Can science make faith become obsolete? In your research, discover the major arguments that have been offered on each side of this debate. What are the strengths and weaknesses of the arguments?

Chapter 1

p. 3   Reprinted with the permission of The Free Press, a Division of Simon & Schuster Adult Publishing Group, from *The Faith Club: A Muslim, A Christian, A Jew—Three Women Search for Understanding* by Ranya Idilby, Suzanne Oliver, and Priscilla Warner. Copyright © 2006 by Ranya Idilby, Suzanne Oliver, and Priscilla Warner. All rights reserved.

p. 13   Reprinted with permission of the author and Michigan State University Press. This work originally appeared in *Fourth Genre*, volume 5, issue 2, fall 2003, published by Michigan State University Press.

p. 29   First published in *Image* magazine. Lindsey Crittenden is the author of *The Water Will Hold You: A Skeptic Learns to Pray*. Harmony Books, 2007. Reprinted by permission of the author.

p. 39   Copyright © 1990 by Tenzin Gyatso, His Holiness, The Fourteenth Dalai Lama of Tibet. Reprinted by permission of HarperCollins Publishers.

p. 47   From *The Spiral Staircase* by Karen Armstrong, copyright © 2004 by Karen Armstrong. Used by permission of Alfred A. Knopf, a division of Random House, Inc.

Chapter 2

p. 61   Scripture quotations (Genesis 3:1–24 and 22:1–18, Deuteronomy 6:1–25, Matthew 5:1–10 and 25:31–40, and Luke 15:1–32) are from the New Revised Standard Version of the Bible, copyright © 1989 by the National Council of the Churches of Christ in the USA. Used by permission. All rights reserved.

p. 63   Scripture quotations (Genesis 3:1–24 and 22:1–18, Deuteronomy 6:1–25, Matthew 5:1–10 and 25:31–40, and Luke 15:1–32) are from the New Revised Standard Version of the Bible, copyright © 1989 by the National Council of the Churches of Christ in the USA. Used by permission. All rights reserved.

p. 66   Scripture quotations (Genesis 3:1–24 and 22:1–18, Deuteronomy 6:1–25, Matthew 5:1–10 and 25:31–40, and Luke 15:1–32) are from the New Revised Standard Version of the Bible, copyright © 1989 by the National Council of the Churches of Christ in the USA. Used by permission. All rights reserved.

p. 69   Scripture quotations (Genesis 3:1–24 and 22:1–18, Deuteronomy 6:1–25, Matthew 5:1–10 and 25:31–40, and Luke 15:1–32) are from the New Revised Standard Version of the Bible, copyright © 1989 by the National Council of the Churches of Christ in the USA. Used by permission. All rights reserved.

p. 69   Scripture quotations (Genesis 3:1–24 and 22:1–18, Deuteronomy 6:1–25, Matthew 5:1–10 and 25:31–40, and Luke 15:1–32) are from the New Revised Standard Version of the Bible, copyright © 1989 by the National Council of the Churches of Christ in the USA. Used by permission. All rights reserved.

p. 69   Scripture quotations (Genesis 3:1–24 and 22:1–18, Deuteronomy 6:1–25, Matthew 5:1–10 and 25:31–40, and Luke 15:1–32) are from the New Revised Standard Version of the Bible, copyright © 1989 by the National Council of the Churches of Christ in the USA. Used by permission. All rights reserved.

p. 71   From Qur'an (1998) edited by Abdul-Haleem MAS. By permission of Oxford University Press.

p. 79   From *Bhagavad Gita,* translated by Barbara Stoler Miller, translation copyright © 1986 by Barbara Stoler Miller. Used by permission of Bantam Books, a division of Random House, Inc.

p. 85   From *Buddhist Scriptures,* translated by Edward Conze (Penguin Classics, 1959), pages 35–36, 37–39, 39–40, 40–41. Copyright © Edward Conze, 1959. Reprinted by permission of Penguin Books, Ltd., U.K.

p. 90   Verses 1 and 13 from *Tao Te Ching* by Lao Tzu, *A New English Version, with Foreword and Notes,* by Stephen Mitchell. Translation copyright © 1988 by Stephen Mitchell. Reprinted by permission of HarperCollins Publishers.

Chapter 3

p. 98   From *God: A Biography* by Jack Miles, copyright © 1995 by Jack Miles. Used by permission of Alfred A. Knopf, a division of Random House, Inc.

p. 103   "The Evolutionary Psychology of Religion" by Steven Pinker was originally presented at the annual meeting of the Freedom from Religion Foundation in Madison, Wisconsin on October 29, 2004. Reprinted by permission of the author. Steven Pinker is Johnstone Family Professor of Harvard University and the author of seven books, including *The Language Instinct, The Blank Slate, The Stuff of Thought,* and *How the Mind Works* (from which the material for this essay was adapted).

p. 114   Excerpt from "Mapping American Adolescent Subjective Religiosity" by Christian Smith, Robert Faris, Melinda Lundquist Denton, and Mark Regnerus. The entire article originally appeared in the 2003 edition of *Sociology of Religion.* Reprinted with

p. 124   "Progress in the Economics of Religion" by Laurence Iannaccone was originally published in *Journal of Institutional and Theoretical Economics*, volume 150, number 4, 1994. Reprinted by permission of the author.

Chapter 4

p. 139   Reprinted with permission from Sojourners, (800) 714–7474, www.sojo.net.

p. 142   Jeff Jacoby, "Atheists' Bleak Alternative," December 13, 2006. Copyright © 2006 The Boston Globe. Reprinted with permission.

p. 146   Reprinted by permission of *Ms.* magazine, © 2004.

p. 159   Statement of the Evangelical Climate Initiative: "Climate Change: An Evangelical Call to Action," www.christiansandclimate. org, reprinted with permission of the Evangelical Climate Initiative.

p. 164   The Cornwall Declaration on Environmental Stewardship, www.CornwallAlliance.org, reprinted by permission of the Cornwall Alliance.

p. 169   Copyright © 2005 by The New York Times Co. Reprinted with permission.

p. 172   © David Frum. Originally published in the *National Post* (Canada), December 23, 2006.

Chapter 5

p. 189   Reprinted with permission of the author. Michael Wolfe is the author of books of poetry, fiction, history, and travel. He has produced several documentary films for Public Television. This article appeared originally on www.beliefnet.com, the leading website for faith, spirituality, inspiration, and more. Used with permission. All rights reserved.

p. 193   Ingrid Mattson, Ph.D., is a professor at Hartford Seminary in Hartford, Connecticut. Reprinted with permission of the author.

p. 198   Paul Davies is director of The Beyond Center at Arizona State University. This article originally appeared in the September 2003 issue of *Atlantic Monthly* magazine. Reprinted by permission of the author.

p. 209   Originally appeared in December 2005 issue of *Atlantic Monthly* magazine. Reprinted by permission of the author.